THE IMPROBABLE

VICTORIA

WOODHULL

Also by Eden Collinsworth

What the Ermine Saw

Behaving Badly: The New Morality of Politics, Sex, and Business

I Stand Corrected

It Might Have Been What He Said

THE IMPROBABLE

VICTORIA WOODHULL

Suffrage, Free Love, and the
First Woman to Run for President

Eden Collinsworth

DOUBLEDAY
New York

Published by Doubleday, a division of
Penguin Random House LLC, 1745 Broadway, New York, NY 10019.

Book design by Michael Collica

Library of Congress Cataloging-in-Publication Data
Names: Collinsworth, Eden author
Title: The improbable Victoria Woodhull : suffrage, free love,
and the first woman to run for president / Eden Collinsworth.
Description: First edition. | New York : Doubleday, [2025] |
Includes bibliographical references.
Identifiers: LCCN 2024050274 (print) | LCCN 2024050275 (ebook) |
ISBN 9780385549578 hardcover | ISBN 9780385549585 ebook
Subjects: LCSH: Woodhull, Victoria C. (Victoria Claflin), 1838–1927 |United States—
Social conditions—1865–1918 | Women—Suffrage—United States—History | Free love—
United States—History—19th century | Women social reformers—
United States—Biography | Suffragists—United States—Biography |
LCGFT: Biographies
Classification: LCC HQ1413.W66 C65 2025 (print) |
LCC HQ1413.W66 (ebook) | DDC 324.6/23092—dc23/eng/20250430
LC record available at https://lccn.loc.gov/2024050274
LC ebook record available at https://lccn.loc.gov/2024050275

penguinrandomhouse.com | doubleday.com

The authorized representative in the EU for product safety and compliance
is Penguin Random House Ireland, Morrison Chambers,
32 Nassau Street, Dublin D02 YH68, Ireland, https://eu-contact.penguin.ie.

To Gilliam, and for Tessa

Tell us all about yourself we pray—
For as yet we can't make out in the least
If you're Fish or Insect, or Bird or Beast.

—from "The Scroobious Pip,"
by Edward Lear

AUTHOR'S NOTE

In writing this account, I made use of a vast array of archival sources, which, as any writer grappling with the past understands, have their limitations, largely due to unjust implicit and explicit biases. Still, I have, when up against the limitations of the historical record, endeavored to accurately understand and re-create the motivations of the historical figures herein.

It began with a plant collection.

1687. A young Anglo-Irish physician by the name of Hans Sloane sailed from Britain for Jamaica to be the personal physician to its new governor. The unfortunate fact that the governor died not long after should not be held against Sloane.

Sloane was also a devoted collector of flora: during his relatively short stay in the Caribbean, he collected one thousand specimens of plants—eight hundred of which were unknown to British academics—and found time enough to marry Elizabeth Langley Rose, the extremely wealthy heiress of sugar plantations. Returning to England with his newly minted wife, Sloane packed a large supply of cacao (some credit him with the invention of chocolate milk), Peruvian bark (from which he would later extract quinine to treat eye ailments), and the many detailed journals he had written. In London, he established a lucrative medical practice catering to its upper classes, serving three successive sovereigns and eventually replacing Isaac Newton as president of the Royal Society.

Throughout his illustrious career, Hans Sloane expanded his collection well beyond plants to include an eclectic assortment of objects and books. That he would become one of the most prolific collectors of his time was due largely to Britain's seagoing trade routes that cut through the Atlantic and Indian Oceans. British imperialism and an international network of correspondents enabled him to amass more than eighty thousand natural objects and ancient rarities, over forty thousand books and manuscripts, and thirty-two thousand coins and medals. Subsidizing what would become one of the most astonishing curiosity cabinets of the age was the combination of his income as a physician, his wife's inheritance, and his ongoing investments in the Royal African Company and South Sea Company, both of which traded in slaves.

Sir Hans Sloane died in 1753 and bequeathed his vast collection to the nation on two conditions: Parliament would pay his executors an amount equivalent to no more than one-fourth the value of the collection, and the collection would be seen by anyone who wished to see it. The powers that be had no problem agreeing to the first proviso, but the second one challenged their belief that scholarship and natural history were activities that should remain with the educated and members of the upper classes. Nonetheless, on June 7, 1753, an Act of Parliament establishing the British Museum received royal assent and the first free, national, and public museum was created with Sloane's collection as its nucleus. In 1759, the museum opened in a seventeenth-century London mansion called Montagu House. It took nearly one hundred years before a permanent building on Great Russell Street was designated. By that time other patrons had donated their personal libraries and the number of manuscripts and books swelled to 520,000. More space was necessary. The solution presented itself when the museum's trustees were informed that there wasn't sufficient sunlight to grow anything in the building's inner courtyard, which had been intended as a garden. Inspired by the Pantheon in Rome, they decided to install a domed edifice in the courtyard to house the museum's book collection.

His Majesty's Treasury granted the funds for an ambitious construction of what, despite its grand scale, would be referred to with English understatement as "the Reading Room." It was opened to the public for special viewings the first week of May 1857, and more than sixty-two thousand visitors came to marvel at what was hailed as one of the great sights of London.

The Reading Room was a masterpiece of mid-nineteenth-century technology featuring modern heating, ventilation, and fire protection systems. Its floor was covered in special material designed to reduce noise. Cast-iron shelves distributed the weight of the books in an area that could accommodate 302 readers seated at thirty-eight tables radiating out from the keyhole-shaped catalog desk. Each table was covered in black leather and had two inkwells sunken side by side: one for quill pens, and one for "steel pens," which were metal nibs in pencil holders.

Members of the public wishing access to the Reading Room after its debut were required to apply in writing and issued a ticket (or not) by the principal librarian.

THE IMPROBABLE

VICTORIA WOODHULL

PART I

Unmarked graves, child clairvoyants, and an ungovernable woman.

A man who never put personal inclination above duty.

Mr. Garnett was sixteen years old when he began his lifelong career at the British Museum's Reading Room. He was so encased in propriety that, even at that young age, he didn't seem to have a first name.

It has been said that there are two distinct systems of problem-solving: the fast-processing way solves quickly but can careen into error; the slower, carefully ordered way grinds out a probable right answer using a more precise method. Mr. Garnett's fondness for order placed him comfortably in the second category. Whenever it was suggested that he might be quibbling over the minutia, he would point out the importance of being as precise as possible. His exactitude was rewarded in 1872—he was given the role of "placer" in the British Museum Library. In 1875 he was promoted to superintendent, with the responsibility of arranging thousands of books on the three separate tiers that circumnavigated the Reading Room.

Despite its staunch utility, the Reading Room would pose a logistical problem for Mr. Garnett when, in 1881, he became the editor of the General Catalogue of Printed Books and discovered that the library's handwritten catalog system had outgrown its allotted space. The Remington Sewing Machine Company suggested the solution was its promising invention—the typewriter. Mr. Garnett rejected the machine because it lacked Latin keys, pointing out that the English language uses the Latin alphabet, but Latin has more variants. Like it or not (and, by and large, Mr. Garnett did not like it), the typewriter was the future. His shortsighted decision to discount it did not, however, prevent his promotion in 1890, when he was given the prestigious title of keeper of printed books at the British Museum.

Mr. Garnett's role at the British Museum placed some twenty-five miles of shelved books and periodicals under his watchful eye.

During the years it took Mr. Garnett to rise to the rarefied upper regions of the British Museum Library, he became a man admired for his amazing power to concentrate his thoughts. Prodigious in output and versatile in range, Mr. Garnett was variously a poet, a writer of short stories, and a biographer. His unerring grasp of his mother tongue and his relish for foreign languages transformed him into a prolific translator of works from Greek, German, Italian, Spanish, and Portuguese. Added to this academic plate spinning were his contributions to several encyclopedias whose editors were grateful for the meticulous nature of his marginal notations.

Mr. Garnett's numerous achievements did not sway his temperament in any one direction—it was constant to an almost metaphorical degree. He had a dislike for surprises and an adversity to conflict. He was dedicated to rational debate and was able to navigate controversy with an evenhandedness that helped him avoid sensationalism. He was committed to courtesy, the ritual by which one person avoids hurting another's feelings by satisfying his own ego. Mr. Garnett never erred against decorum. He seldom raised his voice and believed that a person's highest prerogative was dignity. The library—with its silence and order that removed him from life's disarray—is where he spent most of his time. It situated him within the consoling proximity to books that took him everywhere without the need to ever leave London.

The lives of quiet people are rarely quiet for those living them, and it is possible that Mr. Garnett had fanciful thoughts. We shall never know, for he didn't discuss them or put them to paper. Of one thing we can be certain: he was not a libertine. Eschewing bohemian adventure and foreign travel, he lived in a private apartment within the calming confines of the museum and was at ease in the contemplative company of colleagues, who knew very little about his personal choices other than that he preferred savories over sweets. If forced to socialize outside its intellectual orbit, he would clasp his hands behind his back, offer a polite head nod, and rely on an infallible topic of British conversation—The Weather.

Photographs of Mr. Garnett show a man whose physical appearance was unassuming in every way. He was neither tall nor short, neither fat nor thin. Behind his spectacles were kind eyes—a little sad, perhaps, but kind. His greying hair was side combed in an anguished attempt to cover a spreading bald spot. The wide muttonchops flanking either side of his unremarkable face had an agreement to meet at his chin. His mouth rested in a downward-turned position, suggesting that he didn't partake in a great deal of impulsive levity.

Mr. Garnett's profile was dominated by a forehead that seemed to depict the process of reason itself.

A living master class in consistency, slow to chide, thrill-free, impervious to vulgarity, well-intentioned, discreet and earnest in conviction, uncomplaining, disciplined, acclimated to order—these were the qualities that defined Mr. Garnett as a man with an unblemished record of respectability who regulated his conduct on lofty principles. No one—absolutely no one—could have predicted that, in 1893, he would be accused of libel.

CHAPTER TWO

Mrs. Woodhull, a law unto herself.

Just as unexpected as the accusation of libel levied against Mr. Garnett was the identity of his accuser. The claimant was a fifty-four-year-old American by the name of Mrs. Victoria Claflin Woodhull, who, having lived a controversial life in the United States before moving to London, discovered that the British Museum was cataloging archival material she insisted contained unflattering references to her.

The events Mrs. Woodhull set in motion were preposterous enough that rumor of them surpassed Mr. Garnett's belief until a subpoena was staring him in his flabbergasted face. Had he been wrongfully blamed for committing murder he could scarcely have been more stunned. Years of self-restraint prevented him from showing any visible signs of panic, but he was grateful for being seated behind a desk while reading the summons so that his knees could shake in secret.

Nothing remotely similar had ever happened to Mr. Garnett before and, with no other comparison, he struggled to find his bearings. So bewildering—no, so alien—was the claim that he was convinced his accuser must be deranged. The written material to which she objected appeared in a cataloged pamphlet that featured various news items from America recounting her past life, but he could find no immediate evidence that she'd taken legal action against those very newspapers at the time they ran the stories.

Mrs. Woodhull's solicitor presented the details of her case: the proceedings would be stayed if (1) the museum were to remove the offending publications; (2) the museum's trustees revealed the name of the vendor who supplied the publications to the museum; and (3) if the museum ran a public apology for having circulated libelous material.

"Mrs. Woodhull will incur any inconvenience to obtain justice," was her solicitor's fair warning.

The costs of defending a libel suit in Britain were markedly greater than in America and comparable European countries. Most people on the receiving end of the kind of letter sent by Mrs. Woodhull's solicitor would have relented, not because they had a weak case, but because of the often-crippling expense of fighting the claim. The museum's response was unequivocal: its duty was to provide a wide selection of literature to the public. Acquiescing to any one of the three demands would have profound consequences. As for Mr. Garnett, he deemed it to be an affront to the foundational principles of a public institution. He would not—could not—sanction that the material be withdrawn from the British Library simply because an evidently irrational female objected to it.

The fact that Mrs. Woodhull came from a bizarre, try-anything country with radical individualism at its heart encouraged him to believe that her nationality was the reason for this breach of civilized behavior and reasonable thought. He had not been to America, and the few impressions he had of its people were limited to what he read about them. Mr. Garnett had heard of the legendary Davy Crockett, whose distinctly American attitude was captured in a few short words: "If it's right do it." The French diplomat and political historian Alexis de Tocqueville's book *Democracy in America* suggested that an American's conduct was thought to be a proving ground for character. Charles Dickens embarked on a speaking tour in America and wrote of his admiration for its protean energies and the fact that an ambitious man in possession of a clever idea could become rich, but he came to the conclusion that its overstimulated inhabitants were ill-mannered. Anthony Trollope's mother, Frances Milton Trollope, offered enlightenment on matters pertaining to America in her recently published book, *Domestic Manners of the Americans,* which recounted her travels there. It described the country's raw immaturity and reported tendencies of enthusiastic handshakes, first-name informality, and oversharing. As women often do, Mrs. Trollope assumed that when she judged something or someone to be unattractive, that something or someone should be unattractive to others; still, Mr. Garnett decided it probable that her observations were not ill-conceived. She provided two general warnings: first, that because the foundation stone of liberty in America hinged on the truism that every man is theoretically free to form his own opinions, Americans consider self-importance their birthright; and, second, that they did not share the Englishmen's keen zest to be well-bred.

Despite the benefits that came from his reading about America and its people, Mr. Garnett was certain that there must have been an unknown something else, possibly a hidden depravity, that had stained Mrs. Woodhull's reputation (even by American standards). He put aside his scorn for her and focused on the gravity of the situation after learning that, despite her last name, her litigious English husband was John Biddulph Martin, a partner in the fifth-generation private bank, Martins.

The situation was grave indeed. It was the first time that a suit of libel had been brought against the museum and its esteemed trustees. As the museum's keeper of the printed books, Mr. Garnett was charged with that same crime. Libel covers any published statement alleged to defame a named or identifiable individual in a way that causes loss in their profession or damages their standing in the community. The burden falls upon the accused party to prove that the material deemed libel is, in fact alone, true.

Not only was the American woman seeking damages for libel, she demanded an injunction against further issuance of the material in question.

"I shall not change my course because those who assume to be better than I desire it," she had let it be known.

A trial by jury was scheduled at the Old Bailey—a stalwartly handsome and airless building where the Queen's Bench Division deals with contract and tort (civil wrongs), judicial review, and libel. Mr. Garnett, along with the British Museum and its trustees, would be represented by Britain's attorney general, Sir Charles Russell, QC, who was himself a trustee of the British Museum. Reputed to be the most adept cross-examiner in England, Sir Charles was renowned for his fierce intelligence, powerful recall, and verbal dexterity. Further, he demonstrated confidence in his understanding of the world, an unshakable sense of self-worth, a polite demeanor that belied a steeliness in confronting opponents, unflagging energy, a mastery of both nuance and detailed analysis, and, if needs must, an unsettling stare.

What no one was aware of—and what no one would have believed anyway—was that Victoria Woodhull possessed these same defining traits.

•   •   •   •

The trial began on February 23, 1894.

The Old Bailey was named after the street on which it was located, which follows the line of the original fortified wall (or "bailey") of the City of London. It had been constructed close enough to Newgate Prison to enable easy transfer of prisoners for trial.

On one side of its courtroom was a raised witness box called the dock. Before the installation of gas lighting, mirrors were strategically positioned to reflect the daylight from the windows and onto the individual in the dock; a board was positioned above to amplify his or her voice.

Members of the jury were seated in stalls to the right of the dock and sufficiently close together to consult one another.

Facing the dock on the opposite side of the room and telegraphing authority from a raised platform of equal height was Sir Edward Pollock, a distinguished seventy-year-old judge with the august title of Baron of the Court of the Exchequer.

Seated behind a long table below the dock were clerks and lawyers whose shorthand notes formed the basis of the *Proceedings,* a daily transcript of what had happened in court that lent credence to the suggestion that the history of man is a register of his crimes, follies, and misfortunes.

Relegated to the oak benches in the balcony were members of the curious public and those valiant seekers of truth—members of the press.

Like all aspects of Mr. Garnett's personality, he was set in his ways when it came to his attire. He appeared daily in a pressed white shirt with cuffed sleeves, a subdued silk tie, and dark trousers that fell loosely to his ankles. Not one to chase trends, he wore an out-of-fashion frock coat and a single-breasted waistcoat rather than the newer double-breasted style. His attire the first day of the trial was what it would have been any other day.

Inside the Old Bailey

The imposingly tall Sir Charles cut a dash in the traditional formal court wear of a long black gown that was meant to bring a sense of solemnity to the proceedings. Around his neck and covering his shirt collar was a jabot—a white linen bib the shape of two simple rectangles said to represent the tablets of Moses in the Old Testament. Perching on his head while he ignored the itch it caused was a wig made of whitish-grey horsehair. This, too, had no proven practical purpose but was meant to establish a visual separation between the law and those before it.

Then, of course, there was Mrs. Woodhull. Given what Mr. Garnett considered to be her aggressively unattractive intention to defame the library, it was easy for him to imagine her as a malevolent-looking, odious threat to all things civilized. What walked into the courtroom instead was a dignified woman who had not lost her beauty and vitality to middle age. She was wearing an elegant dress of pigeon grey moiré trimmed with delicate lace and a ruffled flounce. The fresh white rose at her breast added allure without being indecorous. She was of medium height. Her skin was smooth and pale. Distinguishing

her broad face were high cheekbones, an aquiline nose, a full but delicate mouth, and luminous blue eyes. Abundant henna-colored tresses
wound about her shapely head.

Once seated, Mrs. Woodhull's straight posture anchored her as she
gazed out at the sea of men and caught the eye of Sir Charles. The
look she gave him was both detached and penetrating. His response
was to offer a slight smile, which, try as it might, appeared unamiable.

The face-off that would occur between the two could be compared
to an unstoppable force slamming into an immovable object.

Only one was prepared for the collision.

Victoria Woodhull wasn't
remotely what Mr. Garnett
expected her to be.

CHAPTER THREE

Courting danger.

Mr. Garnett had been wrong to imagine Mrs. Woodhull as a bitter, carping creature, but he had been right to believe that the reason behind her accusation of libel was to shed a part of her past. Her barrister explained that she was compelled to clear her name after discovering that the museum had material in its circulation accusing her of immorality.

His opening statement hinted at the drama to come.

"May it please your Lordship, Gentlemen of the Jury, to fully understand the context of this trial, you must permit me to trespass upon your time and describe in sufficient fullness the incidences of the life of this lady in which sorrow has taken no small part."

There exists an unspoken understanding among many English people that any questionable aspect of one's background is not meant to be aired, which is why there was collective dismay in the courtroom when Mrs. Woodhull's barrister began to relay details of his client's primitive upbringing. In what resembled a series of controlled explosions, he laid out the miseries of her hand-to-mouth childhood, describing her indolent parents as "ignorant and violent" people, and volunteering that she had been denied any real education and had often slept in the same clothes she wore during the day.

· · ·

If ever there were a contrast in background, it was that of Mrs. Woodhull's and Sir Charles's.

One advantage after another had paved the way to Sir Charles's privileged station. Authority and responsibility came easily to him; the only thing that didn't was self-doubt. To be clear, Sir Charles was not overly proud of himself. An upper-class Englishman could be proud of his wife, his wine, his property, but not himself. "Gravely confident" is how one would describe him. Yes, of course, he took the charge of libel seriously, but he wasn't prepared to consider Mrs. Woodhull in any way serious, and, even if he had, he was bound to underestimate her for reasons he thought obvious. This was likely not a conscious prejudice on his part—it was more a matter of habit than intent.

A portrait by John Singer Sargent of Sir Charles Russell, the representation of all that is illustriously English. He would be appointed the lord chief justice of England and called Baron Russell of Killowen.

"Am I correct in stating that you minister to the belief in spirits?" was the first question Sir Charles put to Mrs. Woodhull in a cross-examination designed to systematically reveal the facts. A yes from Mrs. Woodhull would enable him to build a straightforward argument that would set him on a course to discredit her claim of libel. A yes was what he was expecting, because there was no other possible answer.

Unfortunately for Sir Charles, his strategy hadn't calculated the likelihood that Mrs. Woodhull also had one. Hers was a game of emotive hide-and-seek. She could play it at a masterly level by deploying creative ambiguity and withholding as much as she shared.

"Spirits have been believed by many people during the course of human history," she replied.

"Are we to assume that you do not reject the notion of the supernatural?" asked Sir Charles.

Mrs. Woodhull reflected for a moment.

"The broader question might be whether there exists anything apart from the tangible." She allowed the suggestion to linger before continuing. "All of us would feel better if we knew what lay beyond the present, and, surely, all of us wish that, whatever that might be, it will place us among those we have loved."

It was more a riddle than an answer.

"So you *do* believe in the supernatural," Sir Charles stated tersely.

Mrs. Woodhull turned her head away from him and toward members of the jury in an unhurried gesture that made him appear to be beside the point.

"We humans live in a world of the flesh and must find a way of reckoning with the impermanence of our existence," she said, speaking directly to the jurors in a warming manner that put them in a pleasant state of expectancy. Her refusal to cohere with Sir Charles's dictated narrative had moved the center of gravity away from him.

"Are you saying that you *do* believe in the supernatural?" he asked again, sounding more irritated than he would have wanted.

Rather than a reply, Mrs. Woodhull gave a spellbinding description of what it felt like to enter an altered state. She portrayed a "condition of exaltation" as if engaged in an earnest conversation with a single friend. She likened the sensation of returning to one's body to the feeling of "suddenly falling from a height, but without harm." She explained that "on the retina of our brain the outline of Truth is revealed to those attuned to the music of the spheres." She shared her hope that, when she died, her soul would live within the world of familiar spirits wherein the natural and supernatural were knit together. Her eyes continued to rest on the jurors and, with companionable ease, she asked them, "What if, under the right conditions, there can be heard their silent footsteps among our loud ones in the here and now?" There was a calculated pause, and then, as if remembering that he was still in the courtroom, she returned her attention to Sir Charles.

"From your line of questioning, I gather it is your belief that spirits do not exist. But I believe they do. And, because I believe they do, you think I have an overheated imagination. You think this because I am a woman, and you are not disposed to entertain the notion that women can be rational beings."

"Are you quite done?" asked Sir Charles with enough condescension to make clear that the concept of rational women did not warrant his consideration.

Mrs. Woodhull stared back at him as though he wasn't paying the right kind of attention.

"No, Sir Charles, I am not done. If I were to match your preconceptions, I would believe that, because you are a man, you deny the existence of spirits because they are inexplicable in the actual conditions of your own knowledge."

She waited a moment for her point to sink in.

"Now I am done," said she.

"We are a *civilized* people in this courtroom, Mrs. Woodhull. Male or female, civilized people depend upon reason to arrive at the right judgment."

"And do not most civilized people believe in God?"

Sir Charles's reply barely made its way through his gritted teeth.

"Of course."

"But human reason does not allow that belief. Something other than plausibility does. Let us agree to employ logic: if you believe in God, you believe in the impossible."

Mrs. Woodhull's well-made argument had crept up on Sir Charles. He was beginning to realize that she was impervious to argument and unfazed by confrontation. Criticism was normal—indeed, even natural—to her. Most people have opinions; fewer have convictions. Mrs. Woodhull was adept at expressing both.

Her belief in an afterlife made Sir Charles anxious that she might question the tenets of the Church of England or—worse still—infringe upon the queen, its titular head. He eased into his next question sideways.

"I understand that you've pursued a series of careers and that, at one time, you were a clairvoyant."

"Not at one time—all the time."

"And still are?"

"And still are," replied Mrs. Woodhull.

The judge leaned forward to hear her elaborate.

"Clairvoyance is a perception of events or people that doesn't come through the channels of our normally recognized senses," she explained. "There are those in this room who believe that the only truth that matters is the truth that can be measured. But what if those people were to imagine throwing a pebble into one side of a body of water—say a pond? The ridges eventually disappear but the vibrations are sent to the other side. The fact that it can't be measured doesn't mean that it doesn't happen. What if those same people would risk thinking outside habit to consider the possibility of a type of communication that is nonphysical, nonspatial, and nonmechanical? And, here, I must include you, Sir Charles."

It felt as if the barometric pressure in the courtroom dropped while Sir Charles's controlled anger turned his face into a thundercloud.

"I do not wish to *imagine* anything, Mrs. Woodhull." His words flicked with anger. "I wish to be informed. The only thing that matters in this trial are fact-based truths."

"The only thing that matters in this trial is what can be believed," Mrs. Woodhull told him. "The fact that you find something difficult to believe doesn't mean it can't be true."

To calm himself, Sir Charles took in a slow, long breath through his nose.

"Rather than venturing into metaphysics, let us address more straightforward issues. I understand that it was your father who launched your career as a clairvoyant."

"This is correct."

"Please describe him for the court."

"My father was a con man, who never passed up an opportunity that didn't require him to work himself. He was a swindler, who used black paint to cover the flaws of the horses he sold. He was a cheat who, after losing at the card table, paid his debts with counterfeit money. Not only did my father force me to perform as a child clairvoyant, he would starve me for days at a time to enhance my performances."

Having decided that disarming frankness would garner respect with the jury, Mrs. Woodhull welcomed their audible gasps.

"You are very blunt," Sir Charles told her.

"I don't see the point in being anything else."

Sir Charles asked Mrs. Woodhull whether her father concentrated his illegal occupations in river towns in order to flee from the authorities by stowing away on timber barges.

"Correct."

"And it occurred to your father that a more effective strategy of escaping the law would be to outwit the authorities rather than to run from them."

"It did."

Sir Charles pressed further.

"Your father became increasingly fond of taking matters to the law over the slightest pretext."

"Yes," came her unconcerned confirmation.

"By reading just enough law to clutter the courts with litigation, he was able to take a stance before being accused."

"All of what you've said is true," she said, free of inhibition.

"Mrs. Woodhull, I contend that you are your father's daughter."

Did she doubt herself? Not a whit. Was there any equivocation to her response? There was not. Her reply took the form of a genial rejection.

"You are wrong," she told him, without elaborating further.

Her breezy denial induced a sort of cognitive dissonance in Sir Charles. Caught on the back foot, his next step was to ask a leading question. Did she believe in free love?

"I never knew that love was anything but free," she responded.

Had she ever been guilty of immorality? he asked.

Mrs. Woodhull explained that from 1870 to 1877 she had been lecturing before the American public, and that, during that same period of time, not a single charge had been made against her character.

Had she written the article on free love, a copy of which the defense wished to enter into evidence?

No, she had not written that article—how could she, it appeared when she was thousands of miles away lecturing.

Had she ever worked in the theater?

It was common knowledge that women who disported themselves on the stage were likely to make themselves sexually available. This was no question at all, but a dog whistle signaling that Mrs. Woodhull was a onetime prostitute.

"Does my question make you uncomfortable?" asked Sir Charles, whose intention was dedicated to that very purpose.

"It would not matter if it did. But, for the moment, I do not remember being on the stage as anything other than a public lecturer," replied Mrs. Woodhull.

"Pray, understand that I am not making it a matter of reproach," Sir Charles volunteered disingenuously. "It was in San Francisco that you performed on the stage."

"If you will allow me to describe the circumstances, I will do so," offered Mrs. Woodhull.

"I think the question is capable of an answer yes or no," pressed Sir Charles. "For the record, you were, in fact, onstage as an actress while living in San Francisco." He was quick to add another slur. "Am I also correct in stating that you have been married twice before?"

It was impossible for Mrs. Woodhull to rebut this fact, but she knew that confirming it would grant permission for everyone in the courtroom to judge her.

"I find your question disappointing. It makes you seem predictable," she said.

"Why would that be?" Sir Charles asked slowly. His dry-mouthed words must have sounded like brittle twigs snapping.

"When a woman is questioned in court it is considered a legitimate part of the defense to make the most searching inquiry into her sexual morality. I realize that I've broken one of the rules by putting words to it, but this kind of concession allows men to go on living with their prejudices. Women make up more than half the British population. What possible harm comes from the suggestion that a more constructive attitude toward them would further this great nation?"

Speech even, gestures few, and without the need of drawing a longer breath as she gathered pace, Mrs. Woodhull had managed to strike a perfect note of candor while invoking Britain as an admirable and great nation. One of the jury members could be seen nodding respectfully. Sir Charles knew that if he was to move against her now, it would appear churlish.

"Is it true that you have seen apparitions?" he asked, retooling his approach for a third time.

It was obvious to Mrs. Woodhull that Sir Charles was setting her up for ridicule, and, being familiar with the rewards that come from charming the right man, she turned toward the judge. The smile that played around the corners of her mouth was as much invitation as deflection.

"Your Lordship, as a matter of fact, there is one appearing to me now."

Like all charismatic people, when Mrs. Woodhull spoke to someone she thought might be helpful, she made him feel (and, with her, it was almost always a him) as if he was the only person who truly mattered. But, despite the obvious dividends of Mrs. Woodhull's charm, the judge was determined not to succumb to her flirtation. Still, the where-is-this-going aspect intrigued him. The tight expression on his face wavered and it appeared that he would allow a momentary diversion of amused curiosity.

"Not a ghostly apparition, I hope," he told her.

"I do not know yet what this one will do, Your Lordship," she said in a dulcet tone. "He is waiting to hear your conclusions."

If there was ever a time for Sir Charles to recapture lost ground, it was then.

"After all that has been said, are you telling me that you *do* believe in messages from the afterworld?" he asked.

"Sir Charles, I don't mean to tell you anything," she said. "It is you, not I, who have been so splendidly educated."

•   •   •

The cross-examination continued between Mrs. Woodhull, nimbly converting her recalcitrant manner into a virtue, and Sir Charles, whose attempts at forcing her to comply with facts were falling short. In one cut-and-thrust instance, when he demanded a more precise answer to a question, she told him that he was requiring too much of them both.

"Like me, Sir Charles, you've arrived at a mature stage in your life. My memories and your interpretation of them are not to be trusted."

It was a brilliant next move from a formidable adversary whose razor-sharp wit more than made up for her lack of schooling. Equally impressive was her refusal to be made uncomfortable by facts; indeed, she appeared not to care whether things were true. Despite Sir Charles's verbal assaults against her—assaults that would have shaken most people—she continued to hold her ground and, if middle distance existed between sincerity and sarcasm, she managed to claim it. There was also the matter of Mrs. Woodhull's insolent confidence. She had the nerve to tell Sir Charles that his "kind of thinking implied damaging absolutes." Infuriating him was the thought that, on this point, she might have been right.

CHAPTER FOUR

The trial's outcome.

When it came time for Mr. Garnett to defend himself, he entered the dock, stood stiffly, looked stony-faced, and explained that the material in question had been placed in the Reading Room according to its rules and regulations . . . that, according to the library's records, there had been only one inquiry about the material in question, which was a pamphlet about Mrs. Woodhull—scarcely a confirmation of wide British interest in the subject. Nonetheless, he had the material locked up in a special cabinet. His role as the keeper of the printed books called on him to provide a wide selection of literature. It was his duty to make available any other published material about Mrs. Woodhull, whose bias deemed it personally unfavorable. On principle, he would not remove any work of value simply because it was called into question based on a personal opinion that ran counter to the purpose of the British Museum Library.

Not a single person in the courtroom would consider questioning the accuracy of the information Mr. Garnett conveyed, but his arid facts were no match for the story of Mrs. Woodhull's life with its lush details. Members of the jury were willing to set aside their insular sense of Englishness to be transported to another place entirely. This left Sir Charles with the unenviable task of convincing them to return to a less enticing reality. His argument was dominated by the iron logic for which he was renowned: i's dotted, t's crossed. He reminded the jury that, as a public institution, the British Museum Library had a duty to make available all literature. He told them that the Reading Room acquired hundreds of publications a year, and that it would take almost as many libel experts to read through them. "Fancy hundreds of experts let loose in the British Museum to scrutinize the books and periodicals, seeking a needle of libel in a bundle of literary hay," he said.

Sir Charles described Mrs. Woodhull as the product of a family that considered litigation as a practiced means of achieving their objectives and, simultaneously, awarded them with the kind of publicity that advanced their nefarious methods of earning income. He pointed out that Mrs. Woodhull had been a lecturer and publisher who, before landing on British shores, had expressed her opinions in America on such headline-grabbing topics as free love and women's rights. He told them that those who dazzle tend to illuminate and obscure the facts at the same time. That Mrs. Woodhull was known in America as a freethinker and that often, those who are the most thin-skinned about criticism are the very freethinkers who deliberately flout societal customs and who are contemptuous of institutions—the very bulwark of a civilization. Mrs. Woodhull had belonged to any and every social reform, no matter the cause and often for her own edification. Controversy was her oxygen. Sir Charles argued that, as someone attracted to high drama, she was happy to provoke it in any way that she fancied, and happier still with its disruptive consequences. By repeatedly confiding in the American press of her own free will, she had put herself indelibly into the public arena.

Mrs. Woodhull was in the business of reinventing her past. The autobiographical stories with which she entertained the courtroom were beguiling, but were they even true? She had once described to the press her happy childhood in a crisply painted white home surrounded by lovingly tended flowers. Sir Charles went so far as to suggest that Mrs. Woodhull had instigated a libel suit against the museum, its trustees, and Mr. Garnett with the sole purpose of absolving her from the embarrassing revelations—true or not—found in the publications in question.

Having frustrated every one of Sir Charles's efforts to force her to admit anything the publications accused her of, Mrs. Woodhull claimed that they were part of an organized smear campaign against her because she was a woman who spoke out against inequality. She insisted that damages, however small, would be satisfaction for the injuries that had befallen her integrity. Sir Charles emphasized that the publications to which Mrs. Woodhull objected had been placed on the Reading Room shelves under statutory power and, at the time they were acquired, it had not been known if, in fact, they contained any libelous material.

The London *Times* reported that it was next to impossible to convey the drama during the four days of the trial's jarring reveals and vicious ripostes. Both parties refused to back down, but, to be fair, neither was entirely wrong. Caught between Martins's family bank and the British Museum—two eminent British institutions—the judge instructed the jury members in a way most likely to satisfy all concerned. He pointed out that "nothing could be graver than anything affecting [Mrs. Woodhull's] character" and that, because she did not desire to put the price of her reputation into her husband's pockets, no heavy damages were asked for. He told them that, equally important was the British Library's "high duty imposed upon it to guard over the interest of the public."

After protracted deliberation, the jury found that the material housed in the British Museum Library to which Mrs. Woodhull objected was libelous by the letter of the law, but that the museum defendants were not plausibly guilty, since it wasn't their duty to have known in advance that the catalog contained libels. To expect that of them in the future would create an untenable state of affairs.

The trial concluded with Mrs. Woodhull being awarded £1 in damages and obliged to pay the museum's legal costs of £508. She decided not to press the case on appeal. When notified of this, the museum trustees breathed a collective sigh of relief.

CHAPTER FIVE

He tries to make sense of what happened.

Mr. Garnett could do nothing to restore the dignity he regrettably lost during the trial, but he was grateful that, shortly after the ruling, there were proposed changes in the law exempting libraries in Great Britain from future libel charges. This, however, did not dislodge his unease that an American woman with no formal education—the daughter of a petty criminal, no less—had attempted to smear his reputation and that of his beloved library. Convinced that Mrs. Woodhull's extravagant peculiarities and outsized aspirations would continue to be a threat in some yet-to-be defined way, he decided to continue to research her background on his own time. In light of the many years of working with archival material found in the Reading Room, he assumed that this would be a straightforward task. He started with the obvious.

The obvious, according to Mr. Garnett, was that Britain had history while America had geography. Adjusting his spectacles, he bent over his desk to study a large map of the United States in order to locate Homer, Ohio, Mrs. Woodhull's recorded place of birth. When he finally found it, he couldn't help but think that the man who named it after the presumed author of *The Iliad* and *The Odyssey* must have had a misplaced sense of grandeur. Homer turned out to be a tiny settlement surrounded by the grasslands of America's Middlewestern frontier. Located some forty miles from the state's capital and situated on a single rutted track less than half a mile long from end to end, the obscure outpost consisted of a handful of houses, a small church, a one-room schoolhouse, and a general store that doubled as the town's post office.

The record of where Mrs. Woodhull was born listed the year of her birth as 1838—a year, Mr. Garnett would have learned, that featured as many remarkable inventions in America as it did violent cruelties: twin brothers from Maine had patented the first steam-powered threshing machine at the same time slavery was driving the economy of the South. Samuel Morse demonstrated his invention of the electric telegraph employing a code made up of dots and dashes at the same time as another Samuel, Samuel Colt, conceived of a multi-shot revolver to improve the chances of inflicting death. Ralph Waldo Emerson published his influential essay "Nature," expressing the relationship between the soul and the surrounding world while some four thousand Cherokee Indians were dying from exposure, disease, and starvation. They had been forcibly removed from their ancestral homelands in the Southeastern United States and relocated in areas designated "Indian Territory," west of the Mississippi River. Among the American notables born that year were Cleveland Abbe, who would become a brilliant meteorologist advocating time zones, and John Wilkes Booth, who would become a second-rate actor and Abraham Lincoln's assassin.

Mr. Garnett wouldn't have been able to locate a record of birth for Mrs. Woodhull's father, Reuben Buckman Claflin—there is none—though census enumerations identify Massachusetts as his place of birth and allowed a near calculation that he and his twin brother were born in 1796—the first two of thirteen children. Mr. Garnett's investigation revealed that Mr. Claflin came from the impoverished branch of a family that had its beginnings five generations earlier when a Scottish mercenary soldier arrived in the New World in 1661. Combing through the little material Mr. Garnett could find on the family, he located a dated photograph of a man referred to as Buck Claflin. Buck was Mrs. Woodhull's father. His pallid face was almost entirely engulfed by a weedy beard. He had a jutted brow and a hawk nose and he wore a black patch over a sightless eye. Had he inspected the photo at closer range, Mr. Garnett would have undoubtedly decided that Mr. Claflin's other eye—the working one—had a nasty glint. Buck Claflin married a woman by the name of Roxanna "Roxy" Hummel in 1825. Mr. Garnett's search for clues about her revealed that she was born to unmarried parents. A photo of her pictured a drably dressed, bone-thin woman with deep lines on her leathery face that made it look like a drawstring purse. She had small eyes and a threadlike, tight mouth that seemed to have been dragged down by what must have been a number of tragedies.

Mr. Garnett was able to take what he discovered about the Claflins in stride until he learned that Roxanna had descended from a colony of German Jews who had married into a tribe of Susquehannock Indians. That would have been when his imagination forced its way past his disciplined mind and began to run riot.

Described by the Europeans as a "giant-like people," the Susquehannocks were among the most formidable Native American tribes of the time.

CHAPTER SIX

Between the dead and the living.

Named after the nineteen-year-old queen of England whose coronation had taken place that same year, Victoria was the seventh of ten
children, six of whom survived until maturity.

She was born a world apart from the gilded rooms of Kensington Palace. The Claflins' unpainted wreck of a one-story wooden
shack was strewn with sleeping mats and beds never made and rarely
changed. The number of people living on the property swelled when
Buck's twin brother, his wife, and their children took up residency in
the barn. The only running water was a nearby stream, and, with no
outhouse, Victoria was forced to dig holes in the ground to relieve
herself. "We were treated with a cruelty that still beclouds the memory of my early days," she recalled during the course of the libel trial,
remembering a childhood of begging for food from the neighbors.
There was an undercurrent of menace in the household to which her
parents contributed equally with their own brand of tyranny. Buck
soaked braided willow switches in a barrel of rainwater, using them to
whip the children flesh-wound raw for no reason. Roxanna—always a
moment away from plunging into crazed psychodrama—would clasp
her children in ecstatic affection, then sadistically torment them and
clap hysterically when they cried. What threatened their very lives
was her belief in mesmerism.

Franz Anton Mesmer was an Austrian physician who practiced in
Europe and somehow managed to project medical authority despite
his habit of wearing lilac taffeta robes during business hours. According to him, there were positive and negative currents passing through a
magnetic fluid in humans, and any blockage to its circulation resulted

in an imbalance that led to physical ailments. Inducing a mesmerized state[1] enabled the practitioner to manipulate the magnetic force and remove the obstacle causing the condition. Restoring this balance required placing the patient in a trance. Once awakened, they had no memory of what had transpired but claimed that their former ills had disappeared.

Roxanna tried her hand at inducing a mesmerized state with her infant children, who suffered from the cholera and typhus that swept through Homer. The fact that two died while she ministered to them did nothing to dissuade her from believing in otherworldly powers. Her own grim childhood had been steeped in superstition: omens of death and illness made themselves known when a dog howled near a window or a fruit tree blossomed in the fall.

Roxanna's mental instability as an adult was fed by a religious fervor. An illiterate who could repeat entire passages of the Bible once read to her, she prayed outside, even in the bitterly cold Midwestern winters, and, when the neighbors complained of her loud, senseless orations, often in German, she insisted that God was speaking through her in a divine language.

Forty years before Roxanna was braying to the night sky invoking God, the Methodist movement seeded itself in the Church of England; after spreading among Britain's working class as a separate denomination, it crossed the Atlantic and fragmented into various forms of worship. Itinerant preachers would seek out people to convert in the more remote frontier locations. Lay preachers known as circuit riders arrived on horseback in rural towns to organize the kind of revival meetings attended by Roxanna. Standing behind a pulpit under a makeshift tent, where damp ground was covered with sawdust, the preacher would conjure visions of fire, brimstone, and spitting oil in the pit of Hell.

"Can you see the fiery billows? Can you hear the yells and groans of the damned roaring under the burning wrath of an angry God?" the preacher demanded to know. Only after the tumult had reached its peak did he dangle the possibility of salvation, "God said those who believeth in me shall be saved!" A rhythmic reply—*Amen!*—would arise in unison from the crowd, arms branching up to the heavens.

Tormented into a transfixed state by the preacher's fiery words, members of the congregation would step forward to confess their sins. The more they confessed, the more they were encouraged. "Those who believeth not in me shall be condemned!" the preacher bellowed. Hallelujahs poured forth from the congregation. Enticed by the promise of spiritual cleansing, Roxanna would rise from the wooden bench, clasp her hands together, pitch her head back, sway her body to and fro, step into the aisle, and—joining the others trembling in unison from ecstatic anguish over past actions—she would repent.

"A loving and kind God have mercy, have pity and take away the stain of my transgressions! Wash me! Cleanse me from guilt! Let me be pure again, for I admit my shamed deed. Create in me a new clean heart filled with right desires! Restore for me the joy of your salvation!"

Emerging from her formerly sinful state—sweat streaming down her face and lips crusted with dried white spittle—Roxanna was born again.

•   •   •

By age three, Victoria had absorbed the rhythms of the evangelical sermons taking place under the tents in Homer. At four, she began to mimic her mother's theatrical outpourings to unseen forces. At five, she described transcendent visits to the netherworld, led by spirit guides. At six—her mind ablaze with imagination—Victoria regaled neighborhood children with folklore and prophecies. What little schooling she was given came in broken intervals, but like Roxanna, she possessed preternatural recall, and like Buck, she had a natural aptitude for mathematics.

While Victoria was teaching herself to read and her mother was being born again and again, her father was becoming familiar enough with the law to learn ways around it. Various get-rich schemes resulted in enough ill-gotten money for him to purchase a gristmill in town that he never actually ran but insured for $500. When it burned to the ground in the dead of winter, suspicion among the townspeople was that he set fire to it for the insurance payment.

Buck wasn't afraid of the law—there was no method of enforcing it in Homer. It was the mob he was afraid of. More precisely, Buck feared the method the townspeople of Homer would use to express their displeasure with him: the planned punishment was an English export—tar and feathering.[2] Tipped off, Buck fled in the middle of the night, leaving his family behind. Days later, it was discovered that, during his brief period of volunteering as the town's postmaster, he'd been steaming open the envelopes of any mail containing money. That stolen money paid for a four-wheeled cart roofed with canvas that he bought in the next town. By the time the Claflins reassembled, Buck was on a one-man crime spree looking for his next easy mark. Thanks to the livery horse he'd borrowed but neglected to return to its owner, he was able to take to the road with his family.

•   •   •

Because, during her testimony at the libel trial, Mrs. Woodhull spoke freely of the afterlife, it is likely that Mr. Garnett's research about her included her fellow American Phineas Taylor Barnum, who'd had an impact on her life at a young age.

P. T. Barnum was a pioneer of staged productions—a genius show-man who had mastered the phenomenon of inventing hoaxes and monetizing them as popular entertainment. It's difficult to understate just how reprehensible his instincts had to be in order to have become rich by the time he was twenty-five.

Barnum exploited an 1835 loophole in New York—a state that had already outlawed slavery—by paying $1,000 (half borrowed) for a twelve-month lease on an enslaved Black woman by the name of Joice Heth. She was blind, paralyzed in one arm and both legs, and had arthritis in her hands. Barnum promoted her as a venerated relic of history, and, billing her as George Washington's 161-year-old former nurse, he exhibited her in a rented room on lower Broadway in New York he called "the American Museum," where he forced her to sing hymns she had purportedly taught Washington when he was a boy. The act proved to be a moneymaker and Barnum booked her in doz-ens of Northeast cities. When she died ten months into the twelve-month lease agreement, he arranged for a two-month public autopsy to demonstrate her actual age. Spectators paid fifty cents each.

Among other exhibitions in Barnum's American Museum were a four-year-old boy, standing not quite two feet high and dressed in a miniature uniform, billed as General Tom Thumb. There was also the embalmed "Feejee Mermaid"—the product of stitching the head and body of a monkey onto the tail of a large fish. Operating with the belief that people were willing to be played as long as they felt that they were getting value, Barnum created a darkened "Moral Lecture Room" in which the "hereafter" could be seen. Muted mood music could be heard as spectral figures emerged to describe life on the other side.

These performances might have been dubious, but they offered a far more optimistic idea of spiritual intervention than the one featuring threats of an unforgiving hellfire. God-fearing people were drawn to the consolation offered in the possibility that the dead were willing to make themselves known in regenerative ways. A flowing conduit to this belief was the recently invented telegraph, erasing the boundaries of time and space with unseen messages sent long-distance through the air. If it was possible to send a message from one place to another far away, what prevented the spirits from doing the same?

Whether they be fraudsters or gifted with precognitive powers, mediums and clairvoyants called their messages "spiritual telegraphs" and followed a similar routine. To frame the spirit world in a way to which the living could relate, it was explained that spirits were capable of sight, sound, sometimes even smell, but that they needed assistance, presumably from the person who was paying money to make the connection.

The "Barnum effect" was the technique of deliberately drawing out the exchange between clairvoyant and her target. Keeping the exchange as general as possible increased the likelihood of chance connections. The clairvoyant might begin incoherently, and, after emerging from a dreamlike state, speak slowly, cautiously, as if listening to an unseen entity. In fact, she was giving herself time to ascertain how the subject was responding: a subtle nod, a smile, a simple shift in body language—these would signal to the clairvoyant if her high-probability guesses were heading in the right direction.

Working to the clairvoyant's advantage was confirmation bias, the human tendency to recall or interpret information in a way that supports one's prior beliefs. If all went according to plan, the subject would make the connections for the clairvoyant rather than the reverse. Some clairvoyants were better than others. The exceptional ones were brilliant at manipulating what was in a subject's mind and playing their truths back to them. Most of the sessions would conclude with a stock "he loves you": the kind of simple message that offered a reassuring farewell from the spirit and, at the same time, confirmed the bias in spiritual beliefs.

It was sheer performance and, by its very nature, a contrivance, but the number of people who suspected clairvoyancy to be fraud was matched by the number of believers, and this gave rise to a broader issue: claiming to be a clairvoyant was one of the few ways a woman could procure a livelihood outside of prostitution.

Capturing the public's imagination were the Fox sisters from Rochester, New York, who could summon a spirit aptly named Mr. Splitfoot. Instructing him to "do as I do," one of the two would clap her hands a given number of times, whereupon the illusive Mr. Splitfoot would repeat the same number of times with a clicking sound. Never mind that the other sister sitting nearby was producing that clicking sound by cracking her toe joints. The sisters were performing their otherworldly powers onstage at seventy-five cents a ticket until P. T. Barnum—marketer extraordinaire—promoted them as child preachers able to communicate with the dead. This they did three times a day for a dollar per person.

News that the Fox sisters were getting rich touring the country was all Buck needed to hear to claim that Victoria, twelve years old at the time, and her younger sister, Tennessee, known as Tennie, were also able to communicate with the dead.

CHAPTER SEVEN

Selling the hereafter.

Buck taught Victoria and Tennie sleight-of-hand tricks. He drilled them on how to interpret facial gestures and to read body language. He schooled them on how to moderate their voices. And, when he thought they were ready to fleece the paying public, he painted the family's covered wagon a vibrant red so that it could be easily seen at a distance and he affixed a large sign on its side.

AMAZING CHILD CLAIRVOYANTS.

Crisscrossing the Midwest in a covered wagon, the family camped on the outskirts of small towns and, if Buck smelled opportunity, he would pay for a notice in the local paper advertising Victoria and Tennie as child clairvoyants scheduled to perform on a single evening. Roxanna would sell tickets in front of the town hall in which a makeshift stage had been constructed. Buck would station himself at the entrance to spot the most gullible looking coming through the door. One by one, he would pull them aside and invite them to write the name of the person they wanted to contact in the afterlife on the back of their ticket.

"Good citizens, we meet here tonight in a time of stress to bring comfort to troubled minds and ease for broken hearts," was how Buck would greet the audience after they were seated and before ushering Victoria and Tennie onto the stage to join him. "I'm proud to say that these two girls, my daughters, will employ their unique facilities to enable you to communicate with those cherished members of your family who are wrongly referred to as 'departed.'"

He would move to the farthest end of the hall and hold up a ticket with a name on the back, pointing out that neither of his daughters was able read the ticket from the stage. One of the two of them would call out a name—not the name on the ticket Buck was holding up, but a name that he knew another customer had written on the back of their own ticket. That name was the one Buck told to Victoria or Tennie before ushering them both onto the stage. "There is a spirit in the room. Is anyone in the audience related to John Smith?" asked whichever of the two girls Buck had given that name.

"That's my son!" or "That's my husband!" came a woman's doleful cry.

So successful were Victoria and Tennie at making perception look like reality that they ended up supporting the extended Claflin family.

Victoria's talent of persuasion made her feel alive, but it was Tennie who enjoyed the public's attention. She kept her manner elusive in a way that suggested different things to different people and drew on her feverish imagination to simulate communicating with spirits. Buck subtracted two years from her already-young age and ran an ad in a Columbus, Ohio, newspaper promoting her telepathic gifts.

A Wonderful Child
Miss Tennessee Claflin

This young lady has been travelling since she was eleven years old, and has been endowed from her birth with a supernatural gift to such an astonishing degree that she convinces the most skeptical of her wonderful power.

She gives information on lost money or property, identifying the person or persons concerned with so much certainty as scarily to leave a doubt of their guilt.

When required, she will go into an unconscious state and travel to any part of the world, hunt up absent friends, and through her, they will tell their inquiring friend their situation and whereabouts, with all the events in life since they last met.

She may be consulted in her room, United States Hotel, High Street, Columbus, from the hours of eight o'clock A.M. to nine o'clock P.M.

Price of consultation $1.00.

Before the ad appeared, Buck visited the city's cemetery and copied information from its tombstones. He might have also purchased a Blue Book that had been compiled by an enterprising local author and provided more fulsome information about local families.

Tennie's thirteen-hour days were made more arduous by the need to feign the belief in spirits when she probably didn't. Victoria might have believed. Superstition was that the seventh child born in a household would possess the gift of second sight and the powers to heal. Victoria was a seventh child and, at an early age, she had insisted that she was visited by an apparition, who, appearing as a nobleman clad in a white Grecian tunic, prophesied that she would emerge from poverty to find "wealth and fame in a city on water crowded with ships" and become "a leader of people."

Victoria's visitation might have been fantasy sowed by an overactive imagination. Her trance might have been nothing more than a welcomed reprieve from a squalid childhood. Perhaps she felt safer in a fictional world. If she did truly believe in an omnipotent world beyond rationality in which thoughts could bring an event to pass, it would have been the same intangible but wholly real belief she had in herself.

Victoria and Tennie survived abusive parents by acquiring a practical shrewdness and a keen sense of self-preservation. Providence

Tennessee Claflin was undisturbed by scruples and beautiful enough to believe that anything she did was right simply because she did it.

played a part by ensuring that they defied genetics—both were as physically beautiful as their parents were ugly. Victoria's beauty was refined; Tennie's was sensuous. Victoria had a tendency to be overly serious; Tennie had a penchant for theatricality.

When it came to the intricacies of human behavior, the two girls were intuitively smart, particularly with men. They had to be. The nineteenth-century patriarchal family in America was based on a premise that the only person recognized by law and public opinion was either the father or the husband, and both had the right to put their children to work. No one objected when Buck installed Victoria and Tennie as mediums in boardinghouse parlors and forced them to work grueling hours.

Spiritualist séances, hands-on healing, fortune-telling—these were the practices that occupied Victoria's dislocated childhood. When the Claflin family was run out of town for their shady activities, Buck would simply relocate them to another town and continue to trade in the currencies of people's needs and wants. This was the disorienting pattern of Victoria's life until the clan returned to Ohio and moved in with the eldest and married Claflin daughter.

CHAPTER EIGHT

For better and, too often, for worse.

Victoria developed a sense of emotional intelligence through the same necessity with which a blind person who, having lost their sight when young, developed acute hearing.

Buck put her to work for months on end until the dank winter weather settled in her bones. By Victoria's accounts, written when she was an adult, she had been a child without a childhood. It was only when her faltering health turned into rheumatism that threatened the family's income that her father sought the services of a doctor—"doctor" being an overly generous description. The medical profession hadn't yet set standards for practice, and training consisted only of reading medical books over the course of a few months.

Twice Victoria's age of fourteen, handsome and unmarried, Dr. Canning Woodhull arrived in Ohio from New York with a surface sheen of respectability. A few short months after he tended to Victoria, she agreed to marry him with the belief that taking a chance as a wife to a man she barely knew was preferable to remaining the abused and exploited daughter of a man she knew too well.

In 1853, the newlyweds left Ohio for Chicago, a growing city that promised Canning more income.

Unacquainted with the city of Chicago—or, for that matter, Illinois—Mr. Garnett would have done what he would do with any subject about which he was not familiar: he researched. He learned that seventeenth-century French explorers and fur traders had seen the territory that would eventually form the Illinois settlement. Their journals included descriptions of the collaborative interactions they had with the indigenous Potawatomi people. That remained the case until Lake Michigan was seen as a crucial link connecting a line of waterways and, arming itself with the excuse of progress, the U.S. government created legislation that forced the Potawatomi people to move onto reservations farther west. What had been the tribe's homeland was sold by the federal government to finance the Illinois and Michigan Canal.

Due largely to the railroads that began to knit America into a more cohesive whole, Chicago was well positioned to take advantage of myriad trade opportunities. Victoria was certain that she would thrive there for no other reason than the prophecy foretold by her childhood spirit guide: that one day she would find wealth in a city on the water.

Thrive in Chicago Victoria did—but only at first, and not for very long. Her marriage to Canning Woodhull delivered on the promise of a prosperous metropolis that hugged the shores of one of the largest known lakes, but Canning proved to be an alcoholic and morphine addict who disappeared for unaccounted stretches. Still a girl herself, Victoria wasn't sure what to expect after he made her pregnant, or what would befall her when she gave birth.

Canning was nowhere to be found when she felt the dull ache of back pain. Muted cramps worked their way into a slow rhythm, and she calmed herself with the tapping of rain against the window. By nightfall, wind gusts from nearby Lake Michigan made the cold-water flat's frigid air turn Victoria's panting into sputtering mists. A woman in the building heard the screams and arrived in time for Victoria's final heave. After the excruciating pain receded, Victoria listened for a baby's cry.

He was alive but listless. She named him Byron, after the admired British poet—a cruelly ironic choice: the baby was born with disabilities and his speech would forever consist of a series of grunts.

Trapped in a system that oppressed her gender in every conceivable way, Victoria's life was dictated, first, by her exploitative father, who capitalized on her talents, then, by her husband, an addict who wasted whatever money she had made until none was left. English common law formed the basis for American law. Neither system provided for the rights of a married woman and almost always crushed any ambitions they might have had for themselves. To take control of her future, Victoria had to take charge of the lives of her husband and son. With unrealistic hope and no idea what she would do when they got there, she decided that they should cross the country and start again. Canning, unemployable in Chicago, went along with her proposition that they move to San Francisco.

Mr. Garnett—a skillful collector of details—calculated the year Victoria left Chicago to be in 1857. That would have made her no older than nineteen. If one were to ask him why he continued researching Mrs. Woodhull despite the resolution of her libel suit against him, he would have insisted that she represented a future threat, though to what he could not say—he only knew that she was an agent of chaos whose motives were unknown and whose actions were unpredictable. Her claims of life-altering spiritual visitations led Mr. Garnett to pursue a wider range of investigation on the subject, which, in turn, introduced him to Joseph Smith.

Smith's past revolved around an assertion that, at eighteen, he had been visited by an angel directing him to a cave not far from his family's home in Western New York. Inside the cave were gold plates on which were inscribed strange characters. He deemed the unknown script to be "reformed Egyptian," which was undecipherable without the aid of magic peep-stones—small, black, shining stones. Smith referred to the stones as "interpreters," whose purpose was to translate and receive revelations. He claimed that he was given two of these seer-stones by another angel, and that, by looking through holes in these stones, he was able to interpret the golden plates. Whether they were the imaginings of a zealot or the spiritual truths of a prophet, Smith's interpretations became the basis of what would become his Book of Mormon—the foundational document for the church he started in a farmhouse with a congregation numbering six people.

With further research, Mr. Garnett would have learned that the Mormons attempted to establish a self-sufficient community in Ohio, but that their isolation earned distrust from the mainstream Christian churchgoers who did an un-Christian thing by tar and feathering Smith. Driven out of Ohio, he led his congregation to Illinois, where they were met by largely unwelcoming Methodists who decided that it was one thing to speak in tongues, and another thing entirely when Mormon men declared that God granted them multiple wives. God might have stopped counting by the time Smith accumulated forty wives, some already married and one as young as fourteen years old. The townspeople, however, had not. They took matters into their own hands and murdered Joseph Smith, thereby accomplishing two things that wouldn't have occurred otherwise: galvanizing the Mormon community and increasing its membership.

I'm certain that Mr. Garnett did his best to clear his mind of any prejudice while giving due consideration to Mormonism, a radically different belief system to his own. However, it is likely he thought that if a person was inclined to wrestle with spiritual issues, that person might more appropriately do it away from the public glare, preferably within a stable institution—the Church of England, for example. It should come as no surprise that Mr. Garnett was a practicing Anglican challenged by the sheer strangeness of a religion based on someone claiming to be God's human spokesperson. And even more difficult to believe: a spokesperson who offered the mythical lure of golden tablets on which were written a script that only that claimant could translate.

That was precisely what Samuel Brannan believed.

Determined to build a Mormon city away from the hostility the church was experiencing in their own country, Brannan, along with some 238 Mormon followers, boarded a ship that embarked from New York City for the Mexican territory of California. During the six months he and his congregation were at sea, the ever-changing United States had gone to war with Mexico. By the time the Mormons sailed into San Francisco Bay, California was no longer part of Mexico, but of America.

Brannan waited in San Francisco for the arrival of another Mormon, Brigham Young, who was leading 150 more Mormons from the Midwest—not by ship, but over four thousand grueling miles in a wagon train. When Young reached Utah and learned of California's vast resources, he reasoned that the state's abundance would attract other settlers likely to turn against the Mormons. It was for that reason that he settled his congregation farther east, near the Great Salt

Lake. Samuel Brannan remained in California and built a personal fortune by servicing the enormous inflow of settlers. His moneymaking endeavors included constructing flour mills and launching San Francisco's first newspaper.

Then something else came up—something that would change everything.

CHAPTER NINE

Fate leads the willing.

On certain rare occasions, history is shaped with very simple tasks by ordinary people in the midst of an average day. In 1848, John Sutter, living in Northern California, paid a carpenter to build a water-powered sawmill along the river that abutted his land. The carpenter found flakes of gold in the streambed.

The first wave of prospectors were men with pioneering experience from western parts of the U.S. Territories. Word spread quickly and, a year later, some three hundred thousand people, referred to in time as "forty-niners," arrived to stake claims on the parcels of land residing on either side of that same river. Coming there on horseback, in covered wagons, and by clipper ships, most expected gold to be located on the surface of the river's silt deposit. They soon discovered that they would have to dig for it.

The gritty willingness to believe what the American West had to offer wasn't confined to those living in America: men came from Mexico, Peru, Chile, Argentina, Hawaii, Australia, New Zealand, Britain, Germany, Italy, Greece, and Russia. France held lotteries to get there. Arriving by ship without any real knowledge of the language, the winners became known as "Keskydees," possibly from the Frenchmen's slang for the invariable phrase *Qu'est-ce qu'il dit?*: "What did he say?"

Samuel Brannan was not one to get his hands dirty digging for gold, but it was gold that swelled his investments to a vast fortune. Mining camps cropped up with names like Red Dog, Angels, and Poker Flat and brought with them every human necessity crying out for ordinary convenience. Brannan had asked the right question: Why mine gold

Early days of California's Gold Rush

when you can sell shovels? He opened a general store. It was soon sell-ing the current equivalent of $150,000 in goods a day, seven days a week. He opened another store, and then a third.

On the other side of the country at the time was Horace Greeley, an economic reformer from the working class, born poor and plainly educated in a small New England town. As a boy, he served as an apprentice at printing businesses before finding employment setting print on a country newspaper. Not much later, Greeley moved to New York, and, when given the chance, he wrote for the journals he put to type. At twenty-three, he borrowed money to launch *The New-Yorker,* a literary magazine.[1] It was a financial failure. Undeterred, he launched a newspaper in 1841, the *New-York Tribune,* instilling it with a progres-sive editorial ethos that reflected his own. At the inexpensive cost of two cents per weekly edition, the *Tribune* gathered a wide working-class appeal in rural towns and became the nation's most influential newspaper.

Greeley was an ardent abolitionist who helped found the Repub-lican Party, but it was as a journalist that he embarked on a cross-country journey to understand for himself what was happening on the other side of the U.S. Territories. The dispatches he wrote along the way ran in the *New-York Tribune*.[2] After returning to the East Coast, his editorial in the newspaper urged communities to part with their young men for the promise of opportunities on the other side of the country.

"Go West, young man, go West and grow up with the country," he wrote. One who did was twenty-nine-year-old Samuel Langhorne Clemens. Born three years before Victoria, Clemens arrived on the West Coast after she did. Some twenty years later, they would both be living in the same city in another country entirely.

Clemens grew up in the backwater of Hannibal, Missouri. He was a printer's apprentice before training as a steamboat pilot on the Mississippi River. "Mark twain" was a boatman's warning that the river was only two fathoms deep—the minimum depth for safe navigation. Clemens appropriated the expression as a pen name in 1863 when he became a reporter in Nevada. It was as Mark Twain that he came to San Francisco after writing a short story based on something he had heard from a bartender. Reprinted in newspapers on both coasts, "The Celebrated Jumping Frog of Calaveras County" launched Twain's career as a writer.

Mark Twain,
by any other name

San Francisco in its original manifestation was a makeshift accumulation of tents and wooden hovels. Victoria and her family arrived there in 1857, seven years after the first gold strike. By that time, its timber mining shacks had given way to brick houses; its mud streets had been paved with cobblestones and lit with gaslights; its harbor, fittingly named Golden Gate—which had been clogged by sailing vessels crowded with newcomers hoping to grab their share of gold— was a model in efficiency loading and unloading passengers and cargo. Samuel Brannan, already rich from commerce, had been made even more so by purchasing three thousand acres in Napa Valley, creating a resort catering to San Francisco's wealthy, and calling it Calistoga.

The gold mined in California generated millions of dollars, but crossing America to get there required five months at least. A start in the spring increased the odds of traveling safely across the Sierra Nevada mountains before the first heavy snowfall. The route on the other side of the range went through the rolling prairies, past graz- ing buffalos numbering in the millions. By the end of the nineteenth century, that number was reduced to only a few hundred. Dooming the buffalo was the U.S. government's post–Civil War solution to what it considered the country's "Indian problem." To make way for the railroads and stagecoach lines, the government forced Native Ameri- cans onto allotted lands, and then it shrank those allotted lands, treaty by reneged treaty. Nearly all the tribes in the Great Plains had lived alongside herds of buffalo. They used the skins for their tents and depended on the meat as a source of food. Killing off buffalo starved the tribes that fought back. Mr. Garnett was not aware of this piti- less fact, but he knew that Buffalo Bill Cody's traveling show toured England and Wales, and that it featured hundreds of Native Ameri- cans performing their own demise by reenacting battles with the U.S. Army.

In his capacity as a historian, Mr. Garnett would have had no choice but to acknowledge the recorded fact that every nation produces atrocities of its own. Buffalo Bill's show—part circus, part rodeo—was a reminder that there was no great power at some point in its history whose elevation was exempt from the exploitation of others, whether those others were living on the same land or, in the case of Great Britain, those living in other parts of the world. True, British imperi- alism had brought progress, but it also led to large-scale decimation of indigenous people and the eradication of their cultures and religions.

As for details of the life Victoria led in San Francisco, the scattered facts Mr. Garnett found were more confusing than revelatory. The method of travel that transported her along with her family may have been a ship but, given the grim state of their financial affairs, how they managed to afford a place to live once they arrived in San Francisco remains a mystery. Records Mr. Garnett unearthed were few and little can be inferred. What was clear was that the San Francisco to which Victoria arrived had become a densely urban, unmistakably Western city teeming with miners, outnumbering women twenty to one. None of those men would have been interested in Victoria as a clairvoyant, but a fair number would have been willing to pay to have sex with her. By Victoria's own account, she was working first as a seamstress and then selling cigars in a saloon. During the course of the libel trial, Sir Charles had forced her to admit that she had been an actress—shorthand for a part-time prostitute.

Just how Victoria had supported her son and a husband lost in a fog of addiction remains her own version of the truth, but, after a year of whatever it required, she decided to return to the East Coast. San Francisco had not been the city surrounded by ships sanctioned by the spirits—the one they foretold would bring her fame and wealth—so it was fortuitous that she had another of her spiritual visitations. This time, the spectral figure took the form of Tennie beckoning her to come home.

CHAPTER TEN

America's fondness for grifters.

During the early years of Victoria's marriage to Canning Woodhull, antislavery activists like Horace Greeley who opposed the expansion of slavery into America's western territories founded the Republican Party.

Believing Abraham Lincoln to be a future obstacle to their own practice of slavery, Southern states threatened secession when he was elected America's first Republican president. To defend their states, young men in the North and South organized independent military units. Ohio—with its central location—remained politically divided by a grassroots element of the Democratic Party that openly opposed President Lincoln's policies.

The year Victoria had settled her family in San Francisco, Buck and his clan were crisscrossing Ohio, traveling from one small town to the next, plying their questionable trade from the back of a wagon. They could hear the muffled rumblings of Union soldiers heading south and, at closer range, the rhythmic sounds of canteens banging against thighs of those marching into what would be the onslaught of America's Civil War.

The war began on April 12, 1861, when Confederate troops fired on Union soldiers at Fort Sumter in South Carolina, and it took only three months to tear the country apart. Death entered the harrowing battlefields with bloody delirium, sustained by the productive capacities of the nation's Industrial Revolution, the output of which produced fatality rates beyond anyone's imagination.

Death offered itself gladly to writers as inspiration. "I saw battle-corpses, myriads of them, / And the white skeletons of young men, I saw them, / I saw the debris and debris of all the slain soldiers of the war," Walt Whitman wrote after volunteering to nurse soldiers and seeing things that he could not unsee. A line from a poem by Henry Wadsworth Longfellow, whose son and nephew were severely wounded in action, describes the bedlam: "Nameless and dateless; sentinel or scout / Shot down in skirmish, or disastrous rout / Of battle."

Like a giant, monstrous wave, Death spread itself over an era that created mass armies ignorant of the transmission of infectious diseases: more than twice the number killed fighting in the Civil War died from tuberculosis, dysentery, malaria, typhoid fever, and syphilis.

During America's four-year Civil War, at least half of those killed in battle or dead from sickness were buried in shallow graves and without identification.

With chances of dying in the war at one in four, the number of men who would never return home grew into the thousands. Neither the Union nor the Confederate army had procedures for notifying next of kin, leaving them to grieve when the observance of grief itself was made impossible. When institutional religions proved unable to provide solace, the bereaved began to turn toward the possibility of an afterlife where the dead were willing to engage with the living.

The invention of the telegraph suggested to some the possibility of communication from across the divide. At the same time, religious revivals offered an alternative to collapsing belief systems. Which was the original disruptor—or was one the consequence of the other?

Few pressed a death-denying possibility of speaking to the dead more convincingly than Buck. When Victoria married, he was left with a single source of income and put Tennie to work, first as a fortune teller who had the gift of communicating with the spirit world, and next as a faith healer with a "clairvoyant eye." Buck added a third swindle to her repertoire after duping a bookseller into allowing him to hold on to a medical dictionary overnight, during which time he copied the physical ailments listed in the book. Rather than buying the book the next morning as was promised, Buck returned the book and used the terms he copied from it to print labels with Tennie's image that would feature on bottles of an elixir.

Roxanna cooked her own potion of vegetable oils in a cauldron behind the wagon. Buck added the moonshine liquor he brewed. In a makeshift assembly line, some of the Claflins glued the labels onto bottles; others filled the bottles with the concoction. Priced at two dollars a bottle, Miss Tennessee's Magnetic Life Elixir for Beautifying the Complexion and Cleansing the Blood guaranteed cures for fever, sore eyes, heart and liver complaints, consumption, inflammatory rheumatism, asthma, and headaches.

The Claflins' traveling medicine show made its way from one small Midwestern town to the next with Buck peddling the miracle elixir from the back of the wagon. By the time any of the customers realized that they had been swindled, the entire Claflin family was already gone.

Charlatans and fraudsters do well in times of transition and change.[1] Buck wasn't the only scam artist selling elixirs. William Avery "Devil Bill" Rockefeller Sr. began as a traveling salesman going by the alias of Dr. William Levingston and identifying himself as a "botanic physician." With capital hard to come by, failing farmers borrowed it from those who had saved it. While Rockefeller was traveling by wagon west across the country selling his elixir, he was also scouting for land deals. He used the profits from the elixir to offer loans to struggling farmers. On his eastward-bound return, Rockefeller would foreclose the loans and take the land from those same farmers who, as was almost always the case, were unable to repay what they had borrowed.

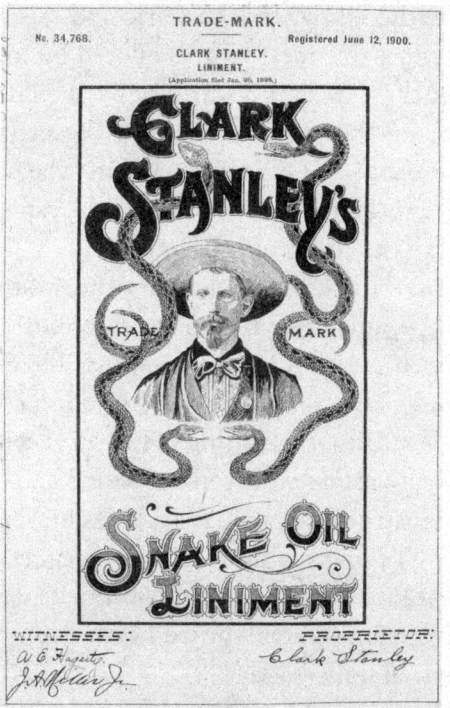

Products on offer at a typical medicine show

(The next generation of Rockefellers took a more respectable route to wealth: his two sons, John Davison Rockefeller Sr. and William Avery Rockefeller Jr., would become Standard Oil cofounders. John Rockefeller is considered by many to have been the richest man in modern history.)

Buck didn't operate on the scale of Devil Bill Rockefeller's heartless opportunism. He remained a sideshow barker, cheating people in mundane moneymaking schemes. At fourteen, Tennie had already been working half her life as a medium; just as she grew, so too did the menu of the services Buck assigned to her. In addition to pimping out his daughter, he built a lucrative sideline business of blackmailing the wealthier customers by acting the distraught father.

Tennie ran away. Buck found her and dragged her back. The Claflins took to the road again and lived off the sick and vunerable in small Midwestern towns by selling home-brewed remedies that probably contained highly addictive laudanum. With no regulation of medical practitioners and disease pathology not yet understood, the treatments available to the ailing were barbaric and rarely effective. A far less painful and affordable method was offered by "magnetic" healers who claimed that they created electricity by the laying-on of hands: the right hand being the positive, the left, the negative force. Buck promoted Tennie as a clairvoyant physician who, charged with an aura that made her a "battery" for spiritual telegraphy, could cure the injured or sick with the touch of her hands.

The more money Buck made cheating the wounded and ill, the more greedy he became, and the more risky his scams. Cancer— puzzling to the medical establishment—was a blank book of opportunity for him and, like a gambler who scorned to count the odds, he ran newspaper ads in Illinois claiming to be "AMERICAN KING OF CANCER" with a guarantee for "cancers killed and extracted in 10 to 48 hours without instruments, pain, or use of chloroform."

Buck rebranded Tennie, claiming that her magnetic touch—if used with a special salve, also for sale—could eliminate dangerous growths beneath the surface. The strategy proved lucrative, with Tennie earning fifty to a hundred dollars a day.

Buck moved his troupe into an abandoned hotel in Ottawa, Illinois, in 1863 and converted its second floor into a cancer infirmary. To make money from the available rooms on the first floor, he placed another newspaper ad offering lessons in what he referred to as the "Cult of Love." Given the number of men and the frequency of their night visits to the hotel, love had little to do with the transactional activities taking place there. However, it would not be charges of prostitution that brought law enforcement to the hotel door. Buck's practice of writing fake testimonials extolling Tennie's successes had run aground when he disclosed the name of a female patient he falsely claimed benefited from his cancer "cure." In reality, the woman was in the last stage of dying from cancer and, with just enough life left to flush him out, she wrote a letter that appeared in the local newspaper. It disclosed the gruesome facts about the Claflin clinic, one being the use of lye in what presumably was Roxanna's diabolical home-brewed treatment.

By the time the marshals showed up at the hotel to raid its second-floor infirmary, the Claflins had fled, leaving behind dying and unfed patients in unspeakable conditions. Tennie had never been able to shake the feeling that it was just a question of time before she would be held to account for her father's foul schemes. She was right, of course. Buck had possessed the foresight to protect himself by registering the cancer infirmary in Tennie's name. It was Tennie who was publicly called out as an imposter "wholly unfit for the confidence of the community," as reported by the local newspaper. It would be Tennie, not Buck, held responsible for what was described as "opening a 'magnetic infirmary' where cancer patients had been literally deserted." When the woman who made the public charge died, it was Tennie who was indicted for manslaughter.

PART II

The thrill of newness.

CHAPTER ELEVEN

Mr. Garnett manages to connect the dots.

Shortly after claiming to have had a spiritual visit from Tennie imploring her to return home, Victoria gathered her family and boarded an oceangoing steamer ship in San Francisco that would take them to New York. In all likelihood, the ship was the property of a company owned and run by Cornelius Vanderbilt. Vanderbilt was a spiritualist. A very rich one.

Roughly twenty years before, a penniless slave by the name of Frederick Bailey, dressed in the sailor's uniform of a free Black seaman, boarded a train in Maryland. Traveling north would take him to freedom.

These circumstances coincided with another: the 1849 arrival in London of politically exiled Karl Marx. Marx would use the British Museum's Reading Room to research and write what would become the bible of communism, *Das Kapital*.

In an era of alternating disarray and regeneration—when anything was possible—the lives of Vanderbilt, Bailey, and Marx would intersect with that of Victoria's.

•   •   •

Dated newspaper clippings led Mr. Garnett to the year that the Claflins escaped the law in Illinois, but it wasn't until he located the recorded birth in New York of Victoria's second child in 1861—Zulu Maud[1]—that he was able to reestablish a timeline of sorts to Victoria's own story. New York as Victoria's destination made sense to Mr. Garnett: when she and her family left San Francisco on a steamer boat, the port in New York was where it would have taken them. He thought it likely that they traveled from New York to Ohio, to rejoin the Claflins. They had relocated there after escaping the authorities in Illinois when Tennie's prodigious output as a spiritual practitioner provided the family the financial means to rent a large house.

Why Victoria decided to reconstitute a life with her parasitic parents was another mystery to Mr. Garnett, but it seemed that this was the time in her life when she finally faced down her father's subjugation and insisted that, to avoid any more run-ins with the authorities, he abstain from placing newspaper ads for medical services and cancer salves. Ever resourceful, Buck placed a sign in the front window of their rented house in Cincinnati.

TENNESSEE CLAFLIN & VICTORIA WOODHULL, CLAIRVOYANTS.

Despite the sign advertising a single service, the neighbors lodged a complaint with the police that the home was also a house of ill repute. (Based on his archival reconstruction of the Claflins' journeys, Mr. Garnett came to the conclusion that, wherever the family took up residence, they brought an open invitation of illicit sex.) Run out of Cincinnati in 1866, the Claflins went to Chicago, where Tennie—whose pleasures were often found in ill-conceived partnerships with men—married a self-described "sporting man" a week after meeting him. She kept her maiden name, certain that its future commercial value would outweigh the unsavory associations it had acquired in two previous states, and abandoned the marriage bed three days after the wedding. Returning with a pocketbook of cash and of the mind that too much sentiment was a deficiency found on the losing side, Tennie showed no contrition for what had been her lucrative foray into prostitution. Instead, she offered to split the proceeds with her husband—but only if he agreed to leave permanently.

Tennie's and Victoria's lives had been controlled entirely by their father, who had leeched off them until they were married. In order to rid themselves of husbands who would do the same, the sisters pooled their resources and purchased a wagon of their own. Unbound by male decrees, they traveled across Tennessee, Arkansas, and Missouri. Victoria, the diviner of hidden meaning, and Tennie, a master of machinations, made a great deal of money as spiritualists who charged to help people heal from the suffering that had been inflicted during the Civil War.

•   •   •

Although he was an otherwise accurate observer of American life, Mark Twain failed to read the zeitgeist when he penned his impression of the spiritualism movement in an article in the *Montana Post*:

"As I have said before, it is safest to stick to the old regular plan of salvation and not speculate in these new and unprospected wildcat religions. I regard spiritualism as wildcat—and shall continue to do so until they get down on it deeper, and show wall-rock on both sides, and prove that they have got a ledge."

Twain's book editor got it right. He wrote to Twain that printing presses were churning out books on the subject.[2] Mesmerism and revivalism had combined to lay a solid foundation for spiritualism in America, and, after gathering millions of followers in a nation of people desperate to learn if their husbands or sons or brothers were still alive after the Civil War, spiritualism crossed the Atlantic, where the performative aspects of it found favor among members of the British upper class. Séances were conducted in the semi-darkness of private houses, where participants sat around a table and joined hands to maintain the flow of energy emanating from the spirit dominion. English high society might have treated these séances like a parlor game, but others took it seriously. Georgiana Houghton developed skills as a medium after attending a séance and spent the next decade producing extraordinary watercolor drawings she insisted she was painting under spiritual guidance. Arthur Conan Doyle, certain that "the unknown and the marvelous press upon us from all sides," set aside Sherlock Holmes to produce more than a dozen books on the subject of spiritualism. Victor Hugo, Rudyard Kipling, and Henry James would dabble in spiritualism, hoping for otherworldly inspiration.

The spiritualist movement in America provided women a dominant role as clairvoyants. Universities barred women from attending, but clairvoyancy didn't necessitate attendance at a university.

Nor did it require permission from church authorities, who prevented women from speaking from the pulpit. In a way that might not have been planned or even predicted, mediumship muted the taboo of women speaking in public and offered an outlet for those savvy enough to recognize a backdoor means to lobby openly for women's rights.

Not all female mediums were feminists, but many spiritualists devoted themselves to reform and advocated women's rights. Tennie and Victoria understood the power dynamics between the sexes and were strategic when it came to what to take from men and what to give in return. A cynic might suggest that the two considered men to be fundamentally utilitarian, and that cynic would have a point. Whether the sisters were inclined to become public advocates for the future of women's rights is difficult to say. It's likely that they were driven by opportunity as much as ideology. The cunning they used to survive a hustler's childhood had become a streak of ruthlessness in their adulthood. If they believed in the cause of women's rights, they wouldn't have allowed it to interfere with a pursuit of the tangible opportunities provided by men.

"Men will not make the changes on their own—they have too much to lose," Victoria once said. "It is my belief that if women were to issue a declaration of independence sexually, and absolutely refuse to cohabit with men until they are acknowledged as equals . . . the victory would be won in a single week."

"Callous" is perhaps too emotive a word to describe how Victoria and Tennie dealt with men. Let us agree to the word "pragmatic."

It was a combination of pragmatism, imagination, and expert guile that Victoria used to circumvent primarily patriarchal obstacles by convincing people that her decisions were not of her own making, but were instructions from spirits. By representing herself as a passive vessel, she was able to prevent anyone from accusing her of being a destabilizing influence. Not just that. She was able to shape her subterfuge by insisting she had no control of the timing of those spiritual visitations.

Eighteen years had passed since Victoria's first claim of being visited by a spirit promising "wealth, fame, a mansion in a city on the water," along with a future in which she would be "a ruler of people." Her second visitation happened in San Francisco, when the apparition took the form of Tennie, who was calling her back to the East Coast. Victoria's third fateful prophecy would take place in St. Louis, Missouri.

CHAPTER TWELVE

A different blueprint for being male.

James Harvey Blood and his younger brother, George, relocated from Massachusetts to St. Louis, Missouri, after the Panic of 1857, a financial meltdown that spread with alarming speed due to a recent invention, the telegraph. By the age of thirty-two James had gained a foothold in the respectable worlds of business and finance as the president of the St. Louis Railroad Company.

Missouri was bitterly divided by the issue of slavery. Some 47 percent of its population were enslaved; at the same time, the state had one of the largest free Black populations. Most whites, particularly in St. Louis, fought against the North in the Civil War. James and George were antislavery loyalists who enlisted in Sixth Volunteer Missouri Infantry of the Union army. When, at the end of the war, James Blood returned to St. Louis, it was as a colonel riddled with wounds. The first bullet hit his right shoulder; another in his right arm; yet another in his left hand. He pried out two more himself from his left thigh with a hunting knife.

The five bullet wounds James suffered in the war testified to his bravery on the battlefield. As a spiritualist, he was able to find comfort in his belief that his fallen comrades in arms lived on. Still, he rarely slept at night, and fought off nightmares when he did. James would have explained this to Victoria in her capacity as a spiritualist healer when he consulted her but, before he could speak a word, she fell into a trance and muttered in a half-conscious state, "We are united by the powers of the air."

Circumstances placed them in a hotel room, so it is likely that also uniting them were bodily fluids.

With his thick glossy hair,
piercing eyes, and a gallant
military bearing, Colonel
James Harvey Blood exuded a
sturdy manhood.

Drawing on her steadfast belief in free love, wherein true marriages
were unions of spiritual affinities, Victoria was certain that she and
James would live together in an alliance of mind, body, and soul.

"I see our futures linked and our destinies bound by the ties of
marriage!" she proclaimed. The fact that both of them were married
to other people at the time didn't seem to be a concern.

By 1865, twelve of Victoria's twenty-six years had been burdened
with a drunk and dissolute husband. Her life-altering decision to run
off with James was unsurprising. James, on the other hand, was con-
ventionally well settled. He was the president of the St. Louis Society
of Spiritualists who enjoyed one of the city's highest salaries, having recently won a three-year term as St. Louis's auditor, a position
that came with his own office in the courthouse. Why would such a
man break every tie by abruptly leaving a wife, children, career, and
good standing in the community? What came to possess him to the
extent that he would forfeit anything of his that had financial value,
including the house, which he gave outright to his wife? A St. Louis
newspaper laid the blame solely on Victoria in an editorial that had a
biblical overlay: "The spell of the enchantress was laid upon him, and
he fell from the path of rectitude." An enchantress? That inclination

would more likely have been found with Tennie, who delighted in the pursuit of men.

It is true that Victoria was never reassuringly domestic. Motherhood did not exalt her; if she felt any regret for not being an active part of their childhood, it didn't extend to self-condemnation. Her childcare arrangements often involved farming out her children to the Claflin clan, and various of its members joined her in St. Louis so that she and James could embark on a journey of their own through the Midwest.

CHAPTER THIRTEEN

Free love, or something like it.

Despite Britain's economic ties with America's Southern states, due primarily to cotton export, its government understood that recognizing the Confederacy would put it on hostile terms with the Union. Britain therefore remained neutral during the Civil War. Its calculation paid off and, at the war's end, it forged a policy of friendship with Abraham Lincoln.

"Malice toward none, with charity for all," was what Lincoln promised to a scarred nation at the end of its Civil War—a promise that was shattered on April 14, 1865, when John Wilkes Booth, gripping a small gun in his right hand and a dagger as backup in his left, fired a bullet into Lincoln's skull. Years later, Walt Whitman wrote *Specimen Days,* his closest thing to a conventional autobiography. In it, he recalled that day: "I remember where I was stopping at the time, the season being advanced, there were many lilacs in full bloom. By one of those caprices that enter and give tinge to events without being at all a part of them, I find myself always reminded of the great tragedy of that day by the sight and odor of these blossoms. It never fails."

Lincoln's assassination and the war's upheaval left a moral void filled, in part, by the ideological movement of spiritualism. Its beliefs of renewal and reform softened the ground for reformers, abolitionists, and feminists. Among its estimated 10 million followers were the poets, writers, and philosophers who began to shift cultural perceptions. Spiritualists tended to define themselves outside of established institutions during a time of inexorable progression, when many questioned whether the past concepts of right and wrong were a burden that should be abandoned.

Most spiritualists were leery of hierarchies—ecclesiastic or civil. Some, living in Northeastern states, pioneered communes of utopian socialism. One such individual, John Humphrey Noyes, embraced the concept of "free love": a reference to Henry David Thoreau's 1842 poem that praised spiritual freedom. Noyes was a progressive reformer who based the term "free love" on a conviction that there was no reason for women to be made unhappy in marriage from the sheer ignorance of sex—or from a husband's ignorance. He also thought that adultery was best left to the people involved, not to the church.

Spiritualists who believed in free love shared two core convictions: there should be no coercion in sexual relationships, and a woman had the right to determine the use of her body. Despite the fact that it was more a social movement than an endorsement of promiscuity, free love was too much for America, a country that was squeamish about sex outside the status quo—sex between a man and a woman in their marital bed that was reproductive in purpose.

John Noyes's open-minded Oneida Community in New York State[1] challenged the contemporary views on gender roles and monogamous marriage. It held to the belief that the enjoyment of sex shouldn't be the prerogative exclusively of men, and that it was absurd to believe virtuous women were incapable of sexual pleasure. In a time when there was no separating the physical act of sex for women from pregnancy, members of the community rightly concluded that for women to have an equal expression in their sexual experiences they must first avoid unwanted pregnancies. Ignoring the public revulsion it inspired, the commune encouraged men to use the withdrawal method of birth control.

James Blood was an intellect, a philosophical anarchist, and a spiritualist who practiced free love. There is little doubt that he introduced Victoria to the unencumbered enjoyment of sex. He also provided a mental framework for her innate intelligence. The money she made on their tour of the Midwest treating the lost souls and torn bodies staggering out of the Civil War enabled James to pay the debt he left behind. Their partnership was one of equals. When they returned to St. Louis, he divorced his wife and Victoria retrieved her children. Tennie joined them when they took to the road, this time for Dayton, Ohio, a city known for its liberalism.

Victoria obtained a divorce from Canning in 1865 and, despite the vagueness of recordkeeping, it seems that, a year later, she was joined with James in a marriage presided over by a Presbyterian minister. The couple moved to Pittsburgh when the North—made rich from war profits—ushered in change. The art of quackery began to lose out to science. Post–Civil War medical standards were imposed by state authorities, the activities of mediums were banned, and courts levied fines against violators.

To avoid being called out for her fraud in the past, the younger of the two Fox sisters admitted that their performances as child clairvoyants had depended on a method of communication similar to that used by prisoners in adjoining cells—a method based on counting tapping sounds. When the mainstream press referred to the hoax as a fatal blow to the spiritualist movement, one of the sisters drank herself to death. The other died eight months later.

Concerned that her own career as a clairvoyant would become less profitable as it became more publicly derided, Victoria journeyed to Galena, Illinois, to meet president-elect Ulysses S. Grant and convince him to hire James as a private secretary. When she returned to Pittsburgh—and it had become obvious that nothing would come of her mission in Illinois—Victoria had another vision, ushered in by the same spirit guide that had appeared to her when she was a child and had prophesied her wealth, fame, and leadership. This time, the apparition bade her to travel to New York, where she would find a house waiting for her in readiness at the explicit address of 17 Great Jones Street.

There was more.

Victoria's ethereal trance featured the image of a brownstone building. As if actually entering through its front door, she could see the furnished interior: first the entrance hall; next, the parlor and library. When she asked the apparition to identify himself, he stretched forth his hand and, with his index finger, began to write letters on the table next to her, spelling out the name "Demosthenes." The letters slowly faded and then vanished altogether, along with the spirit.

Demosthenes was a champion of the Athenian independence and one of Greece's most admired orators. He placed stones in his mouth to improve his pronunciation and recited his speeches by the seashore over the sound of the waves to simulate roaring crowds and to strengthen his voice.

While reading Mrs. Woodhull's written account of this incident, Mr. Garnett must have felt a spasm of admiration. As a scholar of Greek history, how could he not have been impressed? If Victoria truly believed that she was riding on a wave of destiny, Demosthenes would have been the perfect metaphor.

PART III

Among the oddities: gold becomes almost worthless; an American capitalist finances the U.S. publication of Karl Marx's Manifesto; *and women suggest that they are capable of reason.*

CHAPTER FOURTEEN

The richest man in America wasn't nice.

Victoria Woodhull wasn't the only one with visions of the future.

Cornelius Vanderbilt was a practicing spiritualist who built the first of several fortunes in shipping and ended up owning the largest fleet in America. Whether by otherworldly intervention or intuition, he envisioned the nation's growth and was certain that steamships would be replaced by railroads—this because, while the South continued to be fueled by an economy almost entirely dependent on cotton picked by slaves, the North was transforming its wartime industry into the mass production of consumer goods that would require transport.

Between 1863 and 1869, the U.S. government awarded over 100 million acres of land and just as many millions of dollars to support the construction of 1,900 miles of railroad tracks to connect America's heartland. During that time, Vanderbilt's business dealings were underwriting some part of the nation's industrial changes. As his means increased, so did the scope of his ambitions, particularly in New York City. To anyone else, his purchase of land in its Midtown would have appeared to be a counterintuitive decision—until he made sure that Forty-Second Street became the transfer point for all of the railroad passengers arriving in the city.[1]

While New York's population was increasing year to year, the less fortunate crowded onto Manhattan's southern tip in the hopes of supporting themselves and their families. Roaming the muddy streets outside their tenements were barnyard animals that fouled the walkways and fed on garbage. Vanderbilt sensed that the city's affluent would move farther uptown to get away from the encroaching noises and smells. When the state government provided $5 million and eminent domain power to pay the landowners of what would become Central Park, he purchased territory along Fifth, Madison, and Fourth Avenues (eventually called Park Avenue) before the emergence of Central Park's landscaped areas.

Cornelius Vanderbilt showed no interest in the city's poor who might derive benefits from his foresight; his gift of visualizing the future of New York was selfish—so much so that Mark Twain, living in the Northeast, addressed him directly and in writing.

"Go, oh please go, and do one worthy act," pleaded Twain. "Go, grandly, nobly, and give four dollars to some great public charity."

In America, empathy rarely paid. Gumption is what paid: the kind shown by the Dutch West India Company when its 1626 purchase of Manhattan from Native Americans was made with only 60 guilders, an amount equivalent to what would have been about $1,000 today. To Vanderbilt, shame was not a factor. He believed that nothing about America stood in the way of an individual's success, and that those who allowed themselves to become nothing should have no place in it. There was no blot on Vanderbilt's conscience. Why should there be? "Let them do what I have done," was his reply to Twain's appeal. He continued to draw from a bottomless pit of avarice to become the richest man in the country.

The new law of nature in free-for-all American capitalism had only one rule: allow the market to do its job, and if some went under, well, so be it. Striving men were to be admired. The likes of Devil Bill Rockefeller were excused for being ruthless and conniving because being ruthless and conniving was how people got rich.

"It is odd to watch with what feverish ardour [they] pursue prosperity and how they are ever tormented by the shadowy suspicion that they may not have chosen the shortest route to get it," wrote French diplomat and political philosopher Alexis de Tocqueville, casting his gimlet eye on industrious Americans in a hurry.

The bullion coming from California's Gold Rush increased capital in America, and capital, as a lifeline of progress, animated the country's energy. It also created divisions among idealists. Should this be a fair country that looked after its most vulnerable, or one that put its faith in industry and the making of money? There would be no equivocation with Vanderbilt.

"I have been insane on the subject of making money all my life," was Vanderbilt's unapologetic admission to one reporter. Assuming this reporter had done his due diligence, he would have known that Vanderbilt's great-grandfather two times over was a Dutch farmer who, in 1650, emigrated to New Amsterdam (which would later be called New York) as an indentured servant. At the age of eleven, Cornelius—strong-bodied, towheaded, blue-eyed, square-jawed— left school and began to work with his father on the waterfronts of New York, and five years later, he started his own local service ferrying freight and passengers on a shuttle between Staten Island and Manhattan. In an age when American textile mills were developing in the Northeast, only a few railroads existed to transport the goods from Boston to Long Island Sound before connecting with steamboats that continued the journey to New York. Vanderbilt's solution was to increase the number of railroads and thereby own a contiguous method of transporting those goods.

The reporter might also have known that by the early 1840s, Cornelius dominated the steamboat business on the sound and was referred to as "Commodore," and that at the beginning of the California Gold Rush, he pivoted from regional steamboat lines to oceangoing steamships. After amassing the largest fleet in the country, he employed his capital to create a web of railroads across America and increased his fortune by speculating in the New York Stock Exchange, which he didn't hesitate to manipulate. He would have known that Cornelius, possessing not a shred of modesty, named his private railroad "the Vanderbilt," and that his New York Central locomotive, the Commodore, featured headlights decorated with his image—the exact same image engraved on the New York Central stock certificates.

Vanderbilt made money on top of money by feeling the social undercurrents before they were outwardly perceptible. He never told anyone what he was doing until he did it, and one of the few pleasures he took was trampling his competitors. He would lower his prices and, after driving a competitor out of business, jack up his costs again.

He believed he was untouchable. He believed this because he knew it to be true.

"What do I care about the law?" he asked. "Haint I got the power?"

Cornelius Vanderbilt had married his cousin, Sophia Johnson,

when they were both teenagers, and she spent the rest of her life trying to please him. The one time—the only time—Sophia found the
nerve to take a stand against him was when she balked at his demand
that they move from Staten Island to the Washington Square home in
Manhattan. Vanderbilt committed her to a lunatic asylum until she
complied. Her exit strategy from the relentlessly unhappy marriage
was to predecease him. Serving as a pallbearer at her funeral was Horace Greeley.

Even the most cursory knowledge of Vanderbilt would point to a
man of a peculiarly questionable character. He was cutthroat, cunning, crude, hated, and feared. By the same token, he stood by his
word, honored his agreements, and was never a liar. Whether this was
out of ethical consideration or business necessity is up for debate. The
Civil War had been as much an economic struggle as it was a military
one: heaving factories and railroads webbing the North had outper-
formed the agrarian-based South, which perched precariously on a
single revenue source.[2] Vanderbilt fed provisions of money, munitions,
and supplies to the government in Washington. Were his actions proof
of a patriot, or of a savvy operator taking full advantage of the North's
war effort? Progress for its own sake is not a matter of character and,
for good or ill, it took someone like Vanderbilt to forge the cornerstone of America's post–Civil War economy.

CHAPTER FIFTEEN

The two types of gamblers.

Cornelius Vanderbilt would have been the likely owner of the company whose steamship transported Victoria, along with her husband and son, from the West to the East Coast. He was definitely the proprietor of the dark blue railroad car with "New York and Harlem RR" emblazoned in gold on its side that brought Victoria and Tennie to New York City in 1868.

According to Victoria's written account, she and Tennie arrived there at dusk, and, weary from the long journey, made their way to 17 Great Jones Street, where stood a brownstone house matching the one in her prophetic vision. Its interior fulfilled in reality what Victoria had already seen in her trance: the hallway, the parlor—even the furniture—all echoed the visions in her trance. On a table in the middle of the room was a book with a black cover. Its title was stamped in gold: *The Orations of Demosthenes.* According to Victoria, not only did this confirm the identity of her spirit guide, it validated his instructions for her to go to New York.

Victoria's reliability as a witness to even the most likely of circumstances in her life was debatable. Her accounts were defined and then revised by contradictions and qualifiers—so much so that Mr. Garnett almost always found himself lost between what might have been and what really was. He knew that Victoria's explanation of the factors behind her residency at 17 Great Jones Street were not remotely feasible. Nonetheless, he decided that, given that her first home was a wooden shack where she had slept on a filthy mat made of corn husks, the fact of her arrival on the pink-brick doorstep of a respectable dwelling in New York City was secondary to how she got herself there in the first place.

Facing east from the brownstone, Victoria would have seen a building bequeathed as a library by John Jacob Astor, born Johann Jakob Astor, a German-American merchant and investor whose multimillion-dollar fortune had been made primarily in a fur trade monopoly and, farther afield, by smuggling opium into China.

West of the brownstone was Broadway, the city's principal long, wide, bustling street. During the week, it was a thoroughfare for immense charcoal wagons and carriages where scavenging pigs competed with unwashed children foraging for food. On Sundays, the same street was a promenade where wealthy men wearing top hats and women with capes trimmed in ermine crossed paths with the city's beggars.

North was Cooper Union, where, in 1860, Abraham Lincoln gave a speech that gained him important support in New York as the Republican presidential nomination.

South was the financial center where bribes and blackmail played as much a part as banking did. The harbor at the southernmost tip divided the waters into east and west and encased the island of Manhattan.

Regardless of which direction Victoria might have taken to arrive at the edges of Manhattan, she would have looked out on ships and been convinced that the wealth and fame "in a city surrounded by ships" promised by the spirits had finally materialized.

Victoria's parents hoped for fortune, too. Buck and Roxanna wasted little time before arriving on Victoria's doorstep, along with two other family members and their spouses and children. To describe the Claflin household as unruly doesn't capture the half of it. Despite Roxanna's whiplash mood swings, Victoria's loyalty to family members remained absolute. By late 1868, 17 Great Jones Street housed most of her family and served as the location of what Victoria and Tennie advertised as "The Magnetic Healing Institute & Conservatory of Mental and Spiritual Science."

"We have seen one of the clairvoyants," reported one of New York city's newspapers, "and she is beautiful enough to cure anybody. She is young and childish in her manners, with Titian hair, which falls in

rich masses about her head, blue eyes which wear an honest steadfast look, a symmetrical figure which is costumed in excellent taste
and a pretty hand which sparkles with gems. Now we can't see why a
chronic case of heart disease should be cured at all, with such a healing medium. This lady's name is Miss Tennessee Claflin, and while
we admit that there is some power in this art of healing, we confess
that we know nothing only that hopeless people go there, and after a
brief stay of days or weeks, return home cured."

• • •

It was impossible for Mr. Garnett to confirm how Victoria's introduction to Cornelius Vanderbilt came about. The disparate accounts that
he read offered no definitive information and only added to his confusion. He thought it entirely possible that she had traveled to New York
not at the urging of her spirit guide but with the express purpose of
seeking out America's richest man. On the other hand, it was common
knowledge that Vanderbilt was a spiritualist with an eye for young
women, so Buck might have approached him with the intention of
leasing out his two daughters.

Regardless of which Claflin initiated the introduction, the logistics
would have been relatively easy. Vanderbilt spent the working part of

Cornelius Vanderbilt's flinty
gaze could scatter a crowd.

his day playing the stock market in his sparsely furnished one-room office located directly behind his mansion off of Washington Square, not far from Victoria's brownstone on Great Jones Street. Rather than banking on luck, which could easily fail, he relied on information; his open-door policy rested on the belief that someone might show up with an idea for making money that had managed to elude him.

When his long-suffering wife died, Vanderbilt was in his midseventies and still relatively handsome. A destitution of tact was compensated to a degree by an excellent tailor, who ensured that bespoke black suits set off Vanderbilt's well-groomed white sideburns. Having been blessed with an iron constitution, he would occasionally seek sexual occupation with the women who plied their trade near the docks on the East River.

There were two people Vanderbilt actually loved: his mother (dead) and his youngest son, who had attended West Point, fought in the Civil War, and survived the Battle of Shiloh—which had left twenty-three thousand dead or wounded—only to contract and die of tuberculosis there. The fact that Cornelius Vanderbilt was habitually and so obviously dismissive toward his other twelve children undercut Victoria's claim that meeting him for the first time occurred as a result of being "directed by a spirit hand" to his "fatherly care and kindness."

Like Tennie, Vanderbilt was not entirely convinced there were spirits, but neither was he prepared to discount them. He retained a personal medium from Staten Island, a woman by the name of Mrs. Tufts, who allegedly rid him of two spirits who had haunted him. One was a young boy accidently crushed under the hoofs of Vanderbilt's two trotters when he was racing his carriage around the Central Park Reservoir; the other was a railroad worker decapitated under the wheels of a New York Central train. Named the Flying Devil, the speeding train hit the poor man with vicious irony along with lethal force.

The substantial fees Mrs. Tufts charged to perform these services paid for her retirement to Vermont. Vanderbilt wasn't interested in communicating with his wife while she was living, and there was no reason he would do so after she died, but he missed his sessions with Mrs. Tufts, who provided him with monthly updates from his dead mother and son. She also put him in touch on a regular basis with several successful financiers of the past with whom he conferred—or so he said. Chances are that Victoria, aware of these details, would have insinuated as much as was necessary for him to believe that she was a necessary and timely replacement for Mrs. Tufts.

Victoria saw the obvious in Cornelius Vanderbilt—his money. But she also saw his power. Improving the odds of winning over a lonely seventy-four-year-old man was her twenty-three-year-old vivacious, impulsive sister, who had an exuberant sense of pleasure.

One New York newspaper described Tennie as "all verve and vivacity, full of imagination and excitability, very free in her modes of expression." Another wrote that, when she was engaged in conversation, she expressed an enthusiastic openness not only with words but "all over," so much so that "one would think that her whole physical structure was inlaid with a thousand sensitive spiral springs."

Looking so endearingly young and behaving with such careless freedom as she did, it might have been easy to think of Tennie as something other than what she was. Suffice it to say that if few principles were to be found with Vanderbilt, there seemed to be none at all with her. She was unconcerned by the line of work she followed as long as its rewards were tangible. Having found the conditions of New York City streets not to her liking, she decided that her family needed a new carriage, along with two matching white horses and a full-time driver in livery. Vanderbilt could deliver on this.

Given their means-justifying-the-ends agenda, it took very little effort for the sisters to continue their association with Vanderbilt after their initial meeting. Victoria, with her regal beauty and air of higher purpose, replaced Mrs. Tufts as his personal clairvoyant and gave him counsel based on spiritual advice. Tennie, with her expert hands, became his "healer."

The financial arrangement Vanderbilt had with the sisters was generous: he paid Victoria to predict the stock market trends and paid Tennie for her energetic company in and out of bed. It didn't take long before the Claflin household took on a maid, a cook, a governess for Victoria's young daughter, and a nurse for her son.

Vanderbilt's adult children agreed to turn a blind eye to Tennie, who had become a regular feature at their father's house and whom he referred to as "little sparrow." What worried them was Victoria's practice of relaying stock tips to him, claiming that they had come to her from spirits. Vanderbilt's eldest son, Billy, made a point of intercepting any market orders based on her advice until it occurred to him to convert what had been a potential problem into an advantage by reversing the flow of information. Clever Billy advocated stocks to Victoria, who then recommended them to his father. Cleverer still was Victoria, who took advantage of that market intelligence by making sure those same trades were executed on her behalf. Her behind-the-scenes collusion made her a wealthy woman and convinced others that she had amassed her wealth through her own market insights.

Billy was sanguine about the arrangement he had with Victoria, but he remained concerned that Tennie might lure his father into a wholly inappropriate marriage. He decided the best course of action would be to identify another candidate. She was young—not much older than Tennie—and from a venerable but impoverished Southern family. To Billy's relief, his father eloped with the young woman to Canada, leaving Tennie to wonder if the changed circumstances would impact the Claflins' bottom line.

Tennie and Victoria need not have worried. Vanderbilt continued to take the sisters on a rollicking joyride through unregulated capitalism, instructing them to buy as he bought and sell in a time when Wall Street was emerging as a center of the financial world. When he included them in a deal with New York and Harlem Railroad, they walked away with $500,000.

Vanderbilt had made Victoria rich, but not crazy rich. She would do that for herself in the course of a single day in 1869.

The run-up to what would later be dubbed "Black Friday" featured two predatorial financiers, Jay Gould and Jim Fisk, who, by working together the previous year to commit stock fraud and bribery, prevented Vanderbilt from taking control of the Erie Railroad, which was under their ownership. Borrowing from the same playbook of market manipulation, Gould and Fisk turned their sights on Wall Street investors with a plan to corner the gold market.

The spiraling costs of the Civil War had depleted the Union states' reserves of gold and silver coin, which, at the time, was the only legal tender of the United States. In 1862, Congress authorized the issuance of paper U.S. notes in response to an impending financial crisis. Referred to as "greenbacks" for their distinctive color and unredeemable for gold or silver, they constituted the country's first national currency lawfully backed by the credit of the federal government and based on the faith and resources of the nation.

When, in 1869, the post–Civil War dollar weakened, Gould and Fisk bought all the gold they could at a price of $130 per ounce. By the end of that same week, speculators were purchasing gold on credit. Countless others clamored to buy, but the supply had been depleted, and few offered to sell what they had already bought. Gold reached $162 by late morning on September 24. Alarmed that the country's financial structure was being threatened, the government stepped in to protect the nation's economy by flooding the market with the gold stored at Fort Knox. This undercut the market value of gold. It was the first domino to fall. Investors abruptly off-loaded the gold they had already purchased. Pandemonium broke out in New York's Gold Exchange Building in the Wall Street area.

From his onetime perch at the British Museum's Reading Room, Karl Marx had warned about the downside of capitalism as a system. "It must nestle everywhere," he wrote. "Settle everywhere, establish connections everywhere."

Scattered across America were bankers and traders gathered around telegraph wires for the latest readings. When gold dropped to $130 in less than thirty minutes, a frenzied sell-off forced the sale of collateral to meet payments. No fright compares to that on Wall Street: speculators panicked that Friday. Investment houses and banks went bankrupt in the riptide. Hundreds more faced ruin.

In the hours that saw the value of gold plummeting, Vanderbilt put $1 million into stocks to prevent the panic from leaking into his investments. He walked away unscathed, but most others weren't so lucky. Stunned businessmen spilled out through the front doors of the Gold Exchange Building and, zombie-like, wandered in no particular direction.

Victoria waited at the curb in the Claflin carriage Vanderbilt had paid for, gazing out at the bedlam with an expression that gave nothing away. As the price of gold plunged, investors scrambled for collateral to cover their losses by selling their stock for whatever they could get. This pushed the prices down further.

Betting that the market would recover and stock prices would rise,

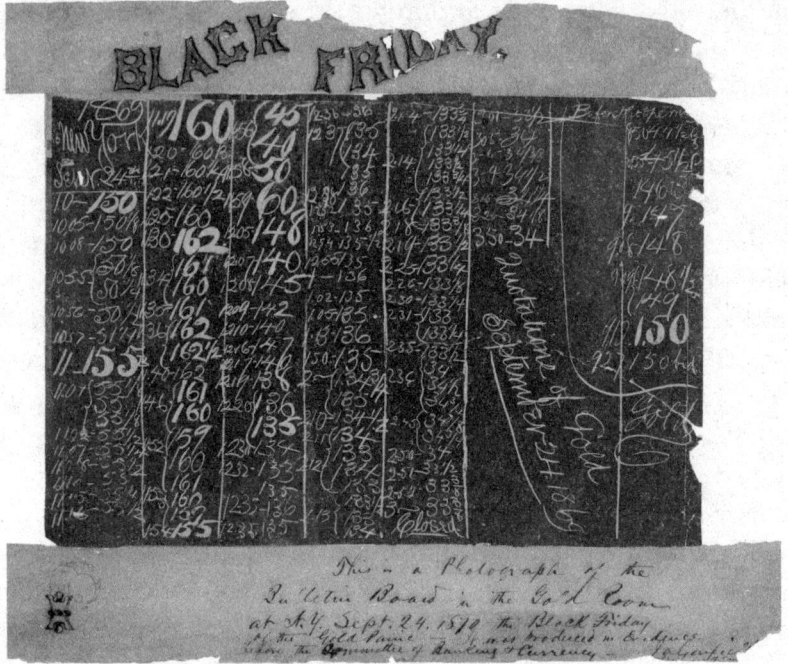

The Black Board from the New York Stock Exchange, showing the tick-by-tick prices of gold trading during the disastrous course of Black Friday

Victoria calmly did the opposite—she bought shares. Women weren't allowed on the trading floor, so Victoria sent men into the building with orders to buy. It would not be the last time men did Victoria's bidding.

There are two types of gamblers: the ones who will risk little money on very high odds, and the ones who risk a fortune on very low odds. All that really matters is how you handle losing. If you let it destroy you, you aren't really a gambler to begin with.

Dozens of investors committed suicide during the forty-eight hours that followed Black Friday. It took seven days for clerks to compile the flood of transactions. Stocks rebounded four months later.

Victoria Woodhull had made a fortune.

CHAPTER SIXTEEN

Women and their money.

The lives of Victoria and Tennie had been assaulted by poverty and every one of its cruel attendants. When their hard-won financial self-sufficiency finally arrived, it came with the acknowledgment of its value.

That women permitted to acquire confidence in their own worth would not willingly agree to shed it was hardly a sublime notion for Mr. Garnett, but neither was it ridiculous. The more he learned of Victoria Woodhull, the more ambivalent his attitude toward her became—not ambivalence as a lukewarm state of the mind, but rather the simultaneity of strong opposing emotions. He was repelled by her willingness to obliterate reason, but he respected her for her fortitude. He was appalled by her refusal to comply with the norms of female amiability, but he admired her for her courage. I suspect that, despite his best efforts, Mr. Garnett couldn't decide what he actually thought of her. The only thing he knew was that she represented a new kind of femaleness. He wasn't sure that this would mean the death of a certain type of maleness, but he was certain that she was a sign pointing away from what his generation of Englishmen had safely assumed about her sex.

There were reasonable grounds for Mr. Garnett to believe that Victoria Woodhull and women like her would want more. Had Demosthenes promised her only wealth, she would likely have cashed in her Black Friday winnings to enjoy an easy life, but she convinced herself that she had been promised fame as well as money. In an effort to utilize the latter in order to acquire the former, Victoria came up with a plan that only she would have thought possible.

At a time when New York was permeated by war profiteers and ruled by a Democratic political machine on the take—when bogus enterprises fobbed themselves off as legitimate businesses, when Wall Street was a snake pit, when quick profits were made and then just as quickly lost on an unpredictable stock exchange—Victoria Woodhull and her sister decided to launch a Wall Street brokerage firm.

Just how it was that they managed to pull it off revealed itself in stages. Mr. Garnett broke them down chronologically:

1. Billy Vanderbilt's ardent hope had been that, once Victoria made her own fortune, she would no longer feel a need to remain within striking distance of his father's. When he realized that this would not be the case, he tried to divert her and her sister with an all-expenses-paid trip to Europe.

2. Victoria put Billy's proposition to work by calling on his father, to whom she extolled the appeal of such a trip. She let it be known that they'd chosen the ship, settled the tickets, packed their trunks, and made all else ready, but that the night before they were to embark, she and Tennie had experienced a shared trance. To embellish the story with an otherworldly flourish, Victoria told Vanderbilt that her spirit guide had advised her not to take the trip and, instead, to secure a seat on the New York Stock Exchange.

3. It could hardly be said that Cornelius Vanderbilt was in the vanguard of feminist support, but when it came to his business dealings, he was an opportunistic investor. Victoria had identified a revenue source he wouldn't have thought of himself: women who possessed the financial means to invest and would likely be more comfortable conferring in that regard with a woman than a man. The logistics of launching a brokerage firm presented quite a few challenges, the first of which was that women were not allowed to be seen, much less to work in the public marketplace of finance. Each seat on the stock exchange was, literally, a numbered chair in which a designated member of the exchange sat during the twice-daily stock auctions. Fortunately for Victoria, a recent change

in stock-exchange membership ruled that a seat could be bought after a member died or resigned.

4. Victoria left Vanderbilt's office with a signed check for $7,000, which would buy a seat on the exchange under Vanderbilt's name but on Victoria's behalf. The check, written by Vanderbilt's hand, was proof that he was her firm's backer. His association would be invaluable on the Street.

5. Victoria passed the check to Tennie.

6. Tennie took the check to Henry Clews, a prominent New York banker. She requested that he open an account for Woodhull, Claflin & Company.

7. Victoria and Tennie waited for word to spread in the city's financial community that Vanderbilt had invested in Woodhull, Claflin & Company.

8. Tennie returned to Mr. Clews and withdrew $1,000 from the firm's account.

9. She took that $1,000 check, payable by Clews's bank, to New York's Fourth National Bank and asked its director to open an account for Woodhull, Claflin & Company. Word that the bank requested Mr. Clews to vouch for the check led to the financial community's belief that it wasn't only Vanderbilt who was backing Woodhull, Claflin & Company—it was also Henry Clews.

•   •   •

Folie à deux is a clinical syndrome whose characteristic feature is the transmission of delusions induced by a primary person to a secondary one, often between close female siblings who have experienced repetitive crises in a dysfunctional family.

Given Victoria and Tennie's habitual way of operating, that definition would set off alarms, except that the sisters were not deluded. They were, however, convinced of their own value and almost always got what they wanted. Man or woman, few people do. Fewer people know how to hold on to it once it's obtained. Victoria and Tennie understood the advantages that came with proximity to men, but they were mindful that the law guaranteed husbands ownership of both the property and the earnings of their wives. To ensure that they retained control of a company they intended to launch, Victoria instructed a lawyer to draw up a contract for James Blood's signature. The document omitted any reference to the fact he was married to her and denied him interest in the firm. Instead, it assigned him a salaried position as the company's silent partner. This meant that, despite having demonstrated his financial dexterity as city auditor of St. Louis, he would not be allowed to make any major financial decisions at the brokerage firm without Victoria's or Tennie's prior approval. None of this seemed to bother him. His own ambitions found a constructive outlet in his role as an adviser.

In 1869, Victoria and Tennie rented a double suite in the Hoffman House, a genteel Midtown hotel and the domain of visiting politicians and financiers. One of the two rooms was kitted out to resemble a drawing room. Prominently positioned on the wall facing its entrance was a large portrait of Cornelius Vanderbilt. Its purpose was to instill confidence among potential clients entering the adjoining room— a solidly established-looking enclave enhanced by the rented books in floor-to-ceiling shelves.

The day Woodhull, Claflin & Company opened for business, Horace Greeley's *New-York Tribune* reported that "the general routine of business in Wall Street was somewhat varied by the mingling in its scenes of two fashionably dressed ladies." The *Sun* warned, "Petticoats Among the Bovine and Ursine Animals." The New York *Herald,* Wall Street's leading paper, was less interested in predicting Victoria and Tennie's financial acumen than it was in commenting on their appearance. No detail was too small: Victoria's weight and shoe size were estimated, and it was pointed out that Tennie might have enhanced her hair with imported ox marrow. One publication conveyed the sisters' sexually suggestive means of soliciting business with a visual code: its illustration showed several overattentive men encircling them.

After being referred to in print as "the bewitching brokers," Victoria and Tennie made the strategic decision to present themselves in ways that looked as businesslike as was possible with wool suits kept to a sober brown palette. Skirt hems reached no longer than the tops of button-up boots—the practical adjustment enabled them to move around the office without the sound of a rustling petticoat. Tennie had her hair cut to a jauntily defiant, androgynously short length.

Tennie, unadorned and
gender-bending

Restyling themselves into a single brand, the two women sent a handwritten note to the *Herald* and enclosed two tastefully engraved business cards in Garamond typeface for Woodhull, Claflin & Company: one with Victoria's name, the other with Tennie's. The note was more invitation than introduction. "We were not a little surprised at seeing our appearance in the Wall Street in your column of today," it read. "As we intend operating as mentioned, we should be glad to make your acquaintance."

The *Herald* dispatched a reporter to the Hoffman House, where Tennie greeted him with an assertive handshake. She explained that Victoria would join them shortly but told him that, in the meanwhile, she would be glad to answer any questions he might have. The reporter suggested that it was understandable that there were questions about two women who sprang from nowhere to become brokers when women weren't allowed to trade stocks . . . and that the only obvious thing about them was that they had a great deal of money. He asked Tennie to confirm that she and her sister were, in fact, doing business as stockbrokers and bankers.

Tennie replied that they had been trading stocks for some time.

Well, no.

"It is a novel sight to see a woman on the Street as a stock operator," the reporter said, taking out his notebook. "Do you find it a challenge?"

"I think a woman is just as capable of making a living as a man . . . My mind is in my business, and I attend to that solely."

No again.

"But stock speculations are dangerous," the reporter pointed out, "and many persons with large capital at their backs have been swamped, as you are aware, and I presume your experience is rather limited."

"I studied law in my father's office six years," was another of Tennie's objectively untrue statements. Gesturing to the portrait of Cornelius Vanderbilt hanging on the opposite wall, she added, "And, besides, we have a strong back."

"Yes, I've been told that Commodore Vanderbilt has been working in the interest of your firm . . . and that you frequently call at his office about business. Is that true?" asked the reporter.

"I know the Commodore," Tennie said, without a hint of the humor that the confirmation deserved.

Victoria glided into the room and, after introducing herself, kept her interview focused on matters pertaining to business. She cited various opportunities she was confident would return substantial profits.

"Entrepreneurs are risk takers, willing to put their reputations on the line in support of an idea or an enterprise," she told him, and then referred to the banking capital at her disposal: "We have made about $700,000 and expect that, when we establish an office, we will do even better." This figure was presumably the combination of accumulated profits from Vanderbilt's tips at one time on railroad stocks, and Victoria's windfall from Black Friday.

The *Herald* interview that appeared the next day was accompanied by a lengthy editorial congratulating the new brokers.

Years of trading from the back of a wagon had given Victoria an understanding of how to handle people and their money, but she understood clearly that what would lure the Street's old guard to her firm would be its connection to Cornelius Vanderbilt. Before they upgraded to new offices, she and Tennie sent their thanks in a letter that layered melodrama, flattery, and spiritualism.

"Commodore, you first extended your hand to aid two struggling women to battle with the world . . . It was you who gave them wise counsel and showed them the shoals and rocks upon which so many men are wrecked; it was you who stood by them when they ventured into the financial heart of the country . . . It was the goodness of your heart, directed by some kind of spirit hand, or else your prescient knowledge of what was to come, that led you to do all this for them."

CHAPTER SEVENTEEN

An affinity for theatricality.

On February 5, 1870, Woodhull, Claflin & Company moved to 44 Broad Street, a block south of Wall Street. The New York *Sun* ran a headline, "New Furor on the Street," and *The New York Times* reported America's financial district had been "aroused" by two "adventurers" resulting in circumstances that "beggared description."

There was no getting around the fact that it had quickly turned into a theatrical extravaganza. Each morning, without fail, a crowd gathered for the arrival of a carriage pulled by white horses driven by a coachman in scarlet livery. Victoria and Tennie would wait for the police to clear a path through the crowd before majestically stepping out of the carriage and sweeping into the building, looking as if they knew exactly where they should be. The ever-increasing number of curiosity hunters required that a guard be stationed at the entrance of the office building and a sign posted on the firm's front door.

ALL GENTLEMEN WILL STATE THEIR BUSINESS AND RETIRE AT ONCE

Changing from spiritual healers to brokers in the financial service sector required restaging. The firm's office was fitted with elegant black marble; its floors were covered with thick carpets. As for stage props, each of the walnut desks represented the individual who would be seated behind it. Victoria's had hers carved with a Greek scroll-and-key design that honored her spiritual guide, Demosthenes. Tennie was petite and delicate; so too was her desk. James's imposing desk was positioned next to a massive Marvin safe, looking every inch a metaphor for the firm's protected and exponentially growing profits.

It was Victoria's idea to section off a back room accessible by a rear entrance restricted to women, and to charge a fixed fee in advance of consultations. Women seeking financial advice were widows, teachers, small business owners, and actresses, along with high-priced prostitutes and their madams who had listened carefully to the idle talk among the tycoons in the city's elegant bordellos. Rarely does karma play out so neatly: Victoria had invaded the male territory of stock speculation where she identified untapped investment capital, the source of which was other women who made their money dealing with men.

Walt Whitman recognized Victoria's impact. Visiting the offices of Woodhull, Claflin & Company, he declared it "a prophecy of the future."

Susan B. Anthony, a figurehead of the women's suffrage movement, heralded their arrival on Wall Street as "a new phase in the women's rights question." Alluding to economic freedom as central to female emancipation, she reported that "instead of making shirts at fifty cents each, these two ladies were using their brains, energy and knowledge of the business to earn a livelihood."

Horace Greeley's *New York Tribune* (whose name forewent its hyphen after 1866) delivered its verdict as a backhanded compliment: "We are so deafened with the demands for unrestricted activities of women, so pestered with claims for the ballot and for office, that it is a pleasure to see a woman do an unexpected and important thing, without iteration and reiteration of her right to do it, and of the injustice, the tyranny of Society in withholding her . . . We commend [this] philosophy to the Woman's Rights Association."

Victoria built on the publicity of the firm by extending its business hours to soirées that showcased prominent businessmen and politicians such as Henry Clews—the banker Tennie had adroitly maneuvered into becoming one of the firm's backers with her request to deposit Vanderbilt's check to launch the firm. Others included were the president of Western Union; President Grant's wartime chief of staff; the president of the Continental Bank; the president of the stock exchange board; and the newly installed managing editor of the *Tribune*, a notably confident man who appeared to move easily among New York's affluent and privileged. Victoria wrote to him the following day. "Accept the thanks of my sister and myself for the generous appreciation in which you held our feelings."

Tennie sent a letter of her own.

"I trust you rested well last night, and that you find yourself refreshed therefrom," was what she wrote, adding a borrowed line from a popular song: "I'm lonely today / I sigh for one smile." Tennie added, "Which I hope to see tomorrow."

Regardless of which men played what roles in advancing the enterprises of Woodhull, Claflin & Company, those already working on Wall Street found it improbable that women would have the natural talent or the professional skills to become brokers. The only thing that would sway their minds was profit.

It took several consecutive months of gains generated by the firm for *The New York Herald* to proclaim that the challenge Victoria and Tennie had undertaken was "far more remarkable than their personal beauty and graces of manner, and these are considerable," adding that "they are evidently women of remarkable coolness and tact, are capable of extraordinary endurance." The *New York Courier* agreed: the two women were "perfectly capable of taking care of themselves."

Other publications with an interest in entertaining their readers were not so fair-minded. Sporting magazines—the nineteenth-century forerunners to contemporary tabloids and celebrity journalism—operated with a conviction that the public was not necessarily interested in accuracy but would always have an appetite for gossip and scandal.

Scandal is not about reporting something. It's about the damage that can be done by the very idea of that something. That's how scandal works. To manufacture the kind of scandal that would sell, the newspapers ran cartoons that recast the sisters' business triumph into a sexualized spectacle.

Having scoured archived articles lampooning Mrs. Woodhull, Mr. Garnett discovered they were dated some twenty years before she brought her libel suit against him and the British Museum. He was at

From the New York Evening Telegraph, February 18th, 1870.

"The Wall Street Hippodrome" from the New York Evening *Tele-gram*, February 18, 1870. Victoria and Tennie are seen as disorderly, dangerous women charging down Wall Street in a chariot of sorts pulled by bulls and bears. The image of the crushed and subjugated men cast the sisters as a threat to the very concept of masculinity.

a loss as to why she hadn't made the same claim against the American publications that had defamed her to begin with.

Had Mr. Garnett been privy to the more personal aspects of Victoria's life at the time, he would have understood that the more immediate challenges of her dysfunctional family, whose past and present members tumbled in and out of her life. Tennie was enjoying a growing number of faceless men who returned with her in the evenings and seemed to melt away unaccounted for in the early hours of the morning. Buck had installed himself at the firm's offices and was passing himself off to reporters as a prominent retired Ohio lawyer. Despite his efforts at a reputational cleaning, he fell back on old habits when he intercepted a runner delivering $30,000 worth of bonds, cashed them in, and pocketed the proceeds.

Victoria's nine-year-old daughter, Zulu Maud, was left at home under the supervision of Roxanna, who was pawning anything of value she could get her hands on, including Tennie's jewelry. Victoria's forty-five-year-old former husband, Canning Woodhull, had moved in, and he wasn't the only alcoholic in the house. Victoria's sister, Utica, had a tendency to drink drugstore bay rum hair tonic when nothing else was readily available.

Victoria's other sister arrived with a husband and their two children, followed by a third sister with her own brood of four. There were three servants, a coachman, a cook, and a nurse to take care of Victoria's son, Byron, who remained unable to clean or dress himself and who communicated more with sounds than words.

When the total number of those living under her roof came to twenty-three, Victoria relocated the ménage to a leased four-story mansion at 15 East Thirty-Eighth Street in the same affluent district and proceeded to spend ostentatious "here I am" money decorating it.

Behind the mansion's imposing façade was a rococo interior groaning under the weight of marble statuary and elaborately framed oil paintings. Venetian glass chandeliers hung in an opulent parlor that opened onto a balcony supported by Corinthian columns. The dining room featured a table that could seat sixteen with chairs upholstered in shimmering satin. Oriental rugs adorned the paneled library. The sound of birds was audible from the conservatory. A massive painted glass dome depicting the loves of Venus looked down from the top of a grand staircase that led to second-floor bedrooms, which were cocooned in plush velvet of various hues.

CHAPTER EIGHTEEN

Karl Marx enters, stage left.

Karl Marx had been exiled from three countries for his political writings when he finally arrived in London in 1849 a stateless refugee who brought with him a wife and young children. Marx had no regular source of income until, in 1851, he accepted an offer by Horace Greeley's *New-York Tribune* to become its foreign correspondent. "Mr. Marx has very decided opinions of his own, with some of which we are far from agreeing," volunteered the fair-minded Greeley, but "those who do not read his letters neglect one of the most instructive sources of information on the great questions of current European politics."

During Mr. Garnett's early years at the British Museum, Marx had frequented the Reading Room to research his concepts of class struggle. Drawing from a draft prepared by German philosopher Friedrich Engels, he wrote *Das Kapital*—a communist manifesto based on the premise that the history of human society is one of the struggles between exploiting and exploited, and that the relentless, omnivorous thing called capitalism was prone to assist one in order to do the other. The work, written in German, passed largely unnoticed, but Mr. Garnett, fluent in the language, would have taken note of it.

The Industrial Revolution had given Britain its flying start as the world's economic capital. Britain's financial base was London, but the subject matter with which Marx engaged came from the city of Manchester. Powering Manchester was the automated loom, which had been built for a commodity everyone wanted and needed: cotton. Humidity was required for cotton to be twisted into thread—it keeps the cotton fibers pliable—which was the reason that the industry settled in Britain's rainy Manchester. By 1871, almost one-third of global

Mr. Garnett was familiar with—and, one might suggest, somewhat proud of—Karl Marx's sources. This is from the admissions register at the British Museum's Reading Room.

cotton manufacturing originated from Manchester and it became the nation's industrial center.

Marx's description of capitalism as a relentless machine crushing the wage earners was quite literally the case with Manchester's cotton mills—brutally demanding taskmasters pushed entire families to spend days tending to the machinery. A man leaning over to adjust a spindle risked losing a finger or hand. A woman's hair caught on a moving belt ripped away part of her scalp. Small children given the task of scavenging loose cotton from beneath the moving machines were sometimes mangled. Deafness from the machines' clatter was a given.

Britain's cotton mills were dubbed "sweating industries" where workers would often be treated as negligible cogwheels. When America followed suit with its own inhumane version of working conditions, Henry George wrote *Progress and Poverty,* a book that investigated the increasing inequity and poverty amid the nation's industrial progress—progress that saw industrialists prospering in the Northeast, while laborers, who had been cut loose from their families in the South and isolated from the traditional network of community, were earning less in wages than they had from working on small farms or in rural stores. James Blood, who likely read the book, was committed to the type of reform aligned with the socioeconomic theories explored by Karl Marx. It was not without reason that the subject of economic inequality was discussed at Victoria's regular open-house evenings.

Cornelius Vanderbilt was a living, breathing embodiment of Karl Marx's belief that capitalism had a tendency toward monopoly, and that successful capitalism drives weaker rivals out of business. James, sincere in his beliefs in a world free of inequity and corruption, managed to find a way around the fact that Vanderbilt's $7,000 seed money enabled Victoria to launch her brokerage firm. James was also somehow able to ignore the disconnect in contemplating issues of the ruling and working classes in a mansion sparkling with gilt. Stephen Pearl Andrews also joined the conversations about reform after Horace Greeley connected him with James. At sixty-one, Andrews looked every bit an apostle of liberal reform: tall, pale, long-bearded, with a permanently furrowed brow and bags beneath his eyes. As a onetime Washington correspondent for Horace Greeley's *New-York Tribune,* he had made himself known to the broader public when that newspaper ran a transcript of a debate he had with Greeley and the renowned philosopher and psychologist William James.

The debate was titled *Love, Marriage, and Divorce, and the Sovereignty of the Individual* and was prompted by the "Matrimonial Causes Act" that had recently passed in English Parliament. It enabled men and women to obtain divorces through a special court. The cost of the procedure was £100, limiting divorce to those who could afford it. While it allowed men to sue for divorce on the simple ground of adultery, a wife could do so only with proof that her husband was guilty of bestiality, bigamy, incest, or rape. During the debate, Andrews put forward the then-radical position that women should be allowed to divorce for the same reason men could. The eminent philosopher and physiatrist William James stood in the middle ground with his army of qualifiers. Greeley argued that marriage should not be dissolved under any circumstance.

To describe Andrews as any one thing would be an injustice. He had been, at various times, a lawyer, a doctor, a philosopher, and a scholar, with indiscriminate curiosity and a mind that reveled in its own omnivorous erudition. He was a linguist who had mastered thirty-two languages and was the author of two French textbooks and one in Chinese. He was a polymath who wrote a jaw-dropping range of essays that included "Comparison of the Common Law with the Roman, French, or Spanish Civil Law on Entails and Other Limited Property in Real Estate"; "Ideological Etymology"; "The Church and Religion of the Future"; and "The Labor Dollar."

Andrews appeared quirky to many; to some, he was innocuously charming, but he was a dedicated reformist committed to interconnected issues. One was the abolition of slavery. When the price of cotton in Texas fell—and with it, the value of slaves—he traveled to England hoping to convince the British antislavery society to advance loans to purchase Texas slaves, and, in so doing, to create a free state.

Andrews failed in his attempt to convince the British antislavery society to advance loans to purchase Texas slaves, but while in England, he became familiar with Isaac Pitman's phonographic reporting (now called shorthand). After returning to America, the autodidact set about devising an improved version of notation system and then wrote a series of instruction books to explain its mechanics.

At the time Horace Greeley introduced Andrews to Victoria, Andrews was living with his wife in a boardinghouse on Fourteenth Street, which doubled as a bohemian meeting ground for the more radical spiritualists mulling over the socioeconomic alternatives proposed by Marx in a time when there was a concentration of immense wealth in the hands of relatively few Americans enjoying vast profits from unregulated industries. New York—a city whose presiding deity was money—was more dishonestly managed than any other. The person enjoying its richest pickings was a great slab of a man with a gouty walk, widely known as Boss Tweed.

William Magear Tweed was the boss of Tammany Hall, a powerful political machine for the Democratic Party that controlled nominations in New York State. With the proviso that they vote for his candidates, he naturalized some forty-one thousand Irish immigrants in a single year. Once his candidates were voted into office, they rewarded the newly installed voters by meeting their needs.

Tweed's political machine replaced the principles on issues around which party politics had previously revolved. The machine's cogs and wheels synched with the interests of the business community. At the height of his political patronage in Manhattan, Tweed was the president of the Guardian Savings Bank; the proprietor of the Metropolitan Hotel; a major stockholder in both iron mines and gas companies; and a board director of the Harlem Gas Light Company, the Tenth National Bank, the New York Printing Company, and the Brooklyn Bridge Company.

Tweed constructed a foundation for corruption by placing himself in a position of access to the city's contractors and funding. He doled out lucrative contracts and expected favors and kickbacks in return; some part of that money was distributed to judges for advantageous rulings. A lower dollar estimate of $20 million has been attributed to Tweed and his ring of associates from their skimming off the top—what the federal government spent on the U.S. Navy in 1870; the higher amount, $200 million, was the equivalent of two-thirds of the entire expenditures of the federal government that year. Not one to forgo increasing his personal income whenever possible, Tweed used his law firm to extort money and bill it as legal services. Among his properties was a mansion on Fifth Avenue worth $2 million that featured mahogany stalls to stable his Thoroughbred horses.

Thomas Nast was an influential caricaturist and barometric reader of whatever was going wrong at the time.[1] The cartoons he drew of Tweed depicted the American incarnation of a corrupt politician.

THE "BRAINS"
That achieved the Tammany Victory at the Rochester Democratic Convention.

William "Boss" Tweed, satirized by
political cartoonist Thomas Nast

Mr. Garnett might have satisfied his English pride by failing to come up with a fraudulent British politician equivalent to the likes of Boss Tweed, but he would have had to acknowledge that Britain's first prime minister, Robert Walpole, once cynically remarked that "every man has his price." Like Victoria, Walpole got rich by taking advantage of an economic crash that ruined so many others by buying shares at their low and selling them at the point the market recovered and returned them to a high. But, according to Mr. Garnett, there was a gaping difference. A man was allowed to straddle the border of questionable conduct while making money as long as it wasn't discussed; a woman doing the same would place herself in opposition to the natural order of things.

CHAPTER NINETEEN

Her talent to provoke.

By the age of thirty-two, Victoria had achieved wealth and prominence. The full prophecy had been "wealth, fame, and the ruler of people," and she set her sights on the last of the three.

On the occasions his wife was out of town, Andrews could be found at Victoria's Thirty-Eighth Street mansion in heady discussions on reform issues. In Victoria, he found a wealthy, self-made, captivating woman with ambition enough to bring his ideological agenda alive. Victoria, in turn, considered Andrews a resource. Convinced that the divination of becoming "a leader of people" would require a more public stage than her recently launched brokerage house, she placed a notice in *The New York Herald*. Written in part by Andrews and dated April 2, 1870, it was newsworthy enough for the *Herald* to splash a headline in large, bold typeface on its first page announcing her presidential run in two years' time. Appearing in the line below was Victoria's bold assertion, "While others argued the equality of woman with man, I proved it by successfully engaging in business . . . I therefore claim the right to speak for the unenfranchised women of the country . . . Having the means, courage, energy and strength necessary for the race [I] intend to contest it to the close."

Among the abundant improbabilities that constituted Victoria's life, announcing her intention in 1870 to stand for president in 1872 was the most improbable. She didn't have the support of a political party. On Election Day, she would still be a year shy of the minimum age of thirty-five laid down by the Constitution to be president. The fact that women were not allowed to hold political office or even to vote was no barricade to Victoria's campaign. Her intention to run for the U.S. presidency had a single purpose: to force a public debate on recent ratification of the Fifteenth Amendment that gave African American men voting rights but withheld the same rights for women.

The announcement that Victoria was running for the presidency was considered too ludicrous to warrant serious consideration, but *The New York Herald* understood the newsstand value of it, and, to keep the story alive, it responded by running its own editorial refraining from questioning Victoria's sincerity in her presidential run, but calling into question its viability.

"Mrs. Woodhull offers herself in apparent good faith as a candidate … There can be no objection to such a competition as this: it possesses the merits of novelty, enterprise, courage and determination … [but] the public is not yet educated to the pitch of universal woman's rights."

James Gordon Bennett was the proprietor of *The New York Herald*,[1] whose nose for a good story led him to offer Victoria a weekly column, "The Petticoat Politician." The column became another platform for Victoria's increasingly controversial polemics, wherein she suggested "taxing vice to provide the means for reformation" and took a stand against the police raids on the city brothels. Blood and Andrews likely shaped and most certainly edited the columns, while Victoria continued to keep her name in the news with tabloid scandal.

Women were not allowed to attend the theater without being accompanied by a gentleman. Victoria commandeered a hotel porter to sit with her. Women were prevented from dining in restaurants after six o'clock in the evening unless accompanied by a man. Victoria and Tennie waited until seven o'clock to appear at the grand New York establishment Delmonico's and drew attention when they seated themselves at a table and attempted to place their order for dinner. The embarrassed waiter retrieved the restaurant's owner, Lorenzo Delmonico, who, making his way to their table through a sea of disconcerted male clientele, handled the uncomfortable circumstances with practiced grace.

"We assumed a gentleman was joining you," is how he explained the staff's error in allowing the two women to seat themselves. Aware that whatever happened next would be reported in the papers, Tennie stood up and left the restaurant. She returned with their coachman, who had been waiting outside. Victoria instructed the coachman to take a seat at their table and ordered dinner for the three of them.

•   •   •

Mr. Garnett had been brought up to believe a woman should never put her foot out farther than she could draw it back. Mrs. Woodhull hunted trouble and didn't care where her foot landed. Exploiting her behavior for dramatic purposes and making spectacles of herself for the political effect—these were the tactics of a woman willing to forfeit respectability. She was arrogant, self-serving, and stubborn: male traits that had no place in womanhood.

The manosphere in New York's Delmonico's restaurant

Stuck in an era not of her choosing, Victoria refused to be restrained by the confinement it placed on her. That alone would not have made her a suffragette, and it was more out of curiosity than a wish to participate that she attended a women's rights meeting the year before she announced her run for president. After listening to the speeches, she decided that a woman's ability to earn money was better protection against the tyranny of confinement than a woman's ability to vote. Even if she were to become an active participant in the movement, Demosthenes had told her she was destined to be famous, which would mean that her place among the women reformers would not be in the ranks, but at the top.

It is possible that Victoria's desire to hasten that prophecy made it necessary for her to become a suffragette, and that her desire to become a suffragette prompted Demosthenes to reappear and inform Victoria (according to her) that "your work is about to begin." That work (according to her) was to put right the wrongs levied against women. A noble aim, to be sure, and one with an emotional truth. But a question nibbles away: Was Victoria self-serving or actually feminist?

Chicken or egg?

CHAPTER TWENTY

A man like no other.

The abolition of slavery in America was kindled largely by a theological debate of human rights among the Quakers, a significant influence during the 1840s. Leading its petition drive was Elizabeth Cady Stanton, the main force behind the 1848 convention of suffragettes in Seneca Falls, New York. During the Civil War, Stanton—in partnership with Susan B. Anthony—encouraged reformers to put women's suffrage to one side in order to work exclusively on the issue of abolition. They were far from the only women focused on the abolitionist movement. Harriet Beecher Stowe activated abolitionists with her 1852 novel, *Uncle Tom's Cabin; or, Life Among the Lowly.*[1]

At the end of America's Civil War there were two camps of thought on women's suffrage: one believed that the time was right for women's enfranchisement; the other, that America, as a nation, would be unwilling to grant a broad range of rights to women for fear it would pull at religious and economic threads and unravel the country's societal fabric. A political consensus was achieved to combine the American Anti-Slavery Society and the Women's Rights Society into a coalition called the American Equal Rights Association. Frederick Douglass—one of the few men who had attended the 1848 Seneca Falls convention—was approached to serve as a member. His wry response: "I have about made up my mind that if you can forgive me for being a negro—I cannot do less than to forgive you for being a woman."

Douglass was born Bailey, of mixed race on a Maryland plantation. At the age of six, he was sent to serve the overseer's relatives in Baltimore. It was unlawful to teach a slave to read: he traded bits of bread with street urchins for their secret reading lessons. At sixteen, he was either given or sold to work for a poor farmer with a reputation of being a "slave breaker."

"I prayed for freedom for twenty years," he would later write, "but received no answer until I prayed with my legs." Bailey boarded a train at a Baltimore depot carrying identification papers obtained from a free Black seaman and dressed in a sailor's uniform that had been given to him. The train crossed into Delaware, another slave state. When Bailey discovered that the rail line hadn't been completed there, he took a steamboat to Philadelphia, a Quaker city and antislavery stronghold with an Underground Railroad. (Neither underground nor a railroad, it was a network of predominantly Black freed men and white abolitionists who hid fugitive slaves fleeing bondage. One of the men who helped Bailey escape to the free state of New York was Mark Twain's father-in-law.)

Bailey arrived in New York in 1838, the year Victoria Woodhull was born. He changed his name to Douglass in honor of a character in a Walter Scott poem, adding an extra "s" for distinction. It was Anna

Frederick Douglass in his twenties, a free man. He would become the most photographed person of the nineteenth century.

Murray, a freed Black slave, who organized his escape and covered its costs. They were married in New York by a Black Presbyterian minister, and, at the age of twenty, Douglass knew freedom for the first time. Years later, he warned that "where justice is denied, where poverty is enforced, where ignorance prevails, and where any one class is made to feel that society is an organized conspiracy to oppress, rob and degrade them, neither persons nor property will be safe . . . Find out just what any people will quietly submit to and you have the exact measure of the injustice and wrong which will be imposed on them."

That Douglass learned to read at the risk of his life gave him a cellular understanding of the power of words. So compelling was the genius of his antislavery writings that it was difficult for even those who saw beyond their prejudices to believe he had actually been enslaved. His response came in 1845 when he wrote *Narrative of the Life of Frederick Douglass, an American Slave,* the first of what would be three autobiographies at a time when millions were still held in bondage. In a hateful turn of fate, that book's bestseller status increased the risk of Douglass's capture and the end of his freedom. With the help of friends and supporters, he escaped slave hunters in America by setting sail for Liverpool, England, where, according to him, it was the first time he was treated not as a color but as a man.

CHAPTER TWENTY-ONE

Slavery as a profit center.

Transatlantic enslavement operated between Europe, Africa, and the Americas with ships that had been outfitted to stow human cargo on their lower decks.

The first leg of the journey—from Europe to West Africa— transported manufactured goods owned by trading companies to West African merchants who sold or bartered the goods to local slavers in exchange for slaves. The ships sailed next to the Caribbean islands carrying human beings chained and forced to lie prone on staked platforms in the ships' hulls: men on the right-hand side; women on the left, boys in the middle. Those who survived the inescapable horror of heat or suffocation were sold as slaves to plantation owners in the Caribbean islands, from whom sugar and molasses were purchased. The ships continued to America, where the last of the remaining European goods and slaves would be sold. American products such as tobacco and cotton were purchased and transported, along with the sugar and molasses from the Caribbean islands, to Europe, with the merchandise to be sold there. British wealth came from the profits its empire reaped from trading in the self-perpetuating business of selling and buying commodities and humans who were considered disposable.

When it came to the business of slavery, Britain trailed behind rivals Spain and Portugal until 1663. By the eighteenth century, the British Empire had become an immense conglomeration of territories in the most distant parts of the world, which were linked by Britain's mastery of the sea. As the world's greatest seafaring nation with ships that numbered more than those in all other nations combined, Britain

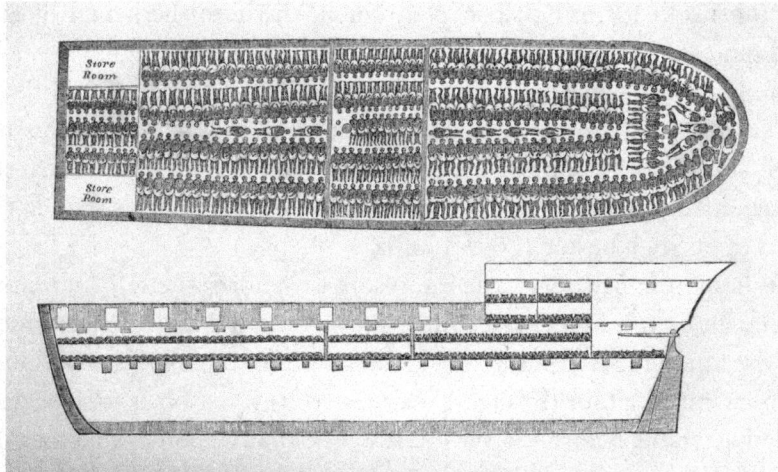

Longitudinal section of a slave ship that stacked humans in the cargo hold.

was able to transport millions of enslaved West Africans to the West Indies to work on British sugar plantations. Caribbean slavery facilitated Hans Sloane's pursuit of the objects and books that became a cornerstone of the British Museum.[1]

Sloane was thought an admirable man, not just for his bequeathal of his collections to the public. He had also donated his salary at London's Christ's Hospital back to that institution. He had supported the Royal College of Physicians' dispensary of inexpensive medications. He was a founding governor of London's Foundling Hospital, Britain's first institution dedicated to the care of abandoned children, in which inoculation was required as a method to prevent smallpox.[2] While living in the Caribbean as a young doctor, Sloane had documented the hideous variety of punishments that befell slaves in Jamaica, noting that, if they rebelled, they were usually punished "by nailing them down to the ground ... and then applying the fire by degrees from the feet and hands, burning them gradually up to the head, whereby their pains are extravagant." For lesser crimes, castration or mutilation ("chopping off half the foot") was the norm. So-called negligent slaves were usually "whipt till they are raw, and some [masters] put on their skins pepper and salt to make them smart; at other times their masters will drip melted wax on their skins, and use very exquisite torments."[3]

Slaves were used and exhausted in the quest of maximum profit for the English until British clergymen, distinguished men of law, and educated older women organized abolition campaigns. Notably, a group of mill laborers in the city of Manchester drafted a letter to President Abraham Lincoln during America's Civil War expressing their support of his antislavery position—this, despite the fact that the blockade imposed on goods from the Confederacy had resulted in the closure of Manchester's cotton mills.

When profit had very little interest in principles, the self-sacrificing act made by the Manchester mill laborers offered a glimmer of hope for the human race, but the spectacular sums of money that continued to pour into Britain through slavery were the reason it took several failed attempts before the slave trade was finally abolished across the British Empire. When Parliament passed the 1833 Abolition Act, the Bank of England compensated some forty-six thousand slaveowners for "lost property." (The total amount came to £20 million, a current value of between £16 and £17 billion.) By 1834, when the 1833 act came into effect, slavery had been abolished in Britain.

Article 1, Section 9 of the American Constitution envisioned the ending of the trade of slaves, but not the institution of slavery. Stephen Pearl Andrews arrived in Liverpool in 1845, determined to convince the British antislavery society to advance loans that would purchase, and thus free, slaves in Texas. That same year, Frederick Douglass set off from Liverpool for a speaking tour in Britain to raise support for the American abolition movement. One of the hundreds of lectures he gave was in Ayr, Scotland, where he recounted his life and the lives of his family in words that became unforgettable.

"I was born a slave. My master's name is Thomas Auld. Besides me, he had other relations of our family whom he counted as his own property, and at this moment I have four sisters and one brother in the same state of degradation and bondage from which I myself have happily escaped. I have a grandmother who has reared twelve children, all of whom have been driven to the Southern slave market and sold."

Over the course of his two years in Britain, Douglass held standing-room-only crowds in thrall with speeches that took from the Bible, Shakespeare, Milton, and Scott. Before he returned to his own country, Douglass's supporters in Britain raised funds to buy his freedom from the man in Maryland who, pursuant to the law in America, still owned him.

In 1848, when Douglass attended the first women's rights convention in upstate New York, he was in favor of women's suffrage. By 1865, the Constitution's Thirteenth Amendment had abolished slavery in the United States. Later, during the debate deciding whether the Fifteenth Amendment gave Black men the right to vote, Douglass feared that linking it with the cause of women's suffrage would result in failure for both. Politics came into play. The Republicans needed Black votes to secure a majority in Congress. Black men—second-class citizens but citizens nonetheless—were granted the right to vote. Native Americans were not considered citizens and denied the right to vote. Women were denied the same right on the grounds that they were not considered capable of reason.

Reformers who had urged women's suffrage felt betrayed by the abolitionists who'd sought and received their backing. What had been a debate became a feud that devolved into a bitter exchange between Douglass and Elizabeth Cady Stanton, who was insulted by what she was convinced was Douglass's condescension. She refused to cede suffrage to African American men before women, and in a downward spiral of argument, resorted to racist claims that those who were "educated" (in other words, white women) deserved to be enfranchised first. She wondered out loud what it was that made wives and mothers the political inferiors to men who couldn't read the Declaration of Independence and ascribed the name "Sambo" to such a man.

Douglass was incensed by the ugly reference, in or out of context. He had witnessed Black men hunted down like animals, whipped to a bloody pulp, and hanged from trees. To his mind, white women would have had to suffer these kinds of horrors for him to give their rights equal urgency. (No mention was made of Black women, including Douglass's first wife, who had met him in Baltimore and emboldened him to escape his slavery. Nor was his second wife considered. She was white, graduated from college, and taught at a school that educated Black men and women.)

Positioned against the New York wing of the women's suffrage movement was the more conservative one in Boston, which agitated for the right to vote but was reluctant to redefine marriage (and least of all a woman's sexual rights). Its president, the popular Brooklyn minister Henry Ward Beecher, ran interference between the two opposing camps of thought. Victoria inflamed passions further when she referred to the Woodhull and Claflin wing of the Woman Suffrage organization and boasted about her success on Wall Street, declaring that "while others argued the equality of woman with man, I proved it."

She continued to claim that she was an ardent suffragette, perhaps because it placed her on a path that she wouldn't have been able to forge on her own. Hers was an impregnable certainty that she would be the one to lead the movement forward. After all, her spirit guide declared that she would become a "leader of people."

To move the prophecy along, Victoria did a very expensive thing. In 1870, she started a newspaper.

CHAPTER TWENTY-TWO

The usefulness of owning the press.

The dominant forces of the American dialogue in the 1870s were its national newspapers. Most were aligned with a political party; all were imbued with the distinct personality of proprietors who set editorial policies. *The Woman's Journal* and *The Revolution* were two such publications. The first was published by Elizabeth Cady Stanton and the latter by Susan B. Anthony. True to its name, *The Revolution* had a more radical agenda.

In New York, *The Evening Post* was a favorite among conservatives, and *The World* was the leading Democratic journal. The go-to paper on Wall Street was the *Herald*. *The New York Times* was known for taking the reporting of events—and itself—seriously. The *Sun* was prone to editorializing. *The Christian Union* was in the tight grip of the popular minister Reverend Henry Ward Beecher, whose sister was Harriet Beecher Stowe. Horace Greeley's New York *Tribune*, whose name forewent its hyphen after 1866, was acknowledged as influential.

A majority of the offices of the New York newspapers were located on Park Row, nicknamed Newspaper Row, near City Hall. The combined number of copies printed daily exceeded 250,000. Entering this crowded field on May 14, 1870 (supported in part by Cornelius Vanderbilt and featuring the inspiring motto of "Upward and Onward") was *Woodhull & Claflin's Weekly*.

Money was spent.

The sixteen-page broadsheet appeared with a large trim size handsomely printed on expensive stock. Its masthead listed Victoria and Tennie in their capacities of editor and proprietor. Designated as its managing editor was James Harvey Blood.

The first issue promised readers that it would be "primarily devoted to the vital interests of the people" and would "treat of all matters freely and without reservation." It declared its support of Victoria C. Woodhull for president "with its whole strength," but reassured readers that it would otherwise be "untramelled [*sic*] by party or personal considerations, free from all affiliation with political or social creeds, and will advocate Suffrage without distinction of sex." It suggested that "the Democratic party has long been only the shade of a name—that the Republican party is effete, and only coheres by reason of place and power; that conservatism is impracticable, while Progress is the only principle worthy of a live, intelligent, independent Journal."

The inseparable names of Woodhull and Claflin arched across the top page of the newspaper.

The first issue of *Woodhull & Claflin's Weekly* featured an installment from a story by French novelist and feminist George Sand, translated from French by Stephen Andrews. His own contribution was an article on Egypt's role in history. There were book and theater reviews, a fashion column, spiritualist topics, sports scores, and financial news. A page was devoted to poetry.

The press response was, on the whole, positive. The *Herald* weighed in with "interesting and agreeable," while *The Standard* found it "a handsome and readable paper." From Philadelphia came more effusive praise with the *Inquirer* reporting that "the new weekly of Mesdames Woodhull & Claflin is one possessing more than ordinary merits."

Not everyone was pleased. Despite her renown as the author of *Uncle Tom's Cabin*, Harriet Beecher Stowe was a bluenose who criticized George Sand, not for her contribution in the newspaper, but for what Stowe identified as her "irregular sex life."

From a business perspective, the *Weekly* got off to a solid start with a print run of several thousand copies. The newsstand cost of ten cents was soon increased and what few copies remained unsold were complimentary to influencers. The operation of the newspaper was divided among its principals: James Blood's management of the brokerage house, Woodhull, Claflin & Company, intermingled with that of the *Weekly*. Victoria assumed the responsibility of its publisher. Tennie's role was to sell advertising space to managers of banks, brokerage houses, and insurance companies. She was also successful in luring certain upscale advertisers such as Tiffany by offering a discounted rate.

By the autumn of 1870, the *Weekly*'s sales increased to a credible twenty thousand copies of predominately out-of-town subscribers at an annual rate of three dollars. Victoria exchanged the newspaper's inspirational motto of "Upward and Onward" with a call to action:

PROGRESS! FREE THOUGHT!
UNTRAMMELED LIVES!

Stephen Pearl Andrews was unleashed and addressed racial injustice, child protection, less rigid divorce laws, and organized labor. He also championed sex education for adolescents, advocated for contraception, and called on testing for sexually transmitted infections in brothels. Interspersed among Andrews's bylined articles, whose opinions almost always raised eyebrows, were the more moderate unsigned ones, which, for example, lobbied for the right of a woman to divorce her husband if there was physical abuse, and her right to honest employment. Presumably, these pieces were written by James Blood.

Despite the fact that there was no political ticket on which Victoria could run for president of the United States, the *Weekly*'s primary purpose remained boosting her as the ideal candidate. Blood and Andrews were able to advance Victoria's platform of social reform in its pages, but to build a constituency from the ground up, she would need the support of a Washington insider. That man was General Benjamin Butler, an influential, cigar-chomping Republican.

Victoria had hopscotched from one male proxy to the next: Vanderbilt had been crucial to her finances; Blood had been indispensable in counseling her on how to marshal her thoughts; Andrews had been an important contributor to her newspaper. Butler would be helpful when it came to Washington politics.

General Butler's reputation during the war had been that of a proactive abolitionist. One of his more resourceful decisions was to declare that, as an officer of the Union army, all of the slaves in the territories he'd captured were free because, according to him, they were "contraband of war." President Lincoln censured him for exceeding his authority, but in the North he was greeted with cheers for his audacious moral stand. After the war, Butler became the congressman from Massachusetts. Like Stephen Andrews, he found his way to Victoria at the invitation of Greeley.

Butler was nothing to look at. He was short, overweight, and spindle-legged. Circumnavigating his bald, spherical head was a fringe of hair that curled upward. He had a droopy mustache, a vulture nose, and eyebrows that branched to the outskirts of his face. What moved him from unattractive to disturbing looking were his eyes. A writer of the time expressed it best: "It was literally eye, not eyes, for the right eyeball seemed to be engaged in some business of its own, as if relieved from regular duty, while the spirit of the man when he looked at you seemed to crouch at the other, and glare out keenly and wryly."

None of this mattered to Victoria. It was Butler's advice she was after and he gave it freely, impressing upon her that suffrage for women would not be won at conventions attended by women, but by lobbying in Washington. And that, rather than campaigning for a new Sixteenth Amendment to the Constitution, she should encourage Congress to consider the premise that women—as "citizens"—already had the right of suffrage. After all, nowhere in the Constitution does the word "men" appear in contradistinction to "women." That the word used is "persons" secures its intent.

James Blood followed the strategy laid out by Butler and ran an editorial in the *Weekly* under Victoria's byline, which set forth arguments designed to prove that the recently written Fourteenth and Fifteenth Amendments enfranchising Black men also enfranchised women, since the language of both amendments directed that all "persons" born or naturalized were citizens with all the rights that were granted to a citizen. The editorial addressed the obvious: that, since women, too, were "persons," it followed that they had those exact same rights. The newspaper included the entire Constitution as an addendum. That, also, was Butler's idea.

Victoria would not have been well-versed on the legal and constitutional precedents cited in the editorial—it was formulated by Andrews, a practicing attorney. The intellect that seeped through its writing came from James Blood. So where was Victoria in all of this? She asserted divine intervention, insisting that, while in a trance and inspired by the spirits, she dictated her thoughts to Blood.

This was precisely how Victoria operated: to avoid being accused of ambition, she claimed that she was no more than a vessel through which an otherworldly force was acting for a greater good.

CHAPTER TWENTY-THREE

Infiltrating the status quo.

Benjamin Butler was certain that he could lead the Republican Party to victory under the two banners of women's suffrage and labor reform. Armed with his confidence in the federal authority of post–Civil War America, he was equally certain that the solutions to both issues would be with the United States Congress. Mark Twain disagreed. His warning for anyone foolish enough to attempt to deal directly with the U.S. Congress came with the easygoing wisdom that was his trademark: "Suppose you were an idiot, and suppose you were a member of Congress; but I repeat myself."

Butler ignored Twain's advice and urged Victoria to construct an argument citing the same points featured in her *Weekly* editorial. The result, likely written by Andrews and almost certainly edited by Butler, was "The Memorial of Victoria C. Woodhull," a declarative document meant to be read out to congressional members. She concluded in the third person: "Your memorialist would most respectfully petition your honorable bodies to make such laws as in the wisdom of Congress shall be necessary and proper for carrying to execution the right vested by the Constitution in the citizens of the United States to vote, without regard to sex."

If anyone was to read the memorial to a congressional committee, insisted Victoria, it should be her, not Butler. He agreed, and a copy was messengered to congressional members in Washington. Tennie traveled there to scout the political terrain and wrangled an invitation to a White House reception attended by President Grant. She made note of how proud he was of his wife and daughter, and both women were the subjects of Victoria's flattery in the next issue of the *Weekly*.

One would be forgiven for thinking that there had been a quid pro quo arrangement when, in the late fall of 1870, Victoria's petition was acknowledged in Washington, and she was invited to put her case in person to the Judiciary Committee of the House of Representatives.

Deliberately or not, Victoria scheduled her trip to Washington at the same time the National Woman Suffrage Association's convention would be taking place. Deliberately or not, she neglected to inform the association's organizers of her appearance in front of the House Judiciary Committee.

Whether women hold other women to a higher standard than they would men is debatable, but while men often deliver their disappointments about women bloodlessly, women convey theirs in a more personal way. Victoria's upstaging the Suffrage Association's convention led to whispers among its members of just how she must have connived it. It took Samuel Pomeroy, a political veteran, to point out that, after twenty-three years, the women's movement was mired in a bog of inaction, and that Victoria had reinvigorated it with fresh ideas. Yes, she might have been disingenuous when she insisted that she "went to Wall Street, not particularly because I wanted to be a broker in stocks and gold, but because I wanted to plant a flag of women's rebellion in the very centre of the continent." Yes, she was reckless, but the fact was that she engineered an unprecedented meeting in front of a congressional committee in order to appeal to them directly on behalf of a woman's right to vote.

Pomeroy offered the suffragists practical guidance: "Men could never work in a political party if they stopped to investigate each member's antecedents and associates. If you are going to fight [for a cause], you must accept every help that's offered."

He convinced the suffrage's old-guard leadership to leave behind their misgivings and uncharitable preconceptions of Victoria and to hear what she had to say.

•   •   •

The morning of January 11, 1871, Victoria and Tennie walked into the congressional chambers and entered a crowded room of newspaper correspondents, curious lawmakers, and those members of the House of Representatives who had already endorsed a woman's right to vote. Waiting for Victoria's arrival there was fifty-year-old Susan B. Anthony, the widely respected proponent of women's rights, who was sensible enough to take Pomeroy's advice.

Victoria was shown to a chair at the end of the long mahogany table where the committee members were already seated. She removed her hat, set it down on the table, and, employing a tactic that was bound to elicit a protective gallantry from the men surrounding her, Victoria apologized in advance for any hesitancy in her manner. When she began to present her memorial, it was in a barely audible voice—this was another of her tactics. It required everyone to listen carefully while she deconstructed the wording of the Fourteenth Amendment. Without referring to notes, she teased out the essence of the amendment by stripping it down to its barest elements before posing two questions, the answers to which were already known: Had the amendment not identified native-born and naturalized persons as "citizens"? And had Congress not forbidden denial of the vote on the grounds of race, color, and previous conditions of servitude? The simple fact was that women were either native born, or naturalized persons, or both.

Victoria laid out her argument by following Butler's strategy, but the emotional authority with which she expressed it was hers alone.

"[Women] are entrusted with the most holy duties and the most vital responsibilities of society; they bear, rear, and educate men; they train and mold their characters; they inspire the noblest impulses in men ... It is by usurpation only that men debar them from their right to vote."

Susan B. Anthony took to the floor with her endorsement. In an article the next day headlined "The Women in Council," *The New York Times* emphasized Victoria's success: "Contemporaries in the woman's rights or suffrage movement have heretofore ignored her, have frowned upon her as an interloper, and have denounced her as unworthy of association ... Now the cry of the suffragans was anthems to Woodhull."

With the *Times*'s benediction came an invitation from Susan B. Anthony to attend the women's convention that was taking place in Washington. Victoria accepted the invitation and, given her success the day before, was asked to join the group's national committee. The nomination process was backed by the majority of rank-and-file members attending the convention, but there was also a bubbling stew of conservative members who were convinced that awarding Victoria a leadership role was irresponsible in light of her notoriety. Gossip, insinuation, and hypotheticals about her fed on the living arrangements she maintained in New York, with a former and current husband under one roof. The questionable relationship she and Tennie had with Cornelius Vanderbilt also came under scrutiny. One of Victoria's fiercest critics, Harriet Beecher Stowe, feared that Victoria's unconventional lifestyle, claims of clairvoyancy, and espousal of free love would detract from the serious issues of suffrage.

Susan B. Anthony held fast against Stowe's criticism of Victoria, and several of the once-reluctant suffrage leaders came to the practical conclusion that Victoria had indeed reignited the cause. Adding to Victoria's credibility was her commitment to pay for a delegation of women to remain in Washington and continue to press the cause. The women planned to appeal to President Grant to pressure the chairman of the House Judiciary Committee for a favorable outcome.

Victoria paved the way for a possible White House seat by writing an editorial in the *Weekly* embellished with superlatives: "[Grant] stands as uncorruptible in his simple honesty, his directness of purpose, his pure integrity." Whether he succumbed to flattery or curiosity, Grant extended an invitation for a meeting. When Victoria was ushered into his office, he rose from his chair and, with more flirtation than conviction, suggested that one day she would be occupying it. Victoria left the White House certain that he could be counted on.

Her optimism had been misplaced. Neither President Grant nor the House Judiciary Committee came through.

CHAPTER TWENTY-FOUR

Democracy . . . just not for everyone.

The House Judiciary Committee rejected Woodhull's petition in a dispatch that pointed out that the authority granting women the right to vote did not reside with the federal government; rather, it was the prerogative of states willing to recognize women as citizens.[1] Woodhull's argument that women were included in the all-encompassing phrase "race, color, or previous condition of servitude" was also rejected. By the same logic, countered the committee, underage and nonresident citizens would be granted the right to appeal to the states to be enfranchised. A resolution was passed discharging the committee from further deliberation.

When Victoria agreed to be interviewed by the New York *Sun* on the outcome, she was aware of the risk of attacking the president for remaining mute. She did it anyway. "[President Grant] has got so many weak men in his Cabinet that he is afraid to do what he knows to be right . . . Politically the administration is throughout weak and corrupt . . . If he had done what he knew to be right at the outset we would have sustained him, and he would have been strong today; but this weakness and cowardice have been his ruin."

To renew her push for congressional action, Victoria remained in Washington and, in her role as the *Weekly*'s proprietor and its major contributor, she requested a seat in the press gallery of the House of Representatives.

"[Woodhull] wanted for some vague and shadowy reason, to be placed especially among the men," was the reaction by an uncomprehending reporter.

The press pass was denied.

Next, Victoria requested the opportunity to address the entire House of Representatives in the House Chamber. When this request, too, was rejected, she appealed to Benjamin Butler, who was unwilling to intervene.

Thwarted by Democrats and Republicans alike, Victoria ran a front-page story in the *Weekly,* announcing "a new party and a newly established third party platform." Appearing above the article was a defiant headline in boldface type.

THE COSMO-POLITICAL PARTY.
NOMINATION FOR PRESIDENT OF THE U.S. IN 1872.
VICTORIA C. WOODHULL

Confident that she could count on women for their votes, she added . . .

SUBJECT TO RATIFICATION BY
THE NATIONAL CONVENTION

The coalition that gathered under the party's umbrella of change included laborers, abolitionists, spiritualists, and suffragists. It proposed an overhaul of the U.S. government, called for abolition of the death penalty, welfare for the poor, national public education, and the establishment of a tribunal to settle international disputes. Incorporated in the party's platform were the points outlined in Victoria's petition that the Judiciary Committee had dismissed, but whereas before she had sought acceptance, now she was demanding it.

"A democracy worth the name cannot be just for men . . . The male citizen has no more right to deprive the female citizen of the free, public, political expression of opinion than the female citizen has to deprive the male citizen."

There had always been a fault line within the women's movement, with one side focused on suffrage causes and the other side willing to tear down institutions that had failed the movement. Victoria was the wedge that split the movement. She formed a third political party whose agenda was in direct opposition to Susan B. Anthony's agenda: a woman's right to vote.

So confident was Victoria that she would be able to count on the suffragists backing her bid for the American presidency that she began to equip herself with a speech, entitled "A Lecture on Constitutional Equity," and made arrangements to rent the largest auditorium in Lincoln Hall, the cultural center of Washington.

When the day arrived and Victoria took to the stage, she identified herself as someone residing in that portion of the people denied the rights of citizens, and then asked a masterly question: If she was not a citizen, why was she expected to pay taxes to the U.S. government?

"I am taxed in every conceivable way," she told the crowded auditorium. "For publishing a paper I must pay—for engaging in the banking and brokerage business I must pay—of what it is my fortune to acquire each year I must turn over a certain per cent."

Victoria steered her speech forward by pointing to the glaring inconsistency of Congress's definition of an American citizen.

"Men fashioned a government based on their own *enunciation* of principles: that taxation without representation is tyranny; and that all just government exists by the consent of the governed. Proceeding upon *these* axioms, they formed a Constitution declaring all persons to be citizens, that one of the rights of a citizen is the right to vote, and that no power within the nation shall either make or enforce laws interfering with the citizen's rights. And yet men deny women the first and greatest of all the rights of citizenship, the right to vote."

Her argument carried logic, but it was her remarkable command of language that compelled the audience to listen. Her understanding of the power of words had come to her as a child living in Homer, while listening to itinerant preachers. She recognized even then that, when spoken out loud and for the sake of performance, words take on cadence and rhythm and pitch and volume. Words, like music, have beats that can move the public in one direction or another.

Victoria held the attention of her audience in Lincoln Hall for over an hour.

The *Washington Chronicle* declared the lecture a triumph, and she returned to New York, where she continued to take her case directly to the public in the pages of the *Weekly* with an appeal to petition Congress for a declaratory law.

Victoria's promise to donate $10,000 to the cause drew praise from a grateful Susan B. Anthony—even more so when Victoria repeated her set-piece speech at New York's Cooper Union. *The New York Times,* which had previously disapproved of Victoria's brazen appearance in front of the Judiciary Committee, acknowledged her power as a leader of the cause. In truth, Victoria had already set about building a broader political base than the one resting on the single issue of women's suffrage. She threw herself into a new round of gatherings in her Thirty-Eighth Street mansion, with attendees that included clergymen, businessmen, congressmen, and members of the press. She produced a book entitled *The Origins, Tendencies and Principles of Government* that sold at the steep price of three dollars a copy and appeared so quickly that it may have been ghostwritten. After Victoria spent the $10,000 that she'd promised to the suffrage cause on brochures that promoted her bid for the presidency and began to sell signed photographs of herself, Susan B. Anthony questioned the direction she was taking. Her commitment to women's suffrage might have begun as an ideology, but it continued as opportunism until it intruded on the suffrage movement itself. By the time Anthony realized that Victoria was running parallel agendas, Victoria had surpassed her prophecy of becoming a "leader of people." She had become a celebrity.

•   •   •

Geoffrey Chaucer wrote his Roman-mythology-inflected poem, *The House of Fame,* between 1374 and 1385. The work comprises two thousand lines and recounts a dream sequence of Chaucer's journey to a glass temple, located at a spot where land, sea, and sky converge. Entering the glass temple, Chaucer discovers that Fame, sitting on a dais, is female. She has countless tongues, eyes, and ears to represent the spoken, seen, and heard. Wings on her heels tell of the alacrity with which she moves. Gathered around Fame's throne are petitioners seeking her favor on behalf of those who have made notable achievements. In Chaucer's dream, the glass temple is built atop a massive rock, but, upon closer inspection, it turns out to be a huge block of ice inscribed with the names of the famous. Certain names have melted to the point of illegibility, as they are outside the protective shade of the House of Fame. This is because mythology, like life, has many properties; sadly, fairness isn't one of them. Fame takes the female form, but there are very few courtiers in her temple promoting women of achievement, which is why fame remains primarily a man's domain. Celebrity, which may be more ambiguous than fame, favors women. Derived from the Latin *celebrem*—a word that implies both celebration and potential "crowding"—celebrity centers on an individual's personality and relies to a large degree upon external scrutiny. Less a destination and more a conferral by the public, celebrity, once bestowed, continues to demand the public's constant attention.

Victoria might not have been familiar with Chaucer's poem, but she had an intimate knowledge of the Bible from her mother, and still, she ignored its warning, "Pride goeth before destruction, and a haughty spirit before a fall."

PART IV

A few simple truths that caused
a great many complications.

CHAPTER TWENTY-FIVE

Flouting convention.

Victoria understood that her run for the U.S. presidency required her to expand her public image from suffragist to humanitarian. The mistake she made was forfeiting the former before cultivating the latter.

In 1871, the National Woman Suffrage Association was prepared to ratify Victoria's position that women be guaranteed the right to vote under the Constitution's Fourteenth and Fifteenth Amendments. The association had planned to do so during its annual meeting at New York's Apollo Hall, but when Victoria took to the stage, she spoke as if the vote for women had already been granted, and that it was the obligation of women to use their vote as a tool to ratify a number of other resolutions. In direct opposition to the wishes of many in the room, she proceeded to explain the platform, point by point, of her new Cosmopolitical Party.

The next day, Horace Greeley wrote in the *New York Tribune,* "We toss our hats in the air for Woodhull. She has the courage of her opinions! She means business. She intends to head a new rebellion, form a new constitution, and begin a revolution."

When several other newspapers referred to the convention as the "Woodhull Convention," Victoria was informed by the movement's elders that she could no longer use the association for her own political ends. Unfazed, she printed the speech she had given at the convention, intending to sell copies of it during upcoming lectures she had already planned in Philadelphia, Pittsburgh, and Chicago.

The time Victoria spent away on that tour left her family dangerously unattended in New York and, never one to miss an opportunity to disappoint, Victoria's mother, Roxanna—who, it should be remembered, was living in a mansion paid for by Victoria and Tennie—attempted to extort money from their friends. In a go-for-broke scheme, Roxanna enlisted Buck to write a threatening letter to Commodore Cornelius Vanderbilt.

Blackmailing Vanderbilt was a serious mistake, but its timing made for a catastrophe.

Vanderbilt's two-year commitment to fund *Woodhull & Claflin's Weekly* was coming to an end at a time when its costs were exceeding its revenues by $300 a week: Tennie had intended to ask him to underwrite a next round of financing for the faltering paper. There was also the brokerage firm's precarious balance sheet: Wall Street investments could yield overnight fortunes, particularly in commodity trading, but those same fortunes could be made worthless just as quickly by the government's shifting monetary policies. Woodhull, Claflin & Company reaped profits from its high-risk investment activities, including margin speculating on gold, until the tide abruptly changed and transactions placed through the firm disappeared, taking the commissions with them.

Vanderbilt, wary by nature, had made an exception in trusting Victoria and Tennie, and that trust was irrevocably shattered when Roxanna attempted to blackmail him. He severed all connections, including the ones that continued to support the *Weekly* and that had held up their brokerage firm. Asked by a reporter about his Wall Street protégés, Vanderbilt replied curtly, "From what I hear, you shouldn't be associated with [them]."

The newspaper and the brokerage firm were both bleeding red ink. It occurred to James Blood that, rather than vying for clients to bank their dollars at the brokerage firm, more could be gained from exposés in the newspaper on the banking community. Victoria, too, perceived a value in the kind of editorial that would cast her as someone admirable, committed to pointing out the corruption and wrongdoing in established institutions, someone working for the good of the people . . . and, when the time came, someone to vote for. She agreed to James's repositioning of the *Weekly* and decided that the front page should be redesigned and a new logo should appear on the paper's masthead. It was a combination of bravado and provocation.

PROGRESS! FREE THOUGHT! UNTRAMMELED LIVES!

Looping in the brokerage firm was the line that ran beneath it.

"Don't Fail to Read the Lady Brokers' Paper!"

Stephen Pearl Andrews propagated his own proposals in the newspaper, the first of which had to do with a land system in which every individual would be entitled to the free use of a proper proportion of the land. He urged a realignment of the educational system and suggested abolishing capitalism's profit-making mandate. The paper's rebooted editorial turned its attention to North Carolina, where state bonds enriched the state's seven railroads at taxpayers' expense. It covered a topic James dubbed "vampire real estate speculation" in New York City and warned of a "bubble," advising anyone holding stocks merely for investment to sell out in time.

The *Weekly*'s crusading exposés placed the journalists who wrote them among the earliest of what would eventually be called "muckrakers," a reference to a character in John Bunyan's classic Christian allegory, *The Pilgrim's Progress*, as a man with the muckrake who rejected salvation to focus on filth. But it was naïve for Victoria to assume she could have it both ways. While she was raising awareness on matters concerning government, business, and public policy, her newspaper was losing advertising revenue from the alienated financial community whose companies the *Weekly* attacked with accusations of alleged malfeasance. The newspaper also began shedding its subscribers, who resented its increasingly revolutionary stance.

Adding its own distress was the continuation of Victoria's simmering domestic life, which boiled over when Tennie, unable to endure her parents after they derailed her relationship with Cornelius Vanderbilt, banished them from the Thirty-Eighth Street residence. Roxanna retaliated. Having lived off the earnings from Woodhull, Claflin & Company under James Blood's supervision, she nonetheless dragged him into court on criminal charges, claiming that he had threatened to kill her.

"I call Heaven to witness," was her clarion appeal to justice the first day in a courtroom packed with the public and journalists. "If God had not saved me, Blood would have taken my life long ago."

James's devotion to Victoria was tested when, under oath, he was left to explain his loosely based marriage in a household that included his wife's first husband and an enthusiast of free love, Stephen Pearl Andrews.

At the end of that first day of the trial—a few short weeks after it chronicled Woodhull's successful speech at the Apollo Hall—the *Herald* was happy to serve its readers speculation about what exactly had been going on among members of the Claflin family.

The general feeling among New Yorkers was that any comment the papers made on Victoria's private life was fair play—after all, she put herself before the public voluntarily and was not ashamed of her conduct. In the early hours of the trial's second day, a queue of people lined up outside the courtroom, hoping for seats inside so that they would learn more about her scandalous lifestyle and unsavory relatives. By the afternoon, reporters were seen prowling around her Thirty-Eighth Street residence hoping to verify that she was living with her former and current husband.

"The fact is a fact," came her unapologetic response. "Dr. Woodhull being sick, ailing and incapable of self-support, I felt it my duty to myself and to human nature that he should be cared for, although his incapacity was in no wise attributable to me."

The trial provided the press and public with two full days of an intoxicating mix of scandal, intrigue, power, and sex. On the third day, exhausted by the drama in his courtroom, the judge opted to reserve judgment.

It seemed that, no matter how terrible the Claflins were to one another, they kept coming back together. Tennie's allegiance to the clan was borne out in the trial's aftermath, when she forgave Roxanna for her reprehensible behavior and addressed the circulated accusation that described the two sisters as seekers of notoriety.

"Do people usually evoke upon themselves continuous persecution, merely to obtain notoriety?" Tennie asked. "Do they consciously invoke the terrible power of the press to crush them, to brand them before the world by every vile and detestable epithet known to language? Do they seek the hoots and jeers of the common multitudes, and the sneer, the upturned noses of the select few wherever they go—merely to become simply notorious?"

Neither hoots and jeers from the public nor seers from the press dissuaded Victoria from her run for the U.S. presidency. "I anticipate criticism," was her prediction. At the very least.

CHAPTER TWENTY-SIX

A serious miscalculation.

To realign her image, Victoria used a different method of messaging it.

An unsigned letter appeared in the *Weekly* dated July 4, 1871, and directed to the leader of the previously named "Cosmo-Political Party."

It read, "A number of your fellow citizens, both men and women, have formed themselves into a working committee, borrowing its title from your name, and calling itself the Victoria League. Our object is to form a new national political organization, composed of the progressive elements in the existent Republican and Democratic parties, together with the Women of the Republic."

In reality, the "Victoria League" didn't exist. The letter, penned by none other than Victoria, had provided her with the opportunity to write a letter in response, which appeared in the next issue of the *Weekly*. To be clear, Victoria made up an entity to endorse herself in a letter that she, herself, wrote and published in the newspaper for which she was the proprietor.

Despite this skillful round-robin of deceit, even the most free-thinking of readers questioned Victoria's future.

Proving a more pressing matter was that Woodhull, Claflin & Company's dwindling clients were unwilling to remain with a firm whose principals took their family brawls to court where possibly anything could be aired. After the trial, the already-faltering firm began its slide toward failure. More bad press would come with the death of Victoria's former husband, Canning Woodhull. The news coverage confirmed his addiction to opium and alcohol and brought renewed attention to her disreputable personal life. Horace Greeley's *Tribune*—having at one time praised Victoria's "high moral worth" and her "sagacious courage"—led the attack. "Let her be the one who has two husbands after a sort, and lives in the same house as them both, sharing the couch of one but bearing the name of the other . . . My conception of the nature and scope of the marriage relation render by conversion to woman suffrage a moral impossibility."

Victoria launched a counteroffensive in her own newspaper.

"[Greeley] has chosen to invade my family sanctum, he will not object to my invading his . . . Mr. Greeley's home has always been a sort of domestic hell."

The Cleveland Leader weighed in: "The unsavory piece of scandal telegraphed from New York could hardly have caused more surprise to anyone who had paid any attention of the record of Mrs. Victoria Woodhull. Her career as a trance-physician in Cincinnati, her brazen immodesty as a stock speculator on Wall Street proclaims her as a vain, immodest, unsexed woman, with whom respectable people should have as little to do as possible. She is a suffrage advocate because being so made her notorious and her paper profitable."

Defiant, Victoria wrote an open letter to *The New York Times* defending herself against the ongoing character attacks: "Because I am a woman, and because I conscientiously hold opinions somewhat different from the self-elected orthodoxy which men find their profit in supporting; and because I think it my bounden duty and my absolute right to put forward my opinions and to advocate them with my whole strength, self-elected orthodoxy assails me, vilifies me, and endeavors to cover my life with ridicule and dishonor. This has been particularly the case in reference to certain law proceedings into which I was recently drawn by the weakness of one very near relative . . . One of the charges made against me is that I lived in the same house with my former husband, Dr. Woodhull, and my present husband, Col. Blood. The fact is a fact. Dr. Woodhull being sick, ailing and incapable of self-support, I felt it my duty to myself and to human nature that he should be cared for . . . My present husband, Col. Blood, not only approves of this charity, but co-operates in it . . . Various editors have stigmatized me as a living example of immorality and unchastity . . . I live in one house with one who was my husband; I live as the wife with one who is my husband."

She could have left it at that, but, instead, reiterated her belief in free love principles as alternatives to rules set by the Establishment and insisted that every man and woman, married or unmarried, had the right to engage in sex with any willing partner. She called out the hypocrisy of her male judges, who "preach against 'free love' openly, practice it secretly." Still not satisfied that she'd done enough retaliatory damage, Victoria continued, "I know of one man, a public teacher of eminence, who lives in concubinage with the wife of another public teacher of almost equal eminence . . . I shall make it my business to analyze some of these lines [*sic*], and will take my chances in the matter of libel suits."

The man Victoria was threatening to expose was the immediately identifiable Henry Ward Beecher. With her veiled reference to him, she was taking on powerful adversaries.

•   •   •

Henry Beecher's father was a preacher, as were all of his five brothers. Two of his sisters were popular writers. A third was active in the suffrage movement. The saying in Boston was that mankind was divisible into three classes—"the good, the bad and the Beechers."

Committed to the abolitionist movement, Beecher had raised money to purchase slaves from captivity in the years leading up to the Civil War. During the war, he sent rifles—nicknamed "Beecher's Bibles"—to the Union army. At President Abraham Lincoln's request, he toured Europe speaking in support of the Union. After the war, he continued to support social reform causes, including women's suffrage.

Beecher was a renowned clergyman of the Plymouth Church in Brooklyn who had a unique oratorical style. At the time Victoria alluded to him in the *Weekly*, he was drawing thousands to the Plymouth Church. Mark Twain, a popular entertainer himself, described Beecher as "howling sarcasm this way and that, discharging rockets of poetry and exploding mines of eloquence, halting now and then to stamp his foot three times in succession to emphasize a point."

Beecher was a trendy figure, and not just behind the pulpit. His books of sermons were prominently displayed in the parlors of the faithful. He was not above endorsing products. That he never suffered from hay fever didn't prevent him from accepting a fee to provide the public with firsthand details about the state of his mucous membranes in an advertisement for Dr. M. M. Townsend's "Remedy for Hay Fever, Asthma and Catarrh." His praise for Pear's soap, "The Famous English Complexion Soap," appeared in newspapers accompanied by his illustrated portrait. The Beecher franchise delivered an astounding $100,000 annually.

It wasn't that he was shilling a hay fever remedy and complexion enhancement, nor was it his expensive choice of attire or, for that matter, his habit of placing opals in the pockets of his velvet jackets so that

"HE TAKES IT PRETTY EASY."

THE REV. HENRY WARD BEECHER ON THE EVENING OF AUGUST 28TH, SITTING AND JOKING ON THE DOOR-STEPS OF HIS RESIDENCE IN COLUMBIA STREET, BROOKLYN, IN COMPANY WITH YOUNG LADIES AND GENTLEMEN, AND WAITING FOR THE INVESTIGATING COMMITTEE.—SKETCHED BY OUR SPECIAL ARTIST.—SEE PAGE 000.

Henry Ward Beecher was known to preach to several of his mistresses every Sunday. Not a good look for a man of God.

he could fondle them. What caught him out was that his fondness for fondling included a number of women.

There was nothing new about Beecher's affairs. For at least a year, rumors of them had echoed within the women's rights movement. Because he was an unlikely looking lover—shortish, lumpish, and in his sixties—something other than his appearance recommended him to the women with whom he had affairs. They included the wife of his protégé and friend, Theodore Tilton.

CHAPTER TWENTY-SEVEN

The benefits of a compliant lover.

Theodore Tilton was a suffrage advocate whom Frederick Douglass described as "a poet and a scholar, brilliant as a writer, eloquent as a speaker." The *St. Louis Globe* referred to him as "unquestionably the most popular young man in America . . . dashing, fearless, truculent, clear-visioned." He had a romantic temperament, a dreamy gaze, and the look of boyish innocence that never fails to attract women. Clean-shaven, immaculately dressed, six feet tall with long wavy auburn hair: it was impossible to find a reference to him that didn't include the word "handsome."

Tilton had been cuckolded in a double betrayal but somehow managed to find a way to put aside jealousy, rage, and humiliation to prevent a scandal by persuading Victoria not to pursue the course of action she had hinted at so publicly. If, according to her, free love was made possible when lovers were united by God-given natural impulses, natural impulses must have kicked in as soon as he walked unannounced through the door of her office.

Within days, she declared him to be a "rare type of man—almost unique," and he said of her that she was one of "the most extraordinary women he had ever met." Neither hid their affair. Tilton stopped going home to his wife and family in Brooklyn, and when he appeared in the mornings at Victoria's breakfast table, her husband, James Blood, didn't complain.

The understanding between the lovers balanced on the tip of an equitable exchange: Victoria agreed to withhold her insinuations about Beecher and Tilton agreed to resurrect her reputation.

The Adonis of freethinkers,
Theodore Tilton

He focused first on Victoria's political agenda. The Woodhull memorial had been composed largely by General Benjamin Butler. To make its issues more accessible, Tilton reframed it in Victoria's own words.

Tilton's next task was to counter the salacious disclosures from Victoria's court case and the press mauling of her that followed. He wrote two thousand words of praise that drew a virtuous circle around her in an essay that took up the entire issue of *The Golden Age,* his political and literary weekly publication.

"She is denounced in the most outrageous manner by people who do not appreciate her moral worth," he insisted. "Her bold social theories have startled many good souls, but anybody who on this account imagines her to stand below the whitest and purest of her sex will misplace a woman who in moral integrity rises to the full height of the highest."

While Tilton was doing what he could to rewrite Victoria's reputation, Harriet Beecher Stowe was busy writing a savagely mocking roman à clef wherein Victoria was its thinly disguised, shamelessly seductive main character who accosts men in their business offices to solicit subscriptions to her newspaper. Informed of this, Victoria decided to publish her biography. James Blood had taken a crack at writing it at one time, but he gave up trying to please her cut-and-paste version of the truth. Tilton would be a more compliant biographer. He attempted to bring pathos to Victoria's life with his own rendition of Victoria's family, beginning with her cruelly demanding and selfish father.

"The whole brood are of the same feather—except Victoria and Tennie . . . For years there has been one common sentiment . . . namely [the two girls] should earn all the money for the support of the numerous remainder of the Claflin tribe—wives, husbands, children, servants, and all . . . They are what my friend Mr. Greeley calls 'a bad crowd.'"

Tilton turned his pen on Buck, who had hurried Victoria into marriage with Canning Woodhull and his lurid way of life. He described the felicitous relationship Victoria had with her current husband, Colonel Blood, as united by "the powers of the air." He wrote of her fateful relocation to New York, and how she and Tennie "won the good graces of Commodore Vanderbilt—a fine old gentleman of comfortable means, who of all the lower animals prefers the horse, and of all the higher virtues admires pluck."

Tilton's draft of Victoria's biography redacted, refurbished, and conflated various accounts in her life, but after reading it, she decided that it lacked the details of her successes as clairvoyant and trance speaker. Spiritualists made up a larger contingency than either the suffragists or the labor reformers and, certain that they would be among her strongest supporters in her run for the presidency, Victoria instructed Tilton to add more references to her spiritual gifts.

"I must now let out a secret," Tilton dutifully added to the book. "She acquired her studies, performed her work, and lived her life by the help (as she believes) of heavenly spirits. From her childhood till now (having reached her thirty-third year) . . . she has entertained angels, and . . . these gracious guests have been her constant companions."

To add a visual dimension, he included a description of her gazing out from the roof of her stately Murray Hill mansion, "communing hour by hour with the spirits."

Tilton referred to James Blood as "a reverent husband to his spiritual wife, the sympathetic companion of her entranced moods." He explained that it was her close bond with James that enabled her divine inspiration. "Every characteristic utterance which she gives to the world is dictated while under spirit-influence, and most often in a totally unconscious state."

To refute any doubts about her authorship of the speeches, editorials, and pamphlets attributed to her name, Tilton added, "The words that fall from her lips are garnered by the swift pen of her husband, and published almost verbatim." He mentioned the trances Victoria experienced as a child and recounted her continued spiritual journey in San Francisco, where the vision of Tennie beckoned her to return to the East Coast; how, arriving in New York, Victoria made her way to Ohio, where the spirit voice had told her she would find her sister; how the reunited Claflin clan took to the road again, this time with a medicine show that featured the two sisters as clairvoyant performers. Victoria's feats in particular ran a gamut of curing the lame and deaf, solving emotional and psychological problems, and, in general, prophesying future events.

Published as a pamphlet in September 1871, *Mr. Tilton's Account of Mrs. Woodhull* sold for ten cents a copy and was met with justifiably bad reviews. *The Tribune* wrote, "If apples are wormy this year, and grapes mildew ... it may be ascribed to the unhallowed influence of Mr. Tilton's life of Victoria Woodhull." A dire prediction was offered by Julia Ward Howe, who had penned the "Battle Hymn of the Republic." "Such a book is a tomb from which no author again rises." *Hearth and Home* magazine took the tomb analogy further by running an obituary: "The brave Theodore Tilton is dead and replaced by a 'pseudo-Tilton' who ... writes insane things about spirits of ancient Greek orators inspiring the meretricious rhetoric of a woman who advocates free love."

•   •   •

Victoria replaced any concern she might have had over her lover's damaged reputation with what was, for her, the happy result. The biography rearranged and even fictionalized a great deal of her life into a bespoke narrative and, as she intended, its detailed account of how she relied on spiritual communication for direction left its mark on the spiritualist communities.

It is possible that Victoria was incapable of bestowing herself on a single thing or person. At the start of her affair with Tilton, she told him that she "foresaw six months of rapture for them." From the very beginning, he had been a lover on borrowed time. Victoria viewed her liaisons with men as impermanent, which is why she could so easily dispense with Theodore Tilton and refocus her attention on James Blood. It made sense that, since Blood was the former president of the St. Louis Society of Spiritualists, she would want him on her arm while she attended the spiritualists' two-day convention in Troy, New York. Despite their noncommittal stance on politics, spiritualists were drawn to reform movements. Victoria came to the convention prepared to discuss the subjects of interest to them.

During the course of the two-day event, resolutions relating to Tilton's rewording of the Woodhull memorial having to do with a woman's right to vote were adopted. Victoria was invited to read her biography (also penned by Tilton) aloud. By the end of the convention, she was elected the president of the American Association of Spiritualists and declared their candidate for the president of the United States.

Expressing her appreciation from the rostrum, Victoria told the crowd that she had been a recipient of heavenly favors ever since she could remember and she was an earnest advocate of the principles of the spiritual philosophy. She thanked the convention for its hand of fellowship.

Upon returning to New York, Victoria repeated her gratitude in a five-column editorial appearing in the *Weekly*, addressing the National Association of Spiritualists directly. She wrote, "I can only regard the fact of your election of me by spontaneous action as your president . . . as an intimation that the great and influential body of spiritualists has arrived at the state of readiness to intervene actively in the political affairs of the country . . . I tell you frankly that I feel myself called upon by the higher powers to enact a great role in connection with this great change. It is not ambition in any sense of the word . . . It is a swelling and overmastering desire for an immense usefulness to my suffering fellow-beings . . . It is an inspiration . . . which I trace and ascribe to spiritual resources . . . and which has in it, the promise of undoubted and unbounded success."

Victoria Woodhull realized that her future would be more promising if she had it all to herself, but what was it that dictated her decisions: impassioned beliefs, or the relentless ambition she so fervently denied having? Perhaps it was a bit of both.

CHAPTER TWENTY-EIGHT

Push becomes shove.

Gathering political backing wherever it could be found, Victoria joined the International Workingmen's Association in New York. Given her determination and drive, it should have come as no surprise to those who knew her—or even knew of her—that she was designated the titular head of the association. Nor would it have been a shock to see that on December 30, 1871, the *Weekly* had become the first publication in the United States to print the English translation of Karl Marx and Friedrich Engels's *The Communist Manifesto.*[1]

When Victoria promised to "advocate the rights of the Lower Million against the Upper Ten," she ignored the indisputable fact that the clients of her brokerage house were members of that "Upper Ten." Not only was she cavorting with communists at the same time she was actively pursuing wealth, her grand ambitions were pushing the communist agenda aside by creating a buffet of her own proposed reforms. Victoria reasoned, for example, that since women were a part of the New York labor force they should be thought of legitimately as laborers. Why not add a woman's right to vote to the association's mandate, Victoria wanted to know . . . and what about including a woman's right to her sexual freedom?

As if her unwelcomed interventions were not disruption enough for the International Workingmen's Association in New York, there were the rolling distractions made by her acolytes. Stephen Pearl Andrews had proposed an international use of a universal language.

The secretary of the central committee sent a concerned letter to Karl Marx describing the disturbance she was causing. "We don't want people to take her ridiculous ideas for the views of this society. The nonsense she's talking about, women's suffrage and free love, might be considered sometime in the future, but the question that interests us as workers is that of labour and wages."

When Victoria let it be known that she had a recent visitation by Napoleon's spirit, Marx decided she was more than just a nuisance. She was an iconoclast whose version of reform was destructively at odds with his ideology and the communist cause. Despite her ground-breaking speeches on labor and the *Weekly*'s original publication of his *Manifesto,* Marx's instructions were to expel Victoria from the International Workingmen's Association.

Unbothered by the rejection, she turned in her party card and refocused her attention on support from freethinking spiritualists. America's broadcast medium, post–Civil War, was the lecture circuit. Victoria embarked on an extended tour that took her to gatherings of spiritualists in Philadelphia, Pittsburgh, Detroit, Cleveland, Chicago, and Buffalo.

Left to her own devices, Tennie decided that she, too, deserved a chance to capture the public's imagination.

•   •   •

The Germans migrated to America in numbers as great as the Irish, and they eventually became the nation's largest non-English-speaking ethnic demographic. It was for this reason that Tennie announced her bid to represent New York's primarily German American Eighth District in Congress. With the ubiquitous Stephen Pearl Andrews as her coach, she launched her campaign in August 1871 and started off with an address to the German-American Progressive Society at New York's Irving Hall.

Speaking to her would-be constituents in halting German— her mother's native language—Tennie incorrectly stated that, even though women weren't allowed to vote they were not forbidden to put themselves forward as candidates. She asked if anyone thought that "things could go worse in the administration of our national affairs than they now do," and suggested that they had very little to lose by trying "the experiment merely of intrusting a woman with the performance of official duties."

It was Tennie's deliberate reference to temperance that brought the most applause: "Just as the religious American has the privilege of going to his church on Sunday, so must the right be equally secure to you to seek your recreation on Sunday . . . and to drink your glass of lager-beer in peace and quietness, as long as you do not disturb the public order."

Tennie's declaration was enough to convince several hundred (presumably beer-drinking) members of the society that she should be the nominee for Congress on behalf of New York's Eighth District. The idea of her as a viable congressional candidate had a quick end, but she was clever enough to take advantage of the brief credit that had been bestowed upon her. She announced her intention to write a book that would encompass her political experience. James Blood and Stephen Pearl Andrews organized and probably wrote most of the material in *Constitutional Equality a Right of Woman*. General agreement among the critics was that Tennie knew a great deal about matters pertaining to the sexes and almost nothing at all about politics. After deciding that scandal was a more effective route to public awareness, she made it known that she would seek the honorary role of commanding an all-Black regiment in Manhattan. A shamelessly outlandish act of publicity? Yes. But it provided a platform to advance her proposition of training women for army combat—a cause that remains relevant to this day.

While Tennie was busy generating public recognition, Victoria spent her time seeking endorsements for her presidential bid. It occurred to her that there was one man in a position to provide a fresh category of voters. Victoria asked her former lover, Theodore Tilton, to act as her intermediary and make arrangements for her to meet Henry Ward Beecher, the very man who, not long before, she had threatened to expose by name for his extramarital affairs. Let it not be forgotten that Beecher had had an affair with Tilton's wife and then enlisted Tilton to convince Victoria not to go public with the fact of it. More remarkable still was that Tilton agreed to Victoria's request.

Putting aside the probability that Tilton's emotional involvement with Victoria had outweighed the peculiarity of her request, she was right to identify Beecher as a hugely valuable asset. His Sunday sermons in Brooklyn were so popular that special ferries—"Beecher ferries" they were called—carried crowds of worshippers there from Manhattan. Certain that Beecher could win her the God-fearing voters, Victoria made it clear to him that, if he refused to endorse her, she would expose his affairs to the public.

Beecher agreed to meet her. Indeed, they met not once but on several occasions and always at a late hour. The liaisons Victoria had with Beecher might not have been a full-fledged affair, but it was enough to confirm that he was a man who practiced free love.

Never one to pass up good material, Victoria ran an article about him in the *Weekly* that outlined one of the many themes of her ongoing lectures. "The immense physical potency of Mr. Beecher, and the indomitable urgency of his great nature for the intimacy and embraces of the noble and cultured women about him, instead of being a bad thing, as the world thinks, or thinks that it thinks, or professes to think that it thinks, is one of the grandest and noblest of the endowments of this truly great and representative man."

Actually, Beecher's nature was not dissimilar to that of Victoria: both were charismatic actors, brilliant at establishing an intimacy with their audiences, who, when the situation called for it, exerted considerable charm; both had grown overly fond of adulation and neither of them were strangers to hubris.

To Victoria, Reverend Henry Ward Beecher was the means by which to relaunch her political career, and she spent the summer of 1871 on a lecture tour. It would culminate with a speech in New York, which, according to the *Weekly*, was "for the express purpose of silencing the voices and stopping the pens of those who . . . persistently misrepresent, slander, abuse and vilify [Mrs. Woodhull] on account of her outspoken advocacy of, and supreme faith in, God's first, last and best law."

The title of the lecture was splashed across the newspaper's pages in capital letters.

"THE PRINCIPLES OF SOCIAL FREEDOM"
INVOLVING THE QUESTION OF FREE LOVE,
MARRIAGE, DIVORCE AND PROSTITUTION.

Victoria rented Steinway Hall, the largest in New York. Giant yellow banners reading FREEDOM! FREEDOM! FREEDOM!

appeared on every side of the building. Printed flyers teased out what to expect at the must-see event: *If it is good in the Religious and Political sphere who shall dare deny that it is good in the SOCIAL SPHERE?*

A speech on the topics of marriage, divorce, and prostitution was too good to pass up and seats at Steinway Hall sold out. Victoria wanted more. She wanted Henry Ward Beecher to introduce her on the stage and, during his introductory speech, she wanted him to publicly declare himself an advocate of social freedom.

Her demands were conveyed with a threatening tone in the letter she wrote to Beecher, the import of which was made abundantly clear: if he refused, she would divulge details of his extramarital affairs. A frantic Beecher conferred with Tilton. Tilton, conversant with the damage Victoria was capable of doing, warned him that not only did Victoria have it in her to reveal his affairs, she wouldn't hesitate to do so in front of a large public audience. He advised Beecher that presiding over her stage appearance would keep her quiet for the time being.

"This may be the last chance to save yourself," was Tilton's warning.

Beecher—in meltdown—agreed to appear by Victoria's side onstage with the understanding that she would never reveal his alleged relationship with Elizabeth Tilton. He also paid for the rental of Steinway Hall, as Victoria had demanded.

CHAPTER TWENTY-NINE

She just couldn't help herself.

Public lectures in America had shifted from being platforms for discourse to something more akin to popular entertainment. On the evening of November 20, 1871—despite the pouring rain—some three thousand people arrived at Steinway Hall for Victoria Woodhull's lecture. Her podium persona was a theatrical rendition of the most provocative issues of the day, and those coursing into the hall welcomed a chance to either call out approval or to hector her.

Every seat on the ground floor and in the two galleries was taken and an overflow of people stood in the aisles. Seated on the stage's platform were Horace Greeley and a number of conservative suffragists from the Boston wing of the movement.

Henry Ward Beecher never showed up. Fortunately for him, Tilton arrived in time to convince Victoria not to expose him. The speech she gave hewed closely to principles she'd rehearsed with Andrews. It underscored "self-ownership" while referencing three inalienable rights set forth in the United States Declaration of Independence: life, liberty, and the pursuit of happiness.

"Individuals have the Constitutional right to pursue happiness in their own way," Victoria told the crowd, and then declared that the laws of marriage and divorce were despotic and "utterly unfitted for an age so advanced upon that."

"Are you a free lover?" was what someone in the audience shouted. Victoria's response was a shell burst of oratory.

"Yes I am a free lover . . . I have an inalienable, constitutional, and natural right to love whom I may, to love as long or short a period that

I can; to change that love every day if I please, and with that right
neither you nor any law you can frame have any right to interfere."

  To refer publicly to the issue of sex was attention-grabbing, but to
advocate sex outside of marriage was enough to silence the audience.
Victoria had aroused the public's curiosity, suspicion, jealousy, envy,
and now rage.

  Political cartoonist Thomas Nast had already noticed the growing
number of suffragists refuting the concepts of free love when Victoria's scandalous speech was reported in the *Herald*. He picked up his
pen and, in one of his vitriolic flashes of wit, depicted the controversial
Victoria Woodhull as Mrs. Satan, drawing her with a sneering face,

Thomas Nast depicted Victoria as Mrs. Satan, who, while promoting
free love, is trying to lure a dutiful wife away from her husband.

a devil's horns, and vulture-like wings. Shown clutching a sign that read "BE SAVED BY FREE LOVE," she was attempting to convince an exhausted woman, who was bent under the weight of her drunken husband while toiling up a steep, rocky path with two infants: one tied to her, the other in her arms.

"GET THEE BEHIND ME, (MRS.) SATAN," reads the caption, with the valiant woman insisting, "I'd Rather Travel The Hardest Path of Matrimony Than Follow Your Footsteps."

A man's perception, surely.

Her provocative lectures, her political stunts, her frequent and sensational trials: Victoria's personal and political lives were one and the same. When objections from other parents forced her to withdraw Zulu Maud from the private school she was attending, it didn't prevent Victoria from forging ahead with plans to run for president. In April 1872—under the false pretense that the announcement had come from the National Woman Suffrage Association—the *Weekly* reported that a meeting would be held on May 9 in Steinway Hall to form a new political party named "the People's Party" and to nominate its candidates for president and vice president. Not only did Victoria mislead the public with her misinformation, but it was obvious that she intended to use the National Woman Suffrage Association's meeting for her own political platform.

"Mrs. Woodhull has the advantage of us because she has the newspaper," was Susan B. Anthony's reaction.

Victoria paid no heed and, on the evening of May 9, arrived at the association's meeting to hold forth on the newly formed People's Party. She recommended that its efforts toward reform should be fused with those of the association, and, when Anthony tried to intercede, Victoria clung to the lectern and continued speaking. Anthony left the stage and ordered the janitor to turn off the gaslights. Nothing, it seemed, could push through Victoria's obstinacy. Standing her ground in the pitch-dark, she announced that the People's Party would meet the next morning at the Apollo Hall. When she left the hall, she took some part of the assembly with her. By severing her link with the suffrage movement, Victoria had made an enemy of Susan B. Anthony.

The "People's Convention" was relocated the following day. Sticking with their strategy of doubling the power of a single impression,

Victoria and Tennie both dressed in black silk. Nearly seven hundred delegates representing twenty-two states and four territories formed a youthful, vibrant, hybrid constituency consisting of faithful *Weekly* readers, spiritualists, communists, and even some of the more radical suffragists.

The first item of business was to rename the gathering the "Equal Rights Party," with the hope that the new name would evoke the unity enjoyed by the Equal Rights Association when it mobilized for suffrage. The ever-useful Stephen Pearl Andrews wrote the political platform. It incorporated a call for women's suffrage, a one-term presidency, reform of the civil service, demands for labor reform (including an eight-hour working day), free trade with all nations, and an end to capital punishment. After a resolution was unanimously adopted, Victoria was invited to address the convention. Her rousing speech was met with shouts of approval.

When, on May 10, 1872, the Equal Rights Party nominated Victoria for president, she claimed to be the first woman to run for the presidency, even though she was younger than the constitutionally mandated age of thirty-five. She also announced that Frederick Douglass would be her running mate for the vice-presidential nomination, even though Douglass was not present and had not been consulted beforehand. In fact, Victoria had never met or spoken to Frederick Douglass. His reaction was a dignified nonresponse.

CHAPTER THIRTY

Sharp truths begin to make dents.

At various times in her life, Victoria had been a sensation, a lightning rod, a concern, a scapegoat, and a target. The nation gave her its full attention when, at the age of thirty-four, she became inescapably relevant as the Equal Rights Party's nominee for president of the United States.

Not all of the attention was favorable. *The New York Times* greeted the news with an attack against her and Tennie.

"Praise or abuse is probably alike welcome to these diffident women. The more prominently the rather ungracious fact of their existence is kept before the public the better their trade is advertised, and the more keenly their vanity pleased."

Looming over Victoria were challenges more serious than her bad press. Profits at Woodhull, Claflin & Company had dwindled—the result not only of Victoria's bad press, but of the firm's high-risk gambles in speculating on margin, which had been disastrous in a volatile market. Advertising in the *Weekly* was draining away, along with the number of its subscribers. Victoria was no longer able to make the payments to cover the newspaper's costs. To keep it afloat, she sold most of the furniture and all of the art in the Thirty-Eighth Street mansion. It didn't stem the losses for very long. Of the difficult choices Victoria was forced to make, suspending the paper was the most upsetting—it had been her access to supporters and the general public.

As Victoria's prospects ebbed away, so too did the support from the men on whom she relied. Horace Greeley disassociated himself from her and accepted the presidential nomination from both liberal Republicans and the Democratic Party. In a stunning rebuke, her former and once-devoted lover, Theodore Tilton, decided to back Greeley. Rubbing salt in that wound was a poem he wrote and published about the aftermath of his affair with her.

> *I clasped a woman's breast,—*
> *As if her heart, I knew,*
> *Or fancied, would be true,—*
> *Who proved, alas! she too!*
> *False like the rest.*

Mr. Garnett was as chivalrous a man as he was a skillful writer. I'm convinced that, had he discovered the poem during the course of his researching Mrs. Woodhull, it would have been difficult for him to decide if Theodore Tilton's ungentlemanly decision to publish the poem exceeded the poor quality of its writing. And had Mr. Garnett discovered the subsequent newspaper interview Victoria gave, I'm certain that he would have felt a slight tug of delight. Asked to comment on the poem, she replied that it was not her habit to read "trashy literature."

Victoria made every effort to keep her declining fortunes secret. That was made impossible when she was evicted from the mansion on Thirty-Eighth Street, which, by then, had been stripped of its furnishings. So disreputable had she become that, shortly after she moved herself and her two children to the Gilsey House—a hotel on Twenty-Ninth Street near Fifth Avenue—the proprietor told her to find other accommodations. Returning to the hotel at the end of that day, she found the family's belongings chucked onto the sidewalk. After a fruitless search for somewhere to spend the night, Victoria and her children ended up sleeping on the floor of the brokerage firm's office on Broad Street. The landlord, made aware that they were camping in the office, increased the rent and demanded full payment for the year.

Adding its own challenge was the filing fee required to put Victoria's name on the state ballots for the November 1872 presidential election. Unlike the established Democratic and Republican Parties, the Equal Rights Party lacked financial resources. Enthusiasm for Victoria's presidential bid died down when those who had attended its convention were asked to contribute to her campaign. James proposed that her supporters lend money to the campaign on the condition that, if Victoria was elected, the money would be repaid. The gilt-edged bonds he had printed went begging. Victoria refused to relinquish her run for the presidency and used donations from the Equal Rights delegates to cover the expenses of renting a house. These living quarters doubled as both the party's headquarters and the brokerage firm's new offices. She wrote a letter to Beecher requesting his help.

"I have submitted to this persecution just so long as I can endure to. My business, my projects, in fact everything for which I live, suffers from it, and it must cease. Will you lend me your aid in this?" she asked.

After Beecher dismissed Victoria's letter as "whining," she did not have to wait long for another of her out-of-body experiences. While onstage during the September convention of spiritualists in Boston, there was, according to her, "overwhelming gusts of inspiration . . . from I know not where . . . made, by some power stronger than I," and she disclosed the details of Beecher's secret love affair with Theodore Tilton's wife.

It was quite a performance.

Pausing only to push back her hair, which had fallen into disarray, Victoria spoke of free love as its own justification while admitting to the affairs she had had. The sole reason she was denouncing Beecher's affair, she told the audience, was to disclose his hypocrisy.

"It is a paradox of my position that, believing in the right of privacy and in the perfect right of Mr. Beecher socially, morally and divinely to have sought the embraces of Mrs. Tilton, or of any other woman or women whom he loved and who loved him . . . I still invade the most secret and sacred affairs of his life, and drag them to the light and expose him to the opprobrium and vilification of the public . . . What I do is for a great purpose."

Not entirely.

Victoria's outpouring of moral duty produced several positive out-
comes for her, and her alone. The story of Beecher's affair with Tilton's
wife traveled quickly and worked to her favor among her core voters.
She was reelected president of the American Association of Spiritualists. Her multicity lecture tour sold out and its proceeds reactivated
the *Weekly*. Its publication in October 1872, known as "scandal issue,"
revealed Beecher's affair with Tilton's wife and was featured in an
eleven-inch column under the headline:

THE BEECHER-TILTON SCANDAL CASE
THE DETAILED STATEMENT
OF THE WHOLE MATTER
by Mrs. Woodhull

Citing falsehoods, slander, and conduct unbecoming of a Christian
minister, Victoria's article included detailed accounts behind the alle-
gations that Beecher was secretly practicing the free-love doctrine
that he was denouncing from the pulpit.

*"I propose . . . aggressive moral warfare on the social question, to begin in
this article with ventilating one of the most stupendous scandals which has
ever occurred in any community," she explained. "I refer to . . . [the] conduct of
Rev. Henry Ward Beecher in his relations with the family of Theodore Tilton.
I intend that this article shall burst like a bomb-shell into the ranks of the mor-
alistic social camp . . . He has, in a word, consented, and still consents to be a
hypocrite. The fault with which I, therefore, charge him, is not infidelity to the old
ideas, but unfaithfulness to the new."*

The issue cost ten cents when it hit the newsstands dated November 2. By that evening, people were paying $2.50 a copy. When the first
edition of 100,000 sold out, enterprising others who had managed to
purchase a copy began renting it for a dollar a day; 150,000 new copies
were printed and sold.

The *Weekly*'s "scandal issue" besmirched the entire Beecher family, whose noble stock of writers, reformers, and clergymen had
become moral standard-bearers for middle-class Americans. Victoria's vengeance-is-mine approach failed to take into account that
post–Civil War tolerance had given way to a social conservatism, and

that criticism levied at anything that might weaken the family unit—believed to be the foundation of a stable society—was now frowned upon. Her disclosures about Beecher might have granted her a degree of short-term satisfaction, but they led her into unpredictable and dangerous territory.

CHAPTER THIRTY-ONE

Jail time.

Despite the fact that both of her parents considered blackmail a sensible source of income, Victoria's threat to expose Beecher had nothing to do with extracting money from him. True, manipulation was baked into Victoria's genetic code, but, according to her, it was the spirits who had commanded her to force Beecher to answer for his hypocrisy. "To preach the doctrine, you must live the life," was how she put it.

The spirits might have commanded Victoria to right Beecher's wrongs, but it was her rage that egged the spirits on. (Beecher wouldn't be the only man Victoria would deride publicly—Theodore Tilton would also answer for his betrayals. She had not forgotten the poem he wrote about their affair.) Mr. Garnett likely wondered whether Victoria would have made her fatal mistake of exposing Beecher if, as Beecher had promised, he'd gone to the Steinway Hall to introduce her . . . or if, when she became destitute, he'd given her money. And why, Mr. Garnett might have also wondered, had James Blood—with his background as an accountant—failed to do a cost-benefit analysis before Victoria brought Beecher into disrepute? Of all people, James must have understood the financial risks.

Money was certainly what was driving Beecher's end of the equation. The profits enjoyed by his backers were dependent on his popularity. Being exposed as an adulterer would impact the number of his parishioners and, thus, deplete the take from his collection plate. It would threaten the subscription base of his newspaper, *The Christian Union,* along with its advertising revenue. The credibility of his bestselling book of sermons would be called into question by the disclosure that the book's editor was one of his extramarital conquests.

Businessmen who invested in Beecher went on the offensive with arrangements to prepay for copies of the *Weekly* and instructed the newspaper's mail room to post the copies in the mail. The rest they left to Anthony Comstock.

•   •   •

Anthony Comstock was a Connecticut-born man who was known to be overly close with his mother with whom he shared a religious fervor. He had fought on two fronts during the Civil War: one was in the infantry for the Union; the other was as a devout Christian facing down the powers of evil. His self-assigned duty to warn fellow soldiers about the moral errors of masturbation made him unpopular.

At the war's end, Comstock married an older woman (who might well have reminded him of his mother) and they settled in New York, where Comstock believed God had sent him to face down "the mouth of a sewer in the middle of a swamp." He had always been suspicious of literature, insisting that, in short, it "defiles the body, debauches the will, destroys the memory, sears the conscience, hardens the heart, and damns the soul."

While earning a living as a dry goods salesman, he took to trolling bookstores looking for what he considered to be lewd material that bred lust and "inflamed the imaginations of young men." By claiming that certain books were "feeders to brothels," he was able to justify supplying the police with information on particular bookstores to raid.

Comstock paved a wider path to righteousness by enlisting the Young Men's Christian Association (YMCA) to join the cause. When he announced his intention of achieving moral purity by "weeding God's garden," the YMCA—seeing the need to create distance from Comstock's fanaticism—assisted him in establishing a separate entity, the New York Society for the Suppression of Vice. As its president, Comstock put himself in charge of monitoring anything he perceived as offensive, and thus dangerous to the public. When the society was chartered by the New York State Legislature, its agents were granted the right of search, seizure, and arrest. They were also awarded 50 percent of whatever fines were levied.

Seeking more authority, Comstock volunteered to forgo a salary in order to be made a special representative of the U.S. Postal Service. In that role he gained the legal right to prosecute anyone suspected of the public distribution of what he considered pornography. The bigger prize was to be had in Washington with the anti-obscenity bill Comstock drafted: it would prohibit the circulation of obscene publications and include contraceptive devices in an inventory of "criminal deeds."

The right half of the seal of the New York Society for the Suppression of Vice depicts a man in a top hat (sartorial shorthand for respectability) throwing banned books into a blazing bonfire. On the left is a marshal, who, equipped with indignation and a billy club is pushing a handcuffed man into a jail cell. Both men were shown achieving worthy goals.

In the span of ten years, Comstock went from creepy vigilante, to dangerous crusader, to savvy political insider who made his case by energizing religious extremists and convincing them that he was a voice against evil. His political lobbying and largely church-based support bore fruit when Congress passed what would later be known as the Comstock Act. Had anyone been paying attention, they would have realized that the statute's wording was so loose that even a comparatively repressed American would have been alarmed with what Comstock deemed obscene.[1] The law disregarded the First Amendment and censored all manner of written material, including medical books illustrating the human anatomy. Designating contraceptives illicit made it a federal offense to disseminate birth control through the mail or across state lines. Twenty-four states enacted their own versions of the law to restrict the contraceptive trade on a state level. Connecticut was the most limiting: it legally prohibited the use of birth control by married couples in the privacy of their own bedrooms.[2]

Comstock had become a hydra-headed creature using nefarious means to capture culprits he believed were selling filth. When he received a confirmation that copies of the *Weekly*'s "scandal issue" were being posted by mail, he secured warrants from the U.S. district attorney for the arrests of Victoria and Tennie, charging them with sending obscene literature. The two were detained in front of the *Weekly*'s offices while the police confiscated all issues of the publication and trashed the office's furniture. Word spread of the arrests and, by the time the marshals escorted Victoria and Tennie to the courthouse, a large procession had formed behind them.

Reverend Beecher refused to sue them or the *Weekly* for libel, but Comstock applied pressure. "An example is needed," was the assistant district attorney's reason for setting bail at $8,000 each for Victoria and Tennie, remanded into custody at the Ludlow Street Jail, where Boss Tweed had been incarcerated after his conviction for draining millions of dollars from the city's treasury.

The following morning, the *Herald* characterized Tennie and Victoria (who, at one time, had been the newspaper's popular columnist) as women who "cannot even be classified with unfortunates. It is a greater depth of infamy to which they belong." *The New York Times* ran an editorial pronouncing that "the female name never has been more disgraced and degraded than by these women." Harriet Beecher Stowe took the opportunity to refer to Victoria as "an impudent witch."

Victoria and Tennie's saving grace was that one in the growing number roused by their incarceration was the eccentric millionaire George Francis Train. Due to the space required on steamships for coal and crew requirements, sailing ships were favored for long voyages. Train organized the clipper ship routes that sailed around Cape Horn to San Francisco.

Like Cornelius Vanderbilt, George Train had made his first fortune in shipping. The sheer size of America made it difficult to see beyond it. George Train did. When the time came to pivot to a newer method of transportation, he was instrumental in the formation of the Union Pacific Railroad.

Train was more than a brilliant entrepreneur who claimed to have achieved the goal he set for himself in 1870 to travel around the world in no more than eighty days. He was also an outspoken supporter of women's suffrage, more than willing to pay for Victoria and Tennie's bail. Not wishing to forfeit the publicity of remaining in custody, the sisters turned down Train's offer, but he likely covered the costs of a well-known criminal lawyer, the famously flamboyant William F. Howe, as their chief counsel.

Howe was known to crave the spotlight and nearly eclipsed the two women when he appeared in front of the commissioner wearing a costume featuring plaid pantaloons, a purple vest, and a blue satin scarf held in place with a gigantic diamond pin. The plea he formulated pivoted on the premise that there was no basis for an obscenity charge since everything in the *Weekly* articles in question could be found in the themes of Shakespeare's plays.[3] Howe also pointed out that if any of the words printed in the *Weekly* issue in question could be considered obscene, the transmission of the Holy Bible through the mail would be exposed to the same penalty.

In the end, nothing Howe could do or say would make a difference. Victoria and Tennie were returned to Ludlow Street Jail, where Victoria closed her 1872 presidential campaign on the eve of Election Day from a barren cell with a melodramatic—but nonetheless prophetic—letter to the editor of *The New York Herald*:

"To the public I would say in conclusion they may succeed in crushing me out, even to the loss of my life: but let me warn them and you that from the ashes of my body a thousand Victorias will spring to avenge my death by seizing the work laid down by me and carrying it forward to victory."

Victoria and Tennie were still incarcerated when Republican Ulysses S. Grant swept into office for a second term. Though Victoria's name hadn't appeared on the ballot, she might have received write-in votes from the twenty-two states where the Equal Rights Party had delegates. Although no national tally was kept, she is often credited as the first woman to have stood for president.[4]

After suffering a humiliating defeat in politics, Horace Greeley had hoped to resume his editorship of the *Tribune*. He was met with the news that the value of its stock had fallen while he was campaigning for the presidency. When he learned that a syndicate was coalescing to oust him from his own paper, he took to his bed in despair and sank into a coma from which he never emerged.

It is my belief that Mr. Garnett, being the kind of man he was, could not abide bullies and must have been relieved to read about the American public's backlash against Comstock's moral authoritarianism. He must have been reassured by the American press's collective uneasiness that the government was overplaying its hand by denying a timely trial, and that even the *Eagle* in Brooklyn—a Beecher stronghold—objected that "without being generally known, the people of this country are living under a law more narrow and oppressive than any people with a written constitution ever lived before . . . We can discover no intention on the part of the authorities to try these women at all."

"Sick in body, sick in mind, sick at heart," began Victoria's open letter in the *Herald*. "I write these lines to ask if, because I am a woman, I am to have no justice, no fair play."

Susan B. Anthony put aside their differences and issued a public response. She pointed out the double standard imposed on women by men and added that the same double standard was practiced by women on other women. "This is one of man's most effective engines for our division and subjugation. He creates the public sentiment, builds the gallows, and then makes us hangmen for our sex."

When, finally, Victoria and Tennie were released from custody, Victoria went on the offensive with a post-prison speech, "Moral Cowardice and Modern Hypocrisy; or, Four Weeks in Ludlow-Street Jail." Her intention was to deliver the speech in Boston, home to illustrious members of the Beecher family, but, having received word in advance, the Boston mayor banned her from the city. She gave the speech in an auditorium in Springfield, Massachusetts, instead.

Anthony Comstock, meanwhile, vowed "to do something every day for Jesus," and used a false name to order copies of the *Weekly*'s scandal issue, requesting that they be mailed from the newspaper's New York office to his home in Connecticut. The receipt of the copies was all that was required for him to instruct the New York sheriff's office to prepare warrants for the arrests of Victoria, Tennie, and James Blood. This time, the charge was for distributing obscene matter across state lines under legislation designed to protect the moral probity of the U.S. Postal Service. James was arrested at the *Weekly* office but managed to get word to Victoria that a marshal was on his way to New York's Cooper Institute, where she was scheduled to deliver another of her speeches that evening.

The police, who had been instructed to wait outside until the marshal arrived, joined hundreds of people congregating inside the hall, all transfixed while listening to Victoria describe the experience she and Tennie had had in a cramped jail cell. She warned of the misuse of public office and explained the weakness of Comstock's case. She reminded the crowd that the object of his persecution was to prevent the *Weekly* from being published. She claimed that, rather than speaking for the powerless, the church had allied itself with money and power, and she concluded her speech by announcing that she would be deprived of her rights as an American citizen. The marshal arrived and, with a theatrical flourish, she extended her wrists to receive imaginary handcuffs, and he escorted her offstage and returned her to Ludlow Street Jail.

Victoria was thirty-four years old when Comstock had her arrested a second time. He, twenty-eight. They were entirely different creatures but shared the same methods of implementing their goals. Both used public opinion as a lever to secure their reputations and appeal to supporters of their crusades. Like Victoria, Comstock was certain that the means he employed always justified the ends: just as she justified her threat to expose Beecher as a hypocrite, so too did Comstock believe that the entrapment he performed to ensnare her was justified.

When it became obvious that Comstock was determined to destroy Victoria, Benjamin Butler, her onetime mentor and an ally in Congress, came to her defense. His letter of support appeared in the New York *Sun*. This was followed by an editorial he wrote for the New York *Sunday Mercury* pointing out that "it does not seem right that the whole machinery of the Federal Government, with its courts and marshals, should be placed at the beck of a man who has, somehow or other, chosen it for his private business to deprive this woman of her liberty."

The bonds required for the eight separate charges brought against Victoria, Tennie, and Blood amounted to a staggering $60,000 each. When the press began to call out the unprecedented harassment, the Plymouth Church lawyers pressured the judge to settle the long-overdue trial. The prison experience shared by Victoria, Tennie, and James was not unlike roping mountaineers together. Victoria described it in more ethereal terms: "Ours is a trinity . . . to which we are equally devoted . . . We three are one in spirit and purpose, and [therein] lies all the strength we have." The three were tried on the charge of circulating obscene literature.

"In God is my trust," Comstock wrote in his diary the day the judge was set to rule on the case. The judge concluded that the statute as originally drafted applied only to books and pamphlets, and not to newspapers. His instructions to the jury were to return a not-guilty verdict.

Comstock's response? He made sure that his legislative oversight would be corrected with a new provision.

CHAPTER THIRTY-TWO

Counting the losses.

Women's suffrage and the labor movement had soured on Victoria; she was no longer invited to their conventions and gatherings. Her role as president of the national spiritualist organization had been taken away when, as a keynote speaker at its 1873 convention in Chicago, she criticized its members for their failure to support her with donations when she emerged from prison broke.

Victoria's repeated arrests left her in dire financial straits when her health—at a perilously low ebb from the months she was held in a damp jail cell—prevented her from riding the drafty trains required for an income-producing lecture circuit. Determined to recoup at least some of the financial losses she'd suffered from her incarceration, Victoria petitioned Congress for $100,000—an amount calculated to be a fifth of the lost income suffered from the suppression of the *Weekly* from the actions brought about by Comstock. When, in 1874, nothing had come of her efforts, Victoria gathered her strength and returned to the lecture circuit with James. Tennie would arrive in advance in each of the tour cities to bargain for the halls, arrange lodgings, and prepare the press. Victoria's daughter, Zulu Maud, remained in school. James's younger brother, George, managed the *Weekly* and did what he could to take care of Victoria's disabled son, Byron.

When it became clear to James early in the tour that Victoria's standard root-and-branch lecture relating to ills of business and government wasn't attracting the large crowds that were expected, he recommended that she switch to one on the forbidden subject of sex. Her nebulously titled lecture, "Tried as by Fire; or, the True and False, Socially," proved to be a moneymaker. Groups paid $280 to hear

Victoria explain why, according to her, sexuality was a "physiological basis of character." She referred openly to female orgasm, but was careful to put it in the context of sex education for men and women— a kind of proto-family-planning program. The most lucrative results came from the women-only audiences she charged to learn about birth control. Earnings from that lecture alone supported the family and kept the *Weekly* afloat.

While it is true that Victoria made a valuable contribution by educating young women about sex when they otherwise would have had no information, it is also true that she was promoting her belief that "healthy children could only be produced by healthy parents" and that impregnation should occur "under perfect conditions of love" and with "mutual consummation." According to her, these conditions would alter the laws of heredity by preventing the negative traits of physical or mental deficiencies. For the first time, she referred publicly to Byron—more precisely, to Byron's impairments—insisting that they were the result of a pregnancy forced upon her by an alcoholic husband when she was still a girl. For a woman to own and control her body "is what it means to be virtuous," Victoria told her audiences, asserting that the improvement of human society would only result from the conscious will of women to select when and with whom to reproduce. That claim, suggesting a connection between women's roles as mothers and the improvement of future generations, was a precursor to what would become the powerful and dangerous concept of eugenics.

•   •   •

Cornelius Vanderbilt and George Train became tycoons in a time when the railroad industry was the largest employer in the United States outside agriculture, and the government's land grants were paving the way for some thirty-three thousand miles of new track to be laid.

Speculation produced an infusion of investment for ancillary facilities that included docks and factories until 1873. That was the year it became obvious to those speculating that the capital funding the country's endless construction was failing to produce the quick returns they had anticipated.

Railroad shares were the first to fall in a collapsing house of cards. The market went into cardiac arrest, and President Grant ordered that no stocks be traded for ten days so that the economy could be given a chance to stabilize. By 1874, one in seven people in New York was unemployed. Dozens of the city's banks and Wall Street firms had failed, including the already-struggling Woodhull & Claflin brokerage company.

Victoria continued to tour the country to lecture—not out of passion, but to pay the expenses of her newspaper and to support her two children, her sister, her husband, and the parents she should have discarded years before. Fewer people had money to spend on lectures. Victoria reduced her fee to ten cents a head. She forwent sleep during grueling all-night train rides and traveled ceaselessly from one Midwest city to the next. Lecturing in unheated halls battered her lungs. "It's like someone is tightening an iron band around my chest," she told a doctor, who urged her to pause her commitments until her lungs cleared up.

Returning to New York to recuperate, she was confronted by the never-ending matter of Reverend Henry Ward Beecher. Her decision to expose his past affairs had come at a steep price. "I had no idea in the beginning of the battle I was waging," she admitted.

The first in a series of its aftershocks came when Beecher's loyalists at Plymouth Church—convinced that Tilton would be a reminder of the fiasco—offered to share the expense of sending him and his family abroad. This forced Tilton's hand, and he threatened to go public. That in turn prompted a church hearing, but not until Beecher's influential allies convinced Tilton's wife that she had an obligation to clear Beecher's name. She testified to the church's six-man panel that Beecher's behavior had been above reproach and that it was her husband, a "free lover," who had had an affair with the notorious Victoria Woodhull.

Beecher repaid Mrs. Tilton for her loyalty by insisting that he had not done anything untoward and that she had forced her attentions on him. Tilton brought charges against Beecher for the alienation of his wife's affections. The scandal provided the public with welcome relief from the grim economic climate during what would prove to be one of the most widely reported trials of the century. Just as delighted as the public by the spectacle were the lawyers: Tilton engaged three; Beecher, five.

Mobs jammed the morning ferries from Manhattan to the Brooklyn City Hall, which housed the courthouse. Hawkers set up stalls selling souvenirs and pretzels in front of the officers issuing tickets to enter a courtroom that could only seat three hundred people. The more enterprising camped on the sidewalk overnight to be the first in line and then scalped tickets at a higher price to the well-heeled waiting in carriages that would line up in front of the courthouse, as if in front of an opera house. The trial began in the first month of 1875 and ended six months later with a hung jury. Among the three hundred seated in the courtroom was Mark Twain. Victoria was at the center of both sides of the argument, but neither side dared put her on the witness stand.

The press covering the trial included European newspapers. A French publication misidentified Reverend Beecher's wife as "Madame Breechertow, the mother of Uncle Tom." Some five years before the trial, the *Weekly*'s debut issue featured the first installment of a story by the French novelist George Sand. That past connection might have been the reason Sand conceived a novel about the trial. Sand died before it could be written.

·   ·   ·

Victoria counted down 1876 in losses. Despite the hundreds of women who benefited from her frank lectures on sex, she no longer had the support from suffragists, who had long since come to view her radicalism as a threat to progress. Life on Wall Street as she knew it limped to its end. The labor movement abandoned her. Washington politicians had written her off. She was forced to resign as president of the spiritualists' association. After a tumultuous six years of owning a newspaper, the last copy of the *Weekly* came out in June.

Victoria's marriage was hanging on by a thread. Her partnership with James Blood had been based on mutual goals. With no more brokerage house, no more newspaper, no more collaborative work on reform ideas, and very few lectures left to give, her relationship with him had deteriorated. Adultery was the only basis for divorce in New York—a method Victoria had publicly decried in the past but that she nonetheless employed to divorce Blood.

Victoria was thirty-eight years old and twice divorced. She had been mocked and derided in the public for years. Now she found herself without a devoted man on whom she could rely for instruction, advice, the writing of her articles, the polishing of her speeches, and the editing of her books. *What next?* Victoria and Tennie could have lit up the sky with the number of bridges they had burnt by the time they appealed for financial help in a letter to Cornelius Vanderbilt. He never responded.

During the 1876 Christmas holiday, Vanderbilt's health weakened. Arriving at death's door the first week of the New Year, he requested that the attending minister sing his favorite hymn, "I Am Poor, I Am Needy." It couldn't have been further from the truth. Cornelius Vanderbilt's fortune amounted to $105 million, $5 million more than the U.S. Treasury had in its coffers.

A pool of reporters rented a room directly across the street from his Washington Place mansion and installed a special telegraph line. Vanderbilt died the morning of January 4. His butler hung black crepe on the front door and flags in New York were lowered to half-mast.

•   •   •

Nine-tenths of the total amount of Cornelius Vanderbilt's fortune was willed to his eldest son, Billy. This displeased Billy's siblings, who contested the will with a claim that their father had been mentally incompetent at the time he signed it. Papers filed in court pointed to the questionable decisions Vanderbilt made while under the influence of magnetic healers and the fraudulent phenomena of spiritualism and cited his connections to Victoria and Tennie. If either were to take the stand and testify, a conservative judge might rule against the will's disproportionate distribution in favor of Billy. The principals on both sides didn't reveal the details, but word had it that Billy appeased one brother by agreeing to provide him with income of $1 million placed in escrow in addition to his inheritance, and that he silenced two sisters with an additional $500,000 each. As for Victoria and Tennie, it's likely that Billy, being familiar with the methods used by the two women when his father was alive, decided the prudent course of action would be to cut a deal. Rumor had it that they were paid $200,000 for a written pledge to leave the country without contesting the will.

Victoria had sought fame in America, but she was forced to settle for notoriety. She had sought wealth, but she was willing to accept enough money to pay for four double first-class cabins aboard a liner bound for England. The year was 1877.

BETWEEN TWO PARTS.

•

Federal troops were removed from the American South. Blacks were left to fend for themselves while parades of armed white supremacists prevented them from voting in the 1876 presidential election. Frederick Douglass levied an accusation at the federal government: "You have emancipated us . . . but you turned us loose to the sky, to the storm, to the whirlwind, and, worst of all, you turned us loose to the wrath of our infuriated masters."

•

The cattlemen on the Great Plains continued to dispose of Native Americans until they were nearly gone. The U.S. government continued to make concessions to railroad interests.

•

The Mormon leader Brigham Young became the first territorial governor of Utah. He benefited from an assortment of lucrative commercial ventures and died the richest man in that state.

•

Due largely to the movement's warring factions, issues pertaining to women's rights were sidelined.

•

After Victoria divorced James Blood, he moved to Maine and took an editorial post at one of the local newspapers.

•

Stephen Pearl Andrews embraced a philosophy he called "universology," which stressed "the unity of all knowledge and activities."

•

Ruined from the expense of his unsuccessful lawsuit against Beecher, Theodore Tilton left New York for Paris, where, for the next twenty-four years, he wrote for French publications and nursed his disappointments with absinthe.

•

George Francis Train's claim to have gone around the world in eighty days—true or not—caused a sensation when Jules Verne fictionalized the feat in a novel.

•

P. T. Barnum took General Tom Thumb to London, where he was a hit on the stage in Piccadilly. A command performance before Her Majesty Queen Victoria at Buckingham Palace opened the door for Barnum's introduction of Thumb to further European royalty, including the tsar of Russia.

•

Anthony Comstock expanded his purity campaign to include a range of targets. One was the Art Students League in New York. He had it raided and issued arrest warrants for those involved in the production and publication of its magazine, which had reproduced pictures of nudes the students had painted. When Comstock threatened to suppress Walt Whitman's book *Leaves of Grass,* it piqued public interest and provided a very happy author with steady royalty payments for the first time in his career.

•

Reverend Henry Ward Beecher remained a leader of the Brooklyn community. The Plymouth Church closed ranks and covered all of his legal costs.

•

Mark Twain's *The Innocents Abroad,* a story of his trip with a group of other Americans through Europe and the Holy Land, sold over one hundred thousand copies, and was followed by another successful travelogue, *Roughing It. The Gilded Age* came next, followed by *The Adventures of Tom Sawyer.* As his fame spread, inconsistent copyright laws resulted in unauthorized editions of his works. He produced President Ulysses S. Grant's memoirs through the fledgling publishing house he co-owned with Charles Webster.

PART V

A different life in another country, and a future bearing no resemblance to the past.

CHAPTER THIRTY-THREE

Determined to become respectable.

After a ten-day transatlantic journey, Victoria, her two children, Tennie, and several servants docked in Southampton. The entourage then boarded a train for London's Waterloo station. Penniless the year before, Victoria was able to rent a cream-painted stucco mansion in London's up-and-coming neighborhood of South Kensington. The country to which she emigrated had a single sharp line cutting through its society, designating those who used the two entrances to the house. Tradespeople used the narrow steps from the pavement that led down to the kitchen and servants' quarters. Family members and visitors ascended the building's stone steps to the front door, which opened up into a wide entrance hall. The hall led to two drawing rooms and a dining room, which benefited from a dish lift from the lower-floor kitchen that boasted the modern conveniences of a ventilation system, an asbestos stove with a gas cooking range, and an ice cellar. Upper floors offered four bedrooms. Servants' accommodations were on the top floor.

As for London itself, in an era of great English writers, Charles Dickens was the most passionate observer of its rhythms and drew fictionalized subjects and characters from its street life. He observed that early mornings belonged to the unemployed living in abject poverty, who began their day's task of feeding themselves with whatever they could scavenge. They were followed by less-poor working men and boys hauling meat and fish to the markets. Next came coal wagons, permitted to unload at certain morning hours, shadowed by fruit and vegetable wagons. Right behind them were the shawled seamstresses and milliners' workwomen, bound for the dress factories of the West

End. Rattling sounds from store carts morphed into an interminable rumble from horse-drawn omnibuses taking commercial clerks to their jobs in the banking center. Lastly, the wealthy emerged from their homes and, ushered into privately owned carriages, made their way to their unhurried destinations.

Dickens suggested that "everything that happens . . . shows beyond mistake that you can't shut out the world; that you are in it, to be of it; that you get yourself into a false position the moment you try to sever yourself from it; that you must mingle with it, and make the best of it, and make the best of yourself into the bargain." Victoria had no intention of mingling. For the sake of becoming respectable, she concentrated on making herself into something she had never been—conventional. Replacing her mannish outfits were ruffled dresses. Her hair, in loose curls, she gathered at her neck. She purchased a copy of *Murray's Handbook for Modern London,* from which she learned "never dispute in the street with a cabman," and that, while Saturday was "the aristocratic day for sight seeing," Monday was "generally a work-man's holiday."

After reading her way through books that provided basic information on how she should maneuver around London, Victoria sought more nuanced instructions on the virtues and graces of the English drawing room. One book counseled that "men frequently look with a jealous eye on a learned woman . . . be cautious, therefore, in a mixed company of showing yourself too much beyond those around you." Another advised that "if at any time the society of your husband causes you *ennui,* you ought neither to say so, nor give any suspicion of the cause, by abruptly changing the conversation."

Good manners are, in effect, the succession of details, but the books and periodicals that Victoria studied so diligently neglected to disclose the fact that the type of English people she wanted to win over shrouded their disapprovals in politeness. The phrase "it would be lovely to see each other again" could be rightfully interpreted as "I have no real interest in knowing you"; "forgive me for disagreeing" really meant "I don't approve of you."

It wasn't only the perils of high society that challenged Victoria. She was confronted by the fundamental and resolutely un-American belief of the English that a person was no better than their hereditary position, even sometimes independently from material wealth.

Faced with the country's blatantly class-conscious perspective, Victoria put her mind to the ways a person's position was determined. On the bottom of the tiered population were laborers. Merchants and bankers were in the middle. The aristocrats occupied the upper echelon. But the English insisted on more subdivisions: laborers were divided in half, the lowest in rank being the workingmen. The almost-as-poor artisans were given more social credit and were harder to identify, as they had largely eliminated signs of their trade outside their workshops.

Victoria found it difficult to define the upper layer of the lower class, and even more of a challenge to understand when it was, exactly, that they interfaced with the lowest ring of the middle class. Clerks, for example, were given a higher step on the social ladder than shipbuilders, made so by the fact that it was their brain and not their hands that had come into play. This meant that, even at his poorest, Karl Marx would have been considered middle class.

Having continuously pushed against the boundaries of respectability in America, Victoria was willing to agree to its confines for the sake of a new life. Aware that her success or failure would turn on mastering that which the English upper class considered correct, she learned that she should not be seen in the inelegant posture of bending over a table to blow out a candle. Bearing in mind that dental deficiencies might be more evident than she thought, she learned that she should avoid smiling too widely. When it came to the treacherous implications of actually speaking, London's floating population included all manner of provincial England, but the only proper version of the language was devoid of a regional accent. As an American, Victoria need not have been overly concerned with the implications of an accent, but she nonetheless followed the strictly codified rule of a muted approach accomplished by speaking quietly, stringing together qualifiers, and avoiding superlatives, especially when it came to praise. She was careful that any reference she made to her own accomplishments was unobtrusively dropped into a sentence as a parenthetical. The one rule she remained at a loss to understand was the requirement that any conversation begin with an exchange about the weather. Having lived through tornadoes, droughts, and blizzards in America, it seemed to her that the most striking thing about the weather in England was that there was not very much of it beyond rain. What there was in abundance was smoke. Thick plumes of it poured out of factory shafts, while an ever-growing number of house chimneys contributed climbing clouds of it.

Coal was the culprit responsible for the dingy veil of smoke that prevailed most days. It had been coal that kick-started Britain's Industrial Revolution. Because it was easily mined, it quickly transformed the way the country ran. The vast number of factories consuming coal produced flakes of floating soot that blackened the buildings and streets. It contributed to a constant smog overcast that blurred the time of day, as if London had "gone into mourning . . . for the death of the sun," suggested Dickens. If one imagined that the evenings brought relief from the din, one had only to read the works of Dickens's fellow author Arthur Conan Doyle. Doyle deployed menacing night settings for his Sherlock Holmes novels, wherein London's labyrinthine streets became symbolic analogies for the troubled lives of his characters.

It wasn't just London's brown air by day and the sordidness of its nights—London smelled. Added to the industrialized miasma that stank of carbon and sulfur was the acid odor from the gallons of horse urine that permeated cobblestone streets. Tens of thousands of working horses produced tons of manure a day and relatively little of it was removed by the young boys employed by shopkeepers to dodge between the traffic and scoop it up.

The sheer volume of London's pedestrians was daunting. Never before had Victoria seen so many concentrated in one place. London, the world's largest city, was at the center of the vast, mercantile British Empire that produced and shipped two-thirds of the world's coal and one-half of its iron.

For all of its class consciousness, Britain's pragmatic aristocracy showed a willingness to hobnob with the merchant leadership for one reason alone: the Thames. The Thames was a vital source of the empire's wealth, and if Victoria were to stroll to the fogbound river from her home in South Kensington and take a route through Chelsea, she might walk past the home of another American émigré—bad boy artist James Abbott McNeill Whistler.[1] Expelled from West Point military academy, he quit America for Paris before choosing a house that overlooked the quieter reaches of the Thames. The river's glimmering water served as blue and gold mood music for his nocturne paintings that hinted at ships and bridges that seemed to dissolve in the nighttime atmosphere.

Victoria's otherworldly visitations were occurring less frequently, but she held on to the prophecy foretold by her spirit guide when she was a child promising wealth "in a city surrounded by ships." Cornelius Vanderbilt had facilitated her ambitious pursuits in America—as a Wall Street broker, as the founder of a newspaper, as a presidential candidate. In death, his money gave her the opportunity to begin another life in London . . . a city, without question, surrounded by ships.

CHAPTER THIRTY-FOUR

Doing whatever was required.

The Vanderbilt go-away money enabled Victoria to reestablish herself in London, but maintaining the household required a new source of income.

To her way of thinking, she had been a respected leader of the women's rights movement in America and was therefore well positioned to attract new audiences in Britain. She sought advice from Millicent Garrett Fawcett, a political activist and writer who had attended London's first suffrage public meeting in 1869, and who, two years later, continued to campaign by undertaking an extensive speaking tour of the West Country. Fawcett wrote to Susan B. Anthony in America before responding to Victoria's outreach. Anthony quickly replied, "Let her severely alone. Both sisters are regarded as lewd and indecent."

Rejected by Anthony and ignored by Fawcett, Victoria forged ahead with plans for a six-month tour with her first public appearance in Nottingham, an important center for lace manufacturing. She replaced her previously outspoken endorsements for free love with broader humanitarian goals. Her revised lecture, reverently entitled "The Human Body: The Temple of God," concerned the sacred institution of marriage.

Her shift away from controversial activism proved to be a success. *The Nottingham Guardian* reported that Victoria "appealed in the most impassioned and fearless language to her audience to awaken the responsibilities of life, and especially of maternity."

The tour was scheduled to conclude at London's St. James's Hall. When posters were placed in London's shopwindows advertising the event, *The New York Times* correspondent predicted that "Englishmen and women are not in the habit of talking about the human body in miscellaneous company . . . Mrs. Woodhull is a rather good looking woman and has circulated her picture. She will be sure to receive many letters and have many callers . . . [but they will be] roués in search of a new sensation and over-educated young women."

Proving the correspondent wrong was John Biddulph Martin, a partner in his family's distinguished bank, the oldest in Britain, older even than the Bank of England.[1] John Martin was three years younger than Victoria and had begun working at his family's bank in 1863, the same year she was living in a cold-water flat in Chicago with her alcoholic first husband, Canning Woodhull. At thirty-six, John was one of the most eligible bachelors among the English gentry: Oxford educated, rich, charming, and exceptionally good-looking.

Why was a man who served on the boards of numerous businesses and charitable organizations—whose family counted eleven members in Parliament and centuries of esteem—drawn to attend Victoria's lecture? John Martin might have had personal reasons for seeking out Victoria Woodhull, or so reasoned Mr. Garnett. John's adored sister, Penelope, died a few years before. She had anonymously penned a series of articles on the subject of women's rights. Perhaps, thought Mr. Garnett, it was out of deference to his much-loved sister that John attended Victoria's lecture and requested a backstage introduction to her. Afterward, John scribbled in his pocket diary how much Victoria had fascinated and charmed him. This, too, was not unthinkable to Mr. Garnett.

Before she met John Martin, Victoria had already decided that she would marry a wealthy man from a respected English family, and she had prepared herself for what she realized would be an uphill struggle. Because Anglo-American marriages were frowned upon by the upper classes at the time, Victoria changed her surname from Woodhull to Woodhall, pointing out that the last vowel had been altered to render it uniform with the Woodhall family in the West of England. In the same spirit of orthographic reinvention, her daughter's Christian name morphed from Zulu Maud to Zula.

The upgrade to Victoria's surname made no difference to John Martin's mother, Mary Ann Biddulph Martin, who patrolled the borders of her son's unmarried life. Mrs. Martin rejected Victoria outright. Divorce was anathema among members of the English upper class. Victoria had been twice divorced. She was an American reformer who had advocated free love, and it was not too much of a leap to assume that she had also practiced it.

Not so! Victoria insisted.

"During no part of my life did I favor free love," she wrote in a series of "Life Sketches," articles that whitewashed her life in America. She also paid for a profile in the British publication the *Traveller*, entitled "Martyr Woman," which cast her as a victim of extortion in America. To vindicate herself further, Victoria scheduled a series of talks extolling the nobility of womanhood. She sought out editors of esteemed British publications and represented herself as having been a public personality in America with a spotless reputation. In its December 1880 issue, *The Court Journal* in London published her open letter condemning the unnamed "unscrupulous and corrupt minds" that had wrought the calumny that assailed her reputation. Victoria insisted, "My name is unrighteously associated with what is known as Free Love. No viler an aspiration was ever uttered. No greater outrage could be inflicted on a woman."

The English class to which Victoria would never belong had been taught not to air their dirty laundry in public; not to pry; not to give way to melancholy. Their reward was a self-respect that came from abiding by the rules. These same reserved, outwardly polite people who adhered so rigorously to the upper-class code of behavior enjoyed the forbidden-fruit effect of gossiping about one another, and London's many newspapers and magazines supplied them with the talk of the town.

Despite Victoria's efforts to renounce her former beliefs, the distribution of American newspapers in Britain continued to drip-feed London's upper-class women with Victoria's unsavory backstory. Included among those women was John's mother.

Victoria had built and maintained her celebrity status in America with provocative interviews, controversial political declarations, and a string of contentious lawsuits. She had always been able to rescue herself and her family with the resourcefulness of reinvention. Reinventing herself for the sake of her ambition to marry John Martin, however, was proving to be difficult. Her modified lectures didn't produce the positive result she was after, nor, it seems, did altering the spelling of her name, or circulating a sanitized version of her life to the British press. Doubling down, she published a special edition of *Woodhall & Claflin's Weekly*, "Devoted to the Advocacy of Great Social Questions and for the Higher Instruction and Improvement of Woman." It reprised her argument that, as a public figure in America, she lectured on women's rights but never espoused free love: "I now openly avow, with all the earnestness of righteous indignation, that during no part of my life did I favour Free Love even tacitly."

In her writing, she ruthlessly sacrificed Stephen Pearl Andrews and James Blood, both of whom, she insisted, had authored articles promoting their own radical social ideas under her name while she was miles away on what had been her extensive lecture tours.

"I could not always read ... the contributions [that ran in my newspaper]," she explained. "My lecturing engagements in distant parts of the States, sometimes extending over one hundred nights, prevented such rigid supervision."

• • •

When the first special issue of the *Weekly* in London proved to be its last, Victoria approached another outlet with her fictional narrative. It was an obscure English publication called *The Cuckoo,* and it agreed to publish the letter she'd written accusing Stephen Pearl Andrews of inflicting "moral leprosy" on the city of New York when he launched a free love club there. She explained that when the club was raided, she "became a scapegoat for other evil doings." Victoria wrote a second letter that appeared in the publication the following week with additional denials.

Not all readers of *The Cuckoo* were so unaware of the facts. One wrote a letter of his own complaining that Victoria's "barefaced mendacity has never been exceeded ... Would it be believed that even Mrs. Woodhull would have the effrontery to deny that she ever had sympathy for or was in any way connected with the doctrines of free love?"

The complaint to the publication was answered by another letter, unsigned but presumably penned by Victoria. It informed the readers that Mrs. Woodhull's upcoming autobiography would provide proof that her speeches had been distorted, and that "from the moment Mrs. Woodhull knew Colonel Blood, he adopted toward her a course of deception and treachery. After she had returned from a long southern lecture tour, his conduct was so flagrant that she felt forced to apply for a divorce."

When Victoria's take-no-prisoners tactic failed to provide the hoped-for marriage proposal from John Martin, she created a diversion by announcing that she would run for the presidency in the United States a second time.

Victoria issued a manifesto encouraging "the people of Europe, America, and all the world [to] rally round my right to represent and to work for the people of America and by becoming their president, prove the fact, for the first time in history that they chose as their president, not of necessity a man, but the best person to represent, govern and maintain their rights."

The press was a threat to Victoria's alternative narrative; at the same time, it was her path toward salvation. She had no intention of forfeiting an opportunity to remain in the press after James A. Garfield won the election, and she let it be known that she would enter the 1884 race.

CHAPTER THIRTY-FIVE

Mounting a campaign to get to the altar.

One of the major impediments that stood in the way of Victoria's trip down the aisle had to do with her family members—her father in particular.

Having been left behind in New York to envy his daughter's Vanderbilt windfall, Buck kept his eye trained on a possible payoff of his own. After learning that the youngest of Vanderbilt's sons initiated a lawsuit to wrest an additional $200,000 from the Vanderbilt estate, Buck claimed demands for the reputational damage and financial loss the Commodore caused Tennie—according to Buck, Vanderbilt failed to follow up on his marriage proposal to his daughter. He threatened to testify on the matter in court. After money changed hands, Buck announced his plans to go abroad with his wife instead.

British society has always been seasonally synched to the parliamentary calendar. When Parliament quits the chambers in August, it triggers an exodus from London. The upper classes leave for their country houses; the professionals and businessmen take their family on holidays. August was a month of repose for all in London but Victoria. The news that her parents would be landing on her London doorstep in September accelerated her mission to reimagine her family background.

In order to advance in a country where family pedigree is judged in centuries, Victoria claimed ancient lineage on both sides of her family. When Mr. Garnett read of this, he came to the conclusion that she must have assumed that America was too far away for anyone in England to fact-check, or that she was unfamiliar with *Burke's Peerage*—the book devoted to documenting British ancestry and updated annually. How else could she have thought that she would get away with converting her father from the con man he was to an eminent barrister, who, despite the urging of prominent citizens of the city and state of New York, decided that, rather than to run for the United States Senate, it was more important to visit his beloved daughters in Britain?

Just when Mr. Garnett might have felt sure that he could no longer be surprised by Victoria Woodhull, he discovered that she had printed a brochure in the 1880s authenticated (so she had said) by no fewer than four prominent genealogists (all unnamed) who cited her father as a descendant of Scotland's King Robert III. The brochure also claimed that her mother was of royal German blood.

Victoria's family tree was no tree at all. It was a sprawling, low to the ground bush rooted in America. Her attempts at assigning double-barreled ancestorial credentials was obviously absurd. Yet John Martin—Oxford educated and adept at the business of banking—was somehow persuaded that the rumors about Victoria in England were the result of spiteful gossip generated in America. John knew little about America.

The only way to explain John Martin's lapse of judgment was to understand just how besotted he was with Victoria. He coded his journal with a red asterisk when he spent the night with her and wrote to a friend that "there were only two sorts of women, the ones in whom you lost yourself and the ones in which you found yourself . . . [Victoria] was more alive than anyone I have ever met. Ordinary words don't describe her. When you were with her everything became so thrilling, seemed so worthwhile . . . The commonplace, the dull, the everyday had disappeared."

John confided to his diary, "Strange that under my acquaintance with Victoria my old enemy should have disappeared," presumably referring to a previous condition that limited his capacity to enjoy the full range of sexual pleasure. "Her forbearance in this respect created a debt of gratitude from me and forms perhaps the strongest link between us."

Out of respect for his mother's wishes, John made a point of not being seen with Victoria in public, but, when he rented a house adjacent to her own, she was certain that it placed her closer to the altar. She would do what was needed to convince not just his mother but his entire family that she was respectable enough to deserve the marriage they so actively opposed.

The battle plan Victoria had been using of dissembling about her past was replaced with a frontal attack against Stephen Pearl Andrews, who underpinned much of what she had previously achieved. According to her, she had never practiced free love and Andrews was "the originator of the most immeasurable infamy." She insisted that the articles on the subject of free love that ran in the defunct American newspaper she had founded were published without her knowledge and she accused James Blood of adultery. She even printed a copy of her divorce decree, despite his decade-long loyalty to her. Blood's circumspect response was that "the grandest woman in the world went back on me." When neither the denouncing of her former crusades nor the invention of a "respectable" genealogy advanced her increasingly frantic pursuit of a marriage proposal, Victoria made the mistake of pushing too hard. Mrs. Martin was showing obvious signs of disapproval whenever her son undertook a defense of Victoria.

No man wants to be thought of as a disappointment by his mother. John left Victoria and fled to Spain. When, six weeks later, the two reunited, Victoria began pressuring John again. He broke off their relationship a second time. Convinced that her absence would lure him back, she told him that she would be returning to America for an extensive lecture tour.

In November 1880, Victoria sailed to New York with her mother, sister, and daughter. Her announcements to reporters at the wharf were partly improvised and largely lies. She said that her reception in England "especially among the higher classes was very flattering," and let it be known that her nineteen-year-old daughter, Zula, was engaged to Lord Colin Campbell, son of the Duke of Argyll. Embellishing her story with more misinformation, she told the press that her work for suffrage had been recognized with the founding of Claflin University in South Carolina.

Lord Campbell was in fact engaged, but to a Miss Gertrude Elizabeth Blood, from a high-standing Irish family. There was, in fact, a Claflin University in South Carolina, but it was not named after Victoria or the Claflin clan. Victoria departed for England again before her falsehoods could be laid bare.

Waiting for her on the dock in Southampton was John Martin.

Victoria pushed ahead with her pursuit of a proposal by purchasing her own engagement ring.

As far as Mrs. Martin was concerned, Victoria had gone from being a fitful indisposition to something resembling a barbarian menacing the borders of the Roman Empire, threatening to cross the Danube and the Rhine. Mrs. Martin had had quite enough. She forbade her son to marry what she referred to pointedly as "the American woman." Dutifully, he broke off the relationship again and took a trip abroad a second time. But Victoria saw a glimmer of hope in Mrs. Martin's failing health. Her resourceful next move was to reposition herself as a wife manqué: in one of the daily letters she dutifully sent to John during his absence, she wrote, "God bless my precious husband for sustaining me and aiding me with his wise counsel so that I may not stumble."

Victoria Woodhull's autofictional narrative would prove successful until Henry James began writing his own lethally observant version.

CHAPTER THIRTY-SIX

Beware the novelist.

Henry James was born in 1843, the second of five children. His older brother, William, would become the esteemed American philosopher and psychologist who argued in the pages of Horace Greeley's *New-York Daily Tribune* on the topic of "Love, Marriage and Divorce" with Stephen Pearl Andrews.

The James family was as clad in privilege as the Claflins were mired in poverty. Mrs. James was from a wealthy family, long settled in New York City. Mr. James enjoyed a substantial inheritance left by his father, who had been a successful banker and investor. The James's primary home was on Washington Place in New York, but Henry had been introduced to Europe as an infant and given a transatlantic upbringing that resulted in a fluency in French, Italian, and German. He attended Harvard Law School and left without a degree to write full-time.

Traveling and living abroad, James found an intellectual, artistic, and cultural milieu in which he moved with ease. His inner circle would come to include George Eliot, Charles Dickens, John Singer Sargent, Ivan Turgenev, Gustave Flaubert, and Émile Zola. He was a great friend of Edith Wharton, herself a product of Social Register, old-world New York, whose own novels would also mine the recurring theme of interactions between old-money Europeans and Americans abroad.

James was drawn to Europe by education and instinct. London was the city that won him over. Since the Romans in 50 AD, the city had experienced every human aspiration, suffered almost every possible man-made disaster, witnessed every act of bravery or ignoble gesture.

To James, London was about flamboyance, eccentricity, bravura, and unorthodoxy. When he took up permanent residency there in 1876, the year before Victoria arrived, he wrote that it was "the biggest aggregation of human life . . . the place where there is most in the world to observe."

James might have known of Victoria before he moved to London when he was a student at Harvard in the early 1870s, assuming he attended her public lecture in Boston. Most probably, it was the press in London that provided the source material that fed his novella, *The Siege of London,* about the social and marital interplay between an émigré American woman and an established and monied English family.[1]

Its barely fictionalized main character, named (appropriately) Nancy Headway, was obviously based on Victoria. Nancy is an audacious American beauty who had married and divorced several times—an adventurer with a lurid past who makes her way to New York, where she intends to conquer the city. When her notorious history catches up with her, she departs for London, where she is determined to marry well.

Like Victoria, Nancy handles "many of the productions of the age with a bold, free touch. She picked up ideas," and "took a hint from every circumstance."

Nancy attracts the attention of the wealthy and conservative Sir Arthur Demesne, who moves in the rarefied echelon of British aristocracy and high society. He is weak and colorless; his primary interest is economics. He sends "regularly to his bookseller for all of the new publications on economical subjects, for he was determined that his political attitude should have a firm statistical basis." (It is no coincidence that John Martin's great achievement was his published essay on currency and banking, which was of practical aid in the reform of gold currency.)

Henry's character thinks of himself as "indispensable in the scheme of things—not as an individual, but as an institution." John Martin was the fifth generation in a family firm financing the country's trade and arranging funding for its monarchs—an institution whose founder was regarded as the father of British banking.

As it was with John's initial impression of Victoria, the character Demesne had "never seen anything like Mrs. Headway; he hardly knew by what standard to measure her." In much the same manner as Martin, Demesne fell "very much under the charm," and "he compromised matters by saying to himself that she was only foreign." Like John, the unfortunate Demesne "was fascinated . . . He asked her a good many questions, but her answers were so startling that, like sudden luminous points, they seemed to intensify the darkness round their edges."

Just as it had been with Victoria, Nancy Headway forces herself on Demesne's respectable family, whereupon Demesne's imposing mother confides her impression to a friend: "She's very pretty, and she appears to be very clever; but I don't trust her." Puzzling over her son's infatuation, she adds, "I don't know what has taken possession of him . . . I don't think she's a lady."

"I'm burying my past," Nancy says in conversation. In another, she comments, "You can't be delicate when you're trying to save your life."

Having failed at achieving respectability by altering the facts of her life in America, she changes her tactics and begins to address Demesne with "a sort of conjugal pronoun." Despite Nancy's resourceful pursuit of Demesne, his unyieldingly disapproving mother forbids him to propose. "She had been so much, and so easily, married, that she was full of these misleading references," is how she was described.

In James's *The Siege of London,* Nancy Headway is denied her hoped-for marriage to Sir Arthur but manages to become the wife of a baronet.

At nine a.m. on October 1, 1883, in a small Presbyterian chapel in Kensington, Nancy Headway's real-life counterpart enjoyed a triumph of her own. After six years of relentless attempts to become Mrs. John Martin, Victoria Woodhull finally got what she wanted.

It was a small, private wedding with Buck and Tennie the only witnesses. The marriage certificate referred wrongly to the thrice-married bride as "formerly Woodhull widow," and then, more accurately as the "divorced wife of James Harvey Blood."

CHAPTER THIRTY-SEVEN

Third time married.

John Martin informed his family that he had married Victoria Woodhull, but only after the fact.

John's brother announced that he would never receive Victoria. His sister, Julia, agreed to see Victoria privately but "could not insult my friends by introducing her," lamenting that "[John] is so weak and she is so clever I always feared she would get hold of him." Julia's husband had a less generous attitude: he would treat John and Victoria as man and his mistress, and "cut her when I like and be civil when I like." In case his sentiment was unclear, he added that Victoria was "a harlot, cunning and deceitful."

Good breeding won out when John's mother—Victoria's primary detractor for the previous six years—wrote a letter to the married couple informing them that she would receive Victoria as her daughter-in-law and left the door open at Overbury Court, the family's imposing Georgian-style estate in Worcestershire.

·   ·   ·

While Victoria focused on asserting herself as a respectable wife, her husband's daily routine continued as it had before. John took care of the bank's business and commenced a project of tracing the bank's history, which would eventually provide material enough for a reference book on Britain's financial history. He attended board meetings of various philanthropic organizations and continued his involvement with the Royal Statistical Society.

In February 1884, Mr. and Mrs. John Martin moved to 17 Hyde Park

Gate, one of London's select urban mansions on a small cul-de-sac off of Hyde Park, a 350-acre leafy sanctuary in the heart of London.

A woman seen walking alone in Hyde Park would invite speculation that she was a prostitute. This meant that only women dressed in elegant habits on horseback, or driven in carriages accompanied by a respectable man, could enjoy the park's lush landscapes. What were the odds, wondered Mr. Garnett, that Victoria—who, in her previous life, prostituted herself in one way or another—would appear in Hyde Park as a pampered wife seated next to a respectable millionaire husband in a splendid carriage.

After hiring a household staff that included one of the best cooks in London, Victoria set about renovating the Hyde Park mansion. She decided against the dark and heavy décor of the period and fashioned the mansion's entrance after a Pompeian villa, which featured red frescoed friezes, a sky-blue dome, and the marble busts of Aphrodite and Hermes. A winding staircase led to the resplendent drawing room, bedecked in green silk. Its polished parquet floors showcased white bearskins, and hanging from its ceiling was an ornately carved wooden chandelier with fluttering cupids. In one corner of the room was a recess with a purple velour backdrop behind a large silver statue of Nike, the Greek goddess of victory—another tribute to her spirit guide, Demosthenes. And if Victoria needed another reminder of how far she'd come from a childhood home without so much as an outhouse, the mansion's excessive number of modern bathrooms was that tribute.

The couple's weekends were spent in a sixteenth-century manor house at Bredon's Norton, an unspoiled and largely rural village in Worcestershire, whose estate had been held by the Martin family for several generations.

According to John's journal entry, Victoria was "happy and in good spirits"—her mood having been lifted by uninterrupted cash flow. Playing its part was the marriage's physical intimacy, made obvious by the countless notes Victoria wrote to her husband on personal stationery whose top right-hand corner was engraved with a six-point star bearing the sign of "KISMET," meaning destiny. London's postal service delivered mail in inner London within an hour and a half, and it often was the case that Victoria sent notes to John at his office in the afternoons so that he could read them before he returned home in the evenings. Though Englishmen are not generally in a hurry to share their feelings, John's testimonial to her character appeared in one of his many notes to her when he wrote, "My heart becomes lighter and happier when I turned to you and home," and signed the note, "Your loving boy."

After settling into married life at Hyde Park Gate, the Martins traveled abroad. While in Rome in 1887, Victoria finally met Frederick Douglass, who was on a grand tour of the continent.

"I do not know that she is not in her life as pure as she seems to be," he wrote, but added, "I treated her politely and respectfully."

Despite the use of a double negative, the point Douglass made came across clearly: no matter how and where Victoria presented herself, she was in possession of a louche past. The Martins returned to London amid curious glances and derisive remarks. When it became obvious that John's friends were disinclined to receive her in their own homes, he began to spend absurdly large sums of money seeking disclaimers from those she identified as her detractors.

In a show of extreme husbandly devotion, John secured a letter from Henry James in which James stated for the record that he had had no intention of representing or suggesting Victoria while writing *The Siege of London.* It was a hollow victory. At the time, James was completing another, more substantial work, *The Bostonians,* a novel whose main character was a beautiful daughter of a charlatan faith healer and showman. The woman becomes a public speaker who refuses to filter what she has to say, but nonetheless manages to enchant her audiences so that those who had come to jeer leave converted.

•   •   •

Victoria's reaction to Henry James's *The Bostonians* was to produce a pamphlet entitled *The Human Body, the Temple of God,* which depicted her as a misunderstood reformer and included a selected array of her earlier works, along with a curated selection of U.S. press clippings. This did nothing to enhance her standing in London's society and she decided the situation called for something more substantial.

John obliged her by underwriting *The Humanitarian,* a publication that debuted in July 1892. Handsomely printed in large type on sixteen pages of expensive paper stock, it listed Mrs. Victoria Woodhull (having returned to the original spelling) Martin as editor and her daughter, Zula Woodhull, as associate editor. Its manifesto promised to examine issues through a scientific approach to human development and to focus on various methods of improving society.

Unlike other European countries that suffered from censorship by church or state, Britain encouraged a prolific exchange of ideas in a time when the nation's intellectual climate contributed to its transformation. With *The Humanitarian,* Victoria had unparalleled opportunity to pursue her enthusiasms on a larger canvas. To her credit, she identified forward-thinking contributors, who, regardless of their chosen topics, had a commitment to engage with the new. The essays and articles she published proposed changes that would occur decades later: government services for the poor, laboratories that could analyze food and drink for impurities, accessible birth control, and warnings that cigarettes were lethal to one's health.

According to Victoria, one the many aims of *The Humanitarian* was to "discuss all subjects pertaining to the well-being of humanity." Despite this declaration, she showed no interest in the recently established Fabian Society, a fellowship organization dedicated to that very issue and that incorporated into its ranks the entire spectrum of reformers. George Bernard Shaw had become a member of the fledgling society in 1884. As one of its spokespersons, he warned against scientific dogma. "Beware of false knowledge," said Shaw, "it is more dangerous than ignorance."

Victoria rejected George Bernard Shaw's definition of false knowledge and drew her ideas from an increasingly popular ideology in England that would stray into dubious territory and become known as "eugenics." In 1896, *"A Monthly Review of Sociological Science"* was added to the publication's title, *The Humanitarian.*

CHAPTER THIRTY-EIGHT

A perilous debate.

Francis Galton increased the cachet of science—if not its accuracy—in the 1890s. He was the first person to plot a weather map. His work with fingerprints resulted in the use of print analysis in criminal forensics. But the idea for which he was almost exclusively known was his extrapolation of the doctrines on the evolution of animals expressed by his half-cousin, the biologist Charles Darwin.

Darwin's 1859 publication of *On the Origin of Species* had had a profound sociological impact with theories that undermined orthodox belief in creationism. Eminent thinkers began to argue that scientific solutions could be applied to social issues. "Social Darwinism," as it would come to be called, claimed a scientific foundation that equated an individual's physical health and moral tendencies with his or her inherited predisposition.

Believing that anything—no matter how vague or subjective—could be made measurable with data, Galton was obsessive about collecting it. His mantra was "Whenever you can, count," and it is fair to say that it was Galton who developed the mathematical methods that became the nuts and bolts of statistics. He was enamored with the possibilities the bell curve presented in statistical analysis of quantitative data. Darwin applied it to evolution, so why not human intelligence? Galton asked himself. In a way that anticipated today's social media, he gathered data on the British population's physical characteristics by encouraging people to share their personal details. What is now called scientific racism was then thought to be a positive force.

For her part, Victoria saw an intersection between the eugenics discourse and the rights of women. In *The Humanitarian*, she wrote that "every effort should be made by those who have the true interests of humanity at heart to teach the consequences of ignorance on those who do not have their higher facilities sufficiently developed to have the true interest of humanity at heart."

"To woman, by nature, belongs the right of sexual determination," was what Victoria once said and probably believed. Her commitment to the theories of eugenics was no doubt motivated by her son's impairments and her belief that they were the result of conceiving him with an alcoholic husband. The fact that she conceived a second time with the same man, and that it produced a healthy daughter, made no difference to a way of thinking that gave rise to her endorsement of social engineering.

Victoria was far from the only person in Great Britain drawn to the principles of eugenics. The concept enjoyed a widespread currency in the sciences, crossed the political divide between conservatives and progressives, and made its way into the pages of novels. H. G. Wells, a student of science as well as an author, imagined it in his work of science fiction *The Time Machine*. After reading her essay in *The Humanitarian*, which put forth her belief that eugenics was imperative to secure the health of the nation he wrote to Victoria expressing his admiration.[1]

Victoria as Mrs. John Martin, pictured with her adoring husband

CHAPTER THIRTY-NINE

Tennie's personality begins to pay dividends.

Unlike Victoria, Tennie refused to abandon her personality in order to be accepted by British elites. And so it was not without irony that her lighthearted enthusiasm—her certain irresistible too-muchness—captivated one of the three richest men in England, Francis Cook.

Cook, Son & Co., founded by Francis's father in 1819, warehoused and distributed finished wool, cotton, linen, and silk from the Near East. Thanks to Britain's recently built railroad network, its sales force was able to visit retailers, bringing with them product samples. Profits increased further from the death of Queen Victoria's beloved husband, Prince Albert. The queen's demand for public mourning resulted in a run on black crepe, a mixture of dyed wool and treated silk. By the time Francis Cook became a partner in the firm, it was the largest and the most profitable of its kind in Britain.

Francis had married in 1841, four years before Tennie was born in 1845, and she was still a child when he purchased what was thought to be the most desirable country seat in Europe: the palace and castle of Monserrate in Portugal. Upon restoring the palace, Francis spent half a million pounds improving Sintra, the municipality in which the palace was located. After returning prosperity to a district that had fallen into disrepair, Francis was rewarded by the appreciative King Luis of Portugal with the title of Viscount of Monserrate.

Francis's primary residence was Doughty House, a grand stone and brick home in London built in 1751 that overlooked the Thames. On its walls were priceless masterpieces by van Eyck, Rubens, and Rembrandt—five hundred paintings in all. What seemed to be its

countless rooms housed Italian majolica, ivory, tapestries, bronzes—
and Cook's wife. She was housed there as well.

It is not clear how, exactly, Tennie made the acquaintance of Francis Cook, but, not long after she did, she moved into a luxurious flat in South Kensington and Francis became her most frequent guest. Having never possessed a woman's inclination to sacrifice herself for love, she thought that there was no real point of marriage unless it came with an equitable monetary exchange. Like Cornelius Vanderbilt, Francis Cook was colossally rich. Vanderbilt had been Tennie's sponsor in New York. Cook would become hers in London. Like Vanderbilt, he relied on spirits to guide him. Employing the technique she used on Vanderbilt, Tennie encouraged Cook to speak about himself in order to anticipate what would please him.

"Softly softly catchy monkey" is a proverbial saying among the English that advocates the best way to achieve an end. Tennie was content to wait until Mrs. Cook died. Then she waited for Mr. Cook to emerge from a respectable period of mourning. Still she waited until it was the right time to convince him that his deceased wife had sent a message from the spirit world advising that he should marry her.

On October 1, 1885, some forty-four years after his first marriage, Francis Cook wed Tennessee Celeste Claflin.

When reports of the marriage reached New York, its newspapers pointed out that it had been only eight years since Tennie and Victoria had left America for England in a rush and under suspicions of blackmail, and they had somehow managed to become the wives of two of Britain's wealthiest men. *The World* of New York reprised a few of the more sensational highlights of the sisters' past exploits in America.

Buck died several weeks after the article ran, and Victoria dispatched an open letter to its competitor, the New York *Sun*. "My father, Reuben B. Claflin, died of grief caused by the malicious libel published in the *World* of October 25th," she stated matter-of-factly before asking readers, "Has not our family suffered enough?"

One would have thought that, after years of dealing with the press, Victoria might have known that any accusation levied against one newspaper was an open invitation for another paper to investigate further. *The Chicago Daily Tribune* suggested that it was ridiculous to believe that Buck—a man proven to have been heartless—could have died of grief. It reported that he had been prostrated by paralytic strokes for the previous two years, and that, at eighty-nine, he died a shameless old man under the care of Victoria and her husband at their Hyde Park Gate address.

The *Tribune* article resulted in a poison pen letter, signed anonymously as "Justice," that was sent simultaneously to the lord mayor of London and the Fleet Street press. It read, "A mysterious death occurred on the nineteenth of November . . . of a much respected and honored citizen by the name of Ruben B. Claflin. His papers were spirited away as was the will that is known to have been made by him, including money and bonds . . . His death was sudden. His sickness and burial was [sic] very mysterious. It would be well to have this matter investigated at once by the proper authorities."

Insomuch as Buck died in the home of Victoria and her husband, by inference, the letter accused them both of euthanasia or worse. John Martin posted a reward for the apprehension of the slanderer, but the hunt was called off when suspicion pointed to the habitually operatic Roxanna, who, unable to read or write, must have paid someone to write the letter for her.

Having suffered childhood abuse at the hands of their parents, why, one wonders, would Victoria and Tennie feel any obligation toward them? Why remain close to the two people who leeched off of them, first in New York and then in London? Why minister to their needs? There is no one answer, but just to say that Victoria ensured that Buck was buried in London's illustrious Highgate Cemetery, and, in her remaining years, Roxanna lived in Doughty House under Tennie's supervision and care.

CHAPTER FORTY

Attempting to outwit the facts.

If Victoria Woodhull was the personification of a single word, that word would be "but." She decried the institution of marriage, *but* she was thrice married. She was a spiritualist who spoke out against organized religion, *but* she often quoted the Scripture. She professed to be an ardent suffragette, *but* her views ultimately lost the support of the movement's leaders. She supported the rights of prostitutes, *but* she was an opponent of abortion. She had been a stockbroker and a would-be capitalist, *but* she claimed to admire Karl Marx.

Victoria handled her conflicting tides of loyalty with brutal detachment. It should be pointed out that, in fact, it was she who had divorced James Blood, not the other way around, and, even then, James continued to defend her. Having relied on Victoria as a lodestar, he lost his sense of direction after she left him. She, on the other hand, gave him not even a brief backward glance. He took a position at a local newspaper in Maine and married an older widow with money enough to finance his misguided adventure to Africa, confident he would make a fortune mining gold. Instead, he disappeared into the wilds, where he died from "the fever." His death was recorded as December 29, 1885, but, by the time his body was recovered, it was impossible to assign a reliable date. The remains of James Blood were returned to America to be buried in Brooklyn.

An ocean away, Victoria had no intention of allowing prior entanglements in America to prevent her from advancing in England. Her method of refuting anything that threatened her status was to privately print and publicly distribute pamphlets defending herself. This only succeeded in drawing attention to her past scandals, which were far more interesting to read than her long-winded justifications of them. Determined to offset the ridicule and judgment that continued to be levied against her, she commissioned yet another pamphlet declaring her father to be the scion of "one of the oldest and most aristocratic houses in England" and that "no one of their ancestry was a drunkard, a convict or a pauper." This absurdity no doubt prompted Mr. Garnett to read the written transcript of the libel trial she'd imposed on him and the British Museum. In her testimony, she described her father as a conniving, child-abusing, snake-oil-peddling con man.

While Victoria occupied herself with the distribution of fact-defying, self-laudatory pamphlets, Tennie was overcoming the impairments against her social standing by convincing her husband to endow £80,000 to establish a boarding school for young women in London whose curriculum was devoted to music and the arts.

Queen Alexandra's House, as it was called, was a tribute to the Princess of Wales, who attended its 1884 grand opening, along with her husband, the Prince of Wales. It was hardly unexpected that, on Francis Cook's sixty-ninth birthday, he was elected fellow to the Royal Society of Arts and that, a few short months later, he was made a baronet by Queen Victoria. The news of Tennie becoming an English lady was a gratifying send-off for Roxanna, who died at Doughty House in 1890.

Tennie was able to put her past behind her. Victoria, it seems, refused to. She made a point of subscribing to newspaper cutting agencies in Britain and America. When *The Brooklyn Eagle* dredged up her dubious past, she persuaded her husband to sail with her to America and instigate suit for criminal libel against the *Eagle*.

They returned to Britain empty-handed.

•   •   •

Background research is a manual task. The process doesn't—shouldn't—include imagining the psychological depth of the individual whose background is being researched. I am certain that Mr. Garnett tried to keep his imaginings of Mrs. Woodhull to a minimum. I am equally certain that, mindful that she had squandered the admiration and wealth she achieved in America, he allowed himself to consider why it was that she so persistently challenged her own good luck. Why would a woman of her uncommon intelligence continue to pursue the unattainable goal of becoming president of the United States? She may or may not have justified her first campaign to draw attention to the crusade of women's rights, but why run a second time? Probably the answer Mr. Garnett gave himself was that it had less to do with Mrs. Woodhull's political ambition and more to do with her social ambition. Having married into an upper-class English family, Victoria insisted that there was a cabal blocking her from its polite society and used her past in America as an excuse. She convinced her husband that, if American women would choose her as their representative in the 1892 presidential campaign, any questions about her past would be replaced with present-day tributes. Next, she convinced him to rally support for her third bid for American presidency. For this effort, they would need to cross the ocean again, this time to New York.

New York had been gorging on progress since Victoria's spirit guide, Demosthenes, had led her to the brownstone at 17 Great Jones Street some twenty-five years before. Gas lamps were being replaced by electric lights. There were elevated railroads. The Brooklyn Bridge arched over the section of the Hudson River where once the Sunday "Beecher's ferries" had crisscrossed. John Martin made arrangements to lease a house on Manhattan's West Seventieth Street, which became Victoria's base of operations. Assisting her was her unmarried thirty-one-year-old daughter, Zula, who had accompanied them from London.

Victoria inaugurated her third campaign by launching a U.S. edition of *The Humanitarian* in which she announced, "I have come back to ask my people to put me in the White House . . . it is my destiny to work out the salvation of my country as an individual." She laid out her political platform with a series of articles. The proposals she put forward included revenue and tariff reforms, as well as nationalizing public health; she pushed for an improvement in housing for the poor and encouraged the arts and sciences.

"The uses of government should be to foster, protect and promote the possession of equality," she wrote. "How does the condition of society reply to this standard for government? Is there anything that even approaches to equality in any of the various phases of life? I unhesitatingly answer, no! Look where we may . . . everything is made to turn upon the rights of property, and nothing upon the rights of humanity . . . Hundreds, thousands, aye, millions of human beings, men, women and children, wander the streets of our cities and the highways of our country, hungry, ragged and cold, vainly seeking in this land of plenty, where physical want should be unknown."

References to Victoria's activities appeared almost daily in the other newspapers, and she was asked repeatedly why she was pursuing an impossible-to-win presidential race for a third time when the alternative would have been to enjoy pampered luxury in England. Her response had a self-serving purpose but conveyed a larger truth—one that still resonates: "Our best citizens are intimidated because their reputations might be jeopardized in political campaigns."

Victoria's initial run for the American presidency had backing from the suffragists. That was not the case now. There had not been even the briefest reference to Victoria in Elizabeth Cady Stanton and Susan B. Anthony's extensive book on the history of the suffrage movement. John—ever supportive—paid to print and distribute an expensive leather-bound pamphlet highlighting his wife's role in the suffrage movement.

While nothing of note was accomplished during her campaign in New York for what she was calling the Humanitarian Party, her subsequent foray to Chicago turned into a disaster. The *Chicago Mail*, encouraged by a prominent Chicago clergyman, deciding to revisit her untoward past life in America, delighted in exposing every salacious detail about Victoria and Tennie's adventures in the Midwest: beginning in Homer, progressing to Ottawa and Chicago, Illinois, and then to Cincinnati and then to New York. On and on and on.

The morning after the exposé ran, Victoria's most vigorous protector, John—along with his attorney—arrived at the Criminal Court Building seeking a warrant for the arrest of the editor of the *Mail* for criminal libel.

The editor responded in the next issue of the newspaper.

If this notorious adventuress had remained in the obscurity of her London life, the *Mail* would have had no word to say about her; but when she, heralded by cablegrams . . . has the effrontery to come to Chicago, it is different. This woman, known to be of bad character, remembered in police and detective circles in this city . . . has the hard gall to talk about regenerating and educating the American people . . . [Victoria Woodhull and Tennessee Claflin] need to have their records exhibited to drive them back where they belong.

Victoria had dragged her husband into one incomprehensible legal drama after another and, this time, he had blundered into a hornet's nest. John's $100,000 demand in damages resulted in the *Mail* running a series of two-column articles, providing names, dates, and the circumstances of the Claflin clan's past exploits, beginning with Buck's illegal activity in Homer and continuing in chronological order through Victoria's career as a "trance-physician" in Cincinnati, her "immodesty" as a stock speculator on Wall Street, and the "open, shameless effrontery with which she has paraded her name as a candidate of the Cosmopolitical Party for the presidency in 1872."

"*The Mail* refuses to believe that the women of the United States look on the Claflin sisters as leaders of their movement, as honorable, chaste, respectable persons," it declared. "Such thought is libel on American womanhood. To prevent such an impression of gaining credence in England was the only cause for [the newspaper] to expose the two women."

According to the *Mail,* Victoria was "a vain, immodest, unsexed woman, with whom respectable people should have as little to do with as possible." It told of her life and that of Tennie in New York, providing a gamut that ran from free love to communism, from attempted blackmail and imprisonment on various charges to Vanderbilt's contested will and their sudden departure for England, where—after years of countless efforts and perseverance—both women had somehow managed to corner very rich husbands.

It was when the *Mail* threatened the possibility that the Illinois authorities might revive the almost three-decade-old indictment against Tennie for manslaughter and fraud that John Biddulph Martin, Esq., his wife, and her daughter gathered their luggage and sailed for England. They did not file a libel suit against the newspaper or its editor.

CHAPTER FORTY-ONE

Coming full circle.

If gullibility is closely tied to trust, John Martin's trust in Victoria proved endless.

She was able to convince her husband that none of what had been reported by the American press was true. Next, she convinced him to believe that there was a conspiracy against her by American journalists. And, two months after the debacle in Chicago that ended in a failed libel charge, she managed to convince him to return to America with her so that she could see her presidential campaign through to the finish.

We all delude ourselves at some time or another, but there must have been a point when Victoria had repeated the fabrications of her past so often that they were not only her truth, but that of her husband.

In 1892, twenty-one years after she had traveled to Washington to appear in front of the Judiciary Committee of the House of Representatives and present a case for a woman's right to vote, Victoria returned to Washington's Willard Hotel to gather together fifty women who were prepared to nominate her as the presidential candidate of her Humanitarian Party. John, who likely paid the expenses of fifty hotel rooms, focused his admiration on his wife as she announced that she was also accepting the nomination as a presidential candidate for the National Woman Suffrage Association. It made no difference to Victoria that the association denied having such a candidate, and that, in fact, the association didn't know a single one of the fifty women Victoria insisted had nominated her. What mattered to Victoria was that her name had been linked in print with the National Woman Suffrage

Association and that she had regained her novelty value by having declared herself its presidential candidate.

Victoria returned to Britain with her husband and announced plans for a speaking tour on the topic of "Humanitarian Government" in England, Scotland, and Wales. She launched it at London's St. James's Hall—the same location that was her last stop in the six-month tour she embarked upon when, more than a decade before, she first arrived in Britain. This time, the response to her speech fell flat. She canceled the tour and, in its stead, distributed *Victoria Woodhull: Some Leaves from Her Life*, a pamphlet that reinvented the better part of her career. No author's name was attached to the fact-depleted biographical narrative, but it is safe to say that, if not penned by her, she had hired a professional to write it. She didn't stop at that.

When, in 1893, John Martin was called on to serve as one of the British commissioners of trade to the Chicago World's Fair, Victoria accompanied him to America in order to lecture one last time in New York at Carnegie Hall. Her speech referred to "the crime of propagating children to live upon their betters and become a curse to the human race."

Promoting eugenics as a biological approach to social, economic, and cultural change for the better might have passed for acceptable in Britain, where eugenics was considered a scientific endeavor and discussed as a positive force. But America was a country built on the promise of opportunity, regardless of one's birth and rank. Victoria had not only failed to read the room; she'd ignored the fact she was, herself, a billboard of American triumph over adversity. Three days later, *The New York Times* reported the departure of Mrs. Woodhull from New York.

Unable to expunge her notorious past in America, Victoria returned to recycling a false narrative in England. Intending to commission another booklet commending her past achievements, she hired a man to locate positive press clippings about her that were archived in the British Museum's Reading Room. Located as well were the unflattering articles that had run in the American press. Victoria could do nothing about the excoriating articles, but she was determined to prevent copies from residing in the British Museum's Reading Room.

This was the juncture in Mr. Garnett's forensic research into

Mrs. Woodhull's background that likely returned him to the libel suit she had brought against him. His investigations, diligent as they were, failed to provide any helpful answers. He had learned that she possessed a frightening ambition and a primal desire to be first at what she decided to do; that her counterintuitiveness often contaminated her declared intentions; that she sought celebrity for her undertakings— one might even say that she was a glutton for it—without any deliberation of long-term goals. All of this said, Mr. Garnett was willing to admit to himself (but only to himself) that Victoria Woodhull might be worth admiring. There had been greater clairvoyants, greater spiritualist healers, greater suffragettes, greater newspaper owners, greater Wall Street brokers, greater candidates for the American presidency. But they would need to have been six different people. This did not mean that Mr. Garnett would ever understand her. It certainly didn't mean that he had to like her. He hadn't come all this way in his research to like Mrs. Woodhull. Everything about her challenged his conviction that the sensibilities of women were finer and more fragile than those of men and that, in a civilized world, there should exist the fundamental understanding that men protect women and women uphold their part by being worth protecting. Mr. Garnett was self-aware enough to realize that his propriety, earnest though it might be, could also render him naïve. He understood that, if his attitude remained the same while the culture shifted, he would not have the same relationship with the world for very long. Still, what kind of future would there be, he wondered, if there were more women like Mrs. Woodhull out there . . . women who, dispensing with the role assigned to them, might prove capable not only of protecting themselves but of advancing on their own terms?

PART VI

Public misgivings about the price of progress, the queen dies after sixty-three years on the throne, and Victoria Woodhull makes her thoughts known in written journals.

"You are no doubt aware that my private life in America has been pictured to the public both in America and here by the press with the intent to make people believe me to be a very bad woman. I regret to have inflicted on my friends any account of the sorrow and anxiety I had passed through, owing to the duplicity and treachery of those who should have stood fast by me. I need not say how deeply humiliating to me it was, both privately and publicly, but I feel that the position I currently occupy before the English public demands from me an explanation of my seemingly inconsistent conduct.

"As a fourteen-year-old girl, I supposed that to marry was to be transported to a heaven not only of happiness but of perfection. Whatever my dreams of a romantic love, the sexual act was one of dutiful submission, and rude contact with the facts chased my visions and dreams quickly away. As a young wife, a great wail of agony went out from my soul and, when I found I had given birth to a human wreckage, to a child that was an imbecile, my heart was broken.

"I was divorced from Canning Woodhull for reasons that to me were sufficient. But I was never his enemy. When he appeared, sick and shivering, at the door of my home in Murray Hill in New York City one day, he was by then addicted to morphine as well as alcohol. He had no one to turn to but me, his onetime wife. Considering that my prominence as a broker on Wall Street already had caused controversy, I might well have denied him sanctuary. But that would have been hypocrisy, which I scorn. So yes, there was a period of time I was a divorced woman living under the roof with a previous and a current husband, but allow me to add that the proceeds from my brokerage house at times supported no less than twenty family members.

"As for the interactions between husband and wife, I believe that without sexual desire, you are not men and women. My life has been my own; I have nothing to apologize for and consider my sexual organs nobody's business. What I might have done with them—what I chose to do with them—is my own choice, just as it is for a man. Is it fair to treat a woman worse than a man, and then revile her because she is a woman? In a speech I gave years ago in New York's Steinway Hall, I said something to the effect that I had the right to change my lover every day or night if I choose to do so. The public press, and the public itself, cried out in chorus that I confessed to living an utterly abandoned life—that I live and sleep with an egregious number of men. Of course this was absurd. I was also accused of endorsing prostitution when I wrote an article in my American newspaper the *Weekly* advocating the legalization of prostitution to prevent venereal disease.

"What we are limited to learn determines what we know. I was left to educate myself, but I know enough to be certain that mankind has forgotten the lesson taught by the Hindus five thousand years ago— that to denigrate or to oppress women involves the physical and moral degradation of man. And I know that a nation, in its march onward and upward, cannot publicly choke the intellectual and political activity of half its citizens by narrow statutes.

"'Life, liberty, and the pursuit of happiness' are the unalienable rights that the American Declaration of Independence says have been given to all humans by their Creator, and that governments are created to protect. The uses of all governments should be to foster, protect, and promote the possession of equity. Men in America and England have organized and maintained governments to the utter exclusion of women, and, in so doing, have defrauded women of the one thing that mattered the most. I do not have access to the British Parliament, but, in America, I listened attentively to speeches from many different men—statesmen, legislators, congressmen—and I continue to find in the institutions that they represent anything that excuses the grandiloquent laudations that they often indulge in. I have supported the right for women to vote, which gives the right to women to pursue happiness by having a voice in that government to which they are accountable. I have been the sport of society for my efforts and, in many instances, I have been rejected by the sex I have served.

"Women who wish to be properly educated are forced to endure the reproach they incur by exhibiting to quit the limitations of the ignorance to which society and the law consign them to. If they marry, their husbands own both their property and earnings and are the sole legal guardians of their children. Society has restricted employment opportunities for unmarried women and, if they attempt to retain some dignity by assuming the role of governess, their remuneration is so low as to make it impossible to save enough out of their earnings to provide for sickness or old age. Women's suffrage must succeed. It will succeed for the simple reason that men cannot roll back the rising tide of reform.

"The outcome of the suit I brought against the British Museum some three years ago vindicated me with proof that there was no foundation for the libels against me. Within the British ruling class is the belief that their rank is somehow preordained. Because I was not formally educated, it was thought that I was innately possessed of a less powerful mind. Because I am a woman, it was assumed that I was illogical, impetuous, and rash. Sir Charles Russell underestimated me, but what he didn't understand—what he could never understand—is that being underestimated can be really quite useful.

"I should say that, not long after the trial, my husband fell ill. A severe cold developed into pneumonia and confined him to bed for the first time. The London winter was doing him no good and his doctor suggested that he would recuperate faster in the warm climate. As soon as he could travel, he booked passage on a ship to the Canary Islands. I, too, was poorly and didn't feel up to making the trip . . . it was the only time during our fourteen-year marriage that I didn't accompany him and both of us were very unhappy at him going away on his own. The mail took days and the first of his letters described the strangest country he had even seen . . . that it was nothing but lava beds and extinct volcanoes. The great tragedy was that our subsequent correspondence was not received on time or not at all. This I was made aware of only when John sent a cable pleading me to write. I cabled back, telling him how lonely our dear home was in his absence . . . that I was grateful he was in a more sympathetic climate than London, but that if he wished me to come and return with him he need only to wire me. My letter crossed with one of his that informed me he was sailing for the most remote islands and would be cut off from the world for some ten days, but that he would be home in London with me by the end of the month . . . that it was no longer worth me making the trip to join him. But within a week of my receipt of that letter, news reached me that my husband had gone riding in the mountains, which resulted in a respiratory infection.

"On March 18, 1897, the same day John's father had passed, I received a telegram from John's doctor in the Canary Islands: MARTIN VERY ILL, BUT NO IMMEDIATE DANGER—WILL WIRE AGAIN. But the following day there was a flurry of cables: MARTIN WORSE—IN DANGER; STILL DANGEROUSLY ILL; and then shockingly, MARTIN SINKING—NO USE COMING and, finally, YOUR DEAR HUSBAND DIED THIS AFTERNOON. My darling husband died of pneumonia on March 20th, 1897, never knowing that his father had died two days before. I shall not forgive his family for their slights. I received a formal letter from John's brother containing the most awful details of the embalming arrangements and a payment to ship John's body to England where he would be cremated. In accordance with his wishes, his ashes were to be scattered at sea."

CHAPTER FORTY-TWO

The party's over.

The obituary Victoria wrote for her husband in *The Humanitarian* gave praise for the man, whose last conscious act, according to her, was to make sure that the doctor attending him during the night was kept comfortable with a blanket. She saluted his "innate nobility of character," before casting back to the previous months of his life, which had been "embittered by the cruel persecution which he and his wife had faced together for years."

"His sensitive nature shrank from publicity, but he was always in sympathy with his wife's views," Victoria wrote, and explained that, although her own shattered nerves had prevented her from accompanying him to the Canary Islands for his recuperation, their separation had been three weeks in a marriage of fourteen years. She made reference to her suffering as a result of his family, and, in case a reader hadn't absorbed her point, added that it had been a "perfect union marred only by persecution."

In an unforeseen chain of circumstances, John Martin died seventy-two hours after his father did. As John's sole heir, Victoria inherited the biggest single shareholding in the Martin family bank, the London mansion at Hyde Park Gate,[1] and the country estate, Norton Park, in Worcestershire. By the age of fifty-nine, Victoria had gone from wretchedly poor to independently rich three times.

While the passing of John Martin was mourned in financial circles (with scant mention of his bereaved widow), the public was far more interested in the queen's upcoming Diamond Jubilee; June 22, 1897, would mark the occasion of the sixtieth anniversary of her accession to the throne. It promised to be an elaborate, theatrical pageant.

Arriving in advance of the celebrations was a contingent of the Colonial Indian Cavalry that had encamped in Chelsea, where the public enjoyed wandering among the pitched tents. Two Muslim waiters had also been sent from India to join the legions of others serving the queen and fifty foreign kings and princes attending the banquet at Buckingham Palace.

A telegraphed message was sent to all of the queen's subjects the morning of the 22nd. It read simply, "From my heart, I thank my beloved people. May God bless them."

Escorting her in a procession through London that afternoon was the largest military display ever assembled in the capital; fifty thousand troops marched in two separate columns, one led by the captain of the Horse Guards. At six feet eight inches, he was the tallest man in the British Army—made taller still by his high-plumed helmet. Leading the other column in the procession was the field marshal of Kandahar riding a grey Arabian horse. The imperial force of arms included New South Wales cavalrymen, Canadian hussars, and camel troops from Bikaner.

The headgear alone in the procession was thrilling. Indian lancers were led by a British officer in a white spiked helmet. Hong Kong Chinese police wore coolie hats. The British Guiana police caps were not unlike those of the French gendarmes. Cypriot Zaptiehs wore fezzes. Dayak headhunters from Borneo wore bright cadmium-red pillbox hats.

Crowds craned to catch a glimpse of the open carriage drawn by six snow-white horses transporting the queen from the palace to Westminster Abbey for the service of thanksgiving. After returning to the palace, she appeared on the balcony and was cheered by crowds stretched to the limit. The following afternoon, she attended a party in Hyde Park where some thirty thousand children were each given a meat pie, a piece of cake, and an orange to celebrate the day. Witnessing it all—the military procession, the marching bands, the lavish bunting, the exquisitely attired visiting princes and sultans—was the ubiquitous American, Mark Twain,[2] who had been on one of his lucrative European lecture tours in Europe.

The three-day commemoration would be the most expensive event in British history. Few argued that the queen was unworthy of the money spent. The British Empire had doubled in size during her sixty-year reign. London had become the world's largest city—larger by a quarter than the second most populous city, Peking, two-thirds larger than Paris and five times larger than New York City. It was the imperial capital of an empire comprising nearly a quarter of the earth's landmass and a quarter of its population. That no other country could ship an army across the seas without British consent made it the master of international movement.

"I do not say the French cannot come," remarked the Earl of St. Vincent, Admiral of the Fleet of the Royal Navy and member of Parliament. "I only say they cannot come by sea."

Unlike the Romans they so admired, the British based their empire's expansion on trade rather than conquest. The 1862 Colonial Office List was 153 pages long, encapsulating a realm that stretched west to Canada and east to Australia and New Zealand; it reached to Africa, including Egypt, Nigeria, and South Africa and even farther south to Antarctica. Quite literally thousands of languages and dialogues were spoken in their dominions.

When Queen Victoria ascended the throne, Britain was a rural country with an agricultural economy. By the time of her Diamond Jubilee, Britain had been transformed by industry and was the world's supreme power. There was a collective pride in the empire's steady progress. "Do as we do" was its message to the world. Anglo-Saxon righteousness fueled the conviction that, in the fullness of time, English rule would eventually and benignly lead millions to govern themselves. It was not merely a British right to impose their justice, their principles, their traditions, their method of getting things done. It was a duty.

Selling at a halfpenny, the *Daily Mail* was one of the first British newspapers to popularize its coverage to appeal to a mass readership. Of the jubilee, the *Mail* wrote, "How many millions of years has the sun stood in heaven? But the sun never looked down until yesterday upon the embodiment of so much energy and power."

There is a dangerous habit among the English of underestimating the gravity of any given situation until it's too late. While Rudyard Kipling and Edward Elgar were conveying British supremacy in words and music, while the trumpets sounded, the drums rolled, and the regiments presented arms so splendidly, industrialization was swelling the numbers of the nation's urban poor, widening social division, and the empire was becoming progressively cumbersome and overextended. The old guard would continue to believe that none of this was happening because, in their minds, it shouldn't.

The Boer War was what should not have happened, but did.

•   •   •

Britain's power was tested when it attempted to unite the British South African territories with the Boer republics. Facing off against the British were Boers—Afrikaans-speaking farmers—who were determined to hold on to their independence. War was declared on October 11, 1899. The British public expected it to be over by Christmas. On paper, it was no match: 50,000 irregular Boer fighters were pitted against 450,000 British troops. To the utter dismay of the British, they suffered a series of defeats in the first month alone, and the unprecedented number of casualties required replacement regiments from Canada, Australia, and New Zealand.

The populist tone of Britain's *Daily Mail* fanned patriotism in its own country, while, in Europe, the Boers were hailed as heroic defenders. Lasting for three bloody years—resulting in the death of over sixty thousand people—the Boer War gave the British what Kipling referred to as "no end of a lesson."

To bring the Boers to the negotiating table, the British resorted to brutal tactics, including the internment of Boer civilians—women and children. Those camps were referred to with new language: "concentration camps." The circumstances that led to these camps—indeed, the very idea of them—upended the once unshakable sense of British identity.

CHAPTER FORTY-THREE

Sex becomes everyone's business.

A fellow American, Henry George, was born a year after Victoria. At about the time she left San Francisco, he arrived there with the intention of prospecting for gold and ended up becoming the managing editor for the newly created *San Francisco Times*. His book, *Progress and Poverty*, likely read by James Blood and Stephen Pearl Andrews, investigated what was then increasing inequity and poverty amid America's industrial progress. Its economic viewpoint was grounded in the "Gilded Age," appropriated in name from a novel Mark Twain had written with his friend, Charles Dudley Warner, published some six years before. That term became synonymous with the materialism of the urban wealthy in the post–Civil War years, an era that saw industrialists prospering in the Northeast, while laborers—cut loose from their families in the South and isolated from the traditional network of community—were earning less in wages than they had from working on small farms or in rural stores.

Women, whose families had lost their men to the Civil War and who had been displaced in the aftermath, migrated North to fill positions as seamstresses and factory hands. Because their weekly earnings were no more than two dollars, respectable boardinghouses turned them away for fear that they wouldn't be able to pay the rent. Many of those women resorted to selling sex in alleyways off New York's Greene Street, or in its cigar stores, or even in the upper tiers of the Bowery Theater. An evening for wealthy men typically included a dinner at Delmonico's, followed by vintage brandy and a visit to a brothel.

There were more than twenty thousand prostitutes in New York

City in 1868, the year Victoria opened her Magnetic Healing Institute at 17 Great Jones Street. Among the products she offered was a sponge soaked in vinegar that acted as a contraception device (or so it was hoped) and a clove-based concoction that, when applied, felt warm and gave the impression to a man that the woman was eager. Hefty profits from the Healing Institute were no surprise: prostitution was an integral part of the city. One of the more popular books, *A Gentleman's Guide,* listed the brothels and detailed the services each of them offered. The *Herald,* the leading paper on Wall Street, ran personals that were used as a guide to prostitutes.

The legions of prostitutes in New York were matched only by those in Victorian London. At the time of Queen Victoria's Diamond Jubilee in London—with its pomp and ceremony—great wealth and extreme poverty were a stone's throw away from each other. The rich lived in grand mansions and the poor shared shelter in multifamily tenement dwellings called "rookeries" (the analogy being that, while birds nest separately, rooks do not). Entire families were crammed into single rooms. Drinking water was collected from a dirty street pump and dozens of neighbors shared filthy outdoor toilets.[1]

Urban poverty was a driving force behind the number of prostitutes in London, and here, again, Henry George's economic theory comes into play: it was Britain's Industrial Revolution that created the surplus of labor that drove a large part of the nation's population into towns and cities in search of employment. In the sixty-three years of Queen Victoria's reign, the population of Britain doubled and produced a wealth gap, particularly in London, where the very rich made up 1 percent and the vast majority were poor as a result of job displacement. Those on the bottom rung of the employment ladder were given few options, and women were given even fewer. They were restricted by the types of jobs available to them. Most took on low-paying and arduous work in factories. Others became domestic servants or were employed in dressmakers' shops. Factory worker, house servant, seamstress—no one of the three would have earned enough to feed themselves, much less their children. Charles Dickens cofounded a safe house for prostitutes who had been trapped in unbearable circumstances and wrote that "among the girls were starving needlewomen . . . violent girls imprisoned for committing disturbances in ill-conducted workhouses, poor girls from Ragged Schools, destitute girls who have applied at police offices for relief, young women from the streets . . . domestic servants who had been seduced."

In Victorian discourse, the term "prostitute" referred to lower-class women who, under pressure of poverty, eked out a living with paid-for sex. A "fallen woman" typically referred to the sexually promiscuous from the middle class who bartered sex for advancement, financial or otherwise. A woman in possession of great attraction and considerable charm might be able to make permanent arrangements with one of her wealthy clients and become a mistress. Regardless of the nomenclature, women who received compensation for sex were mopping up the demand for it when its supply could not be found among well-bred single women who had become wives.

Consider those well-bred, single women, whose education bore no real relationship to useful knowledge. They were meant to attract the right kind of man but instructed not to appear too forward in his company in order to avoid evincing a sexual appetite of their own. This imperative had been put forth by Victorian clergymen, who condemned any interest a woman might have in the possible enjoyment of sex as unnatural. It was not only the Church of England that regulated the behavior of women: Queen Victoria, more a "Mother of the Nation" than a participant in politics, represented a kind of domestic femininity that centered on the home and the family, on wifeliness and respectability. A woman's place was at her husband's side, wherever he chose to be or was called on to go, and marriage required her graceful acquiescence to that assigned role. Alfred Lord Tennyson's poem, *The Princess,* spelled it out:

Man for the field and woman for the hearth:
Man for the sword and for the needle she:
Man with the head and woman with the heart:
Man to command and woman to obey.

The English writer, philosopher, art critic, and sexually conflicted John Ruskin stripped the concept down to its nuts and bolts. A sheltered upbringing and a possessive mother propelled him into notions about sublime beauty that turned into a growing preoccupation with what should be expected of women in their ideal state. Ruskin was in his twenties when he met twelve-year-old Effie Gray, a girl for whom everything was decided, including her marriage to Ruskin when she was old enough. Once married, she was expected to devote her life to a man who would never touch her. That their marriage was meant to throw a cloak over the possibility that he was asexual is beside the point: despite the fact that his marriage was annulled after six years on the basis of nonconsummation, Ruskin continued to opine on the ideal state of men and women together. His book *Sesame and Lilies,* first published in 1865, stands as a statement on the natures and duties of men and women. It counsels that the sexes are fundamentally different: whatever a man is, a woman is not. A man's power is active energy, which is why he is the doer. A woman is meek and virtuous, which is why she is a moral guide. Ruskin suggested that it is only by withholding themselves from men that women convert men from brutes to, presumably, something more manageable. He refers to the separate spheres inhabited by men and women and declares that a woman should be "an angel in the house," a reference to the popular poem at the time by Coventry Patmore about the sublime acquiescence of a married woman, whose principal duty is as presider over the sacred hearth, who provides comfort to her husband each evening when he returns from the vulgar world of commerce.

"Great nations write their autobiographies in three manuscripts;— the book of their deeds, the book of their words, and the book of their art. Not one of these books can be understood unless we read the other two. But of the three, the only quite trustworthy one is the last," John Ruskin the art critic wrote. In a different work, he wrote, "The greatest thing a human soul ever does in this world is to *see* something, and tell what it saw in a plain way."

Perception is not a simple and straightforward act of seeing. Ruskin viewed women through the lens of almost exclusively privileged men who questioned what rights an unmarried woman could possibly want or need that an educated and well-connected husband could not supply. Stifling views of married women, whose only destiny was to provide moral support to a husband, led to calls for female emancipation. The most influential thinker on the subject was John Stuart Mill, who issued a written attack on Ruskin's binary perspective of wives and, in general, women's place in Victorian society.

Mill described his accelerated education in his autobiography. He was born in 1806 in London and was taught Greek at the age of three. Next came Latin so that, by the age of eight, he had read the whole of Herodotus and was acquainted with the six dialogues of Plato; by ten, he was reading Demosthenes, which would have pleased both Mrs. Woodhull and Mr. Garnett had they been aware.[2] The long-standing friendship Mill had with Harriet Taylor—herself accomplished—reinforced his advocacy of women's rights. He married her in 1851. Fifteen years later, as a Liberal MP in Parliament,[3] Mill was the first to call for women to be given the right to vote, arguing that "the legal subordination of one sex to the other—is wrong itself, and now one of the chief hindrances to human improvement." He pointed out that he had been elected based on a system that disallowed women from voting. Because that right would have required every political, social, and economic axiom to be reconsidered, his advocacy for change was unsuccessful. It did, however, place female suffrage on the parliamentary agenda, and much-needed debate ensued about women and their roles.

CHAPTER FORTY-FOUR

Women, but newer.

The unifying thread that ran through Victoria's decades in America was what she achieved in public life at a time when her sex made that virtually impossible. She had been the first woman to address a congressional committee; the first to run for the presidency; the first to operate a brokerage firm on Wall Street; and among the first to found a newspaper. As a fervent activist for suffrage and labor reforms, she had advocated for women's right to vote; an eight-hour workday; access to public schooling for all social classes; sex education; and birth control.

Given that she had so valiantly and persistently fought for women's suffrage, why, one might ask, had she decided to become a noncombatant? After her husband's death, she continued to publish *The Humanitarian* but abandoned the controversial subjects of social reform—including women's rights. Instead, she wrote articles concerning horticulture and poetry. Victoria had been a visionary who set a high standard for herself and then tried to force others to accept it. It was due entirely to her own determination that she could rightfully claim to be a self-actualized individual. It might have been that, having endured a wretched childhood, ignominy, and imprisonment, she had no interest or energy to reactivate her commitments as a reformer, or to exhaust herself by challenging social and political institutions. Having been under the collective glare for so long, perhaps she felt she deserved to be excused from the public stage—that she deserved late-in-life contentment. Regardless of the reasons, she stepped aside and let other women push the limits set by a male-dominated society.

While reforms in England had allowed a woman to enter universities and retain property, women were prevented from holding political office and could not vote. If women's suffrage was to succeed in Britain, it would not be from a sense of fairness, but from what the British call "maths." One-third of the nation's workers were women. One-fourth of them were married. The sheer number of women who might impact the efficiency of Britain's thriving industrial economy forced its courts to recognize spouses as separate legal entities with their own rights. Barbara Bodichon was a fine artist who exhibited at London's Royal Academy. She was also a formidable campaigner for women's rights. The pamphlet Bodichon wrote, *A Brief Summary in Plain Language of the Laws Concerning Women*, was the beginning of her continued efforts to help women gain control of their lives. Those efforts culminated in the 1882 Married Women's Property Act, allowing wives and widows to buy, maintain, and sell property separate from that of their husbands.

Among those women who benefited was Sarah Grand, who left her unhappy marriage in 1890 and moved to London, trusting that she would be able to support herself with the money she made writing. Grand used the term "New Woman" in an article describing educated, independent women who challenged the constraints of marriage. Henry James popularized the concept, first with the title character in his novella *Daisy Miller,* and next with the memorable Isabel Archer in his novel *Portrait of a Lady.* Both characters were affluent and spirited American expatriates living in Europe who—despite, or because of, their independent wealth—exercised control over their lives.

Earlier nineteenth-century female novelists had been serious contributors to the male-dominated literary scene: Charlotte Brontë, George Eliot, and Jane Austen. "Men have had every advantage of us in telling their own story. Education has been theirs in so much higher a degree; the pen has been in their hands," declares the heroine of Austen's last novel, *Persuasion,* published posthumously in 1817.

Some seven decades later, the first wave of New Women would feature not only in Sarah Grand's writing, but in that of Florence Farr, whose father had advocated for women's education and professional rights. Farr—with her wide-ranging career as a leading British actress, a women's rights activist, and a journalist writing articles on the subject—was considered the bohemian's bohemian, even within the interconnected world of nonconformist writers and artists. She had an affair with George Bernard Shaw and starred in several of his plays. She became the leader of the Hermetic Order of the Golden Dawn, an occult society with an explicit recognition of gender equality. She was romantically involved with W. B. Yeats and performed his poetry. Her freethinking cabal of friends included Oscar Wilde, freshly returned from his year-long lecture tour in America, and artist Aubrey Beardsley, a leading figure in Aestheticism, another movement that challenged the values of the Victorian mainstream.

Farr enlisted Beardsley to illustrate her first novel, *The Dancing Faun,* published in 1894.

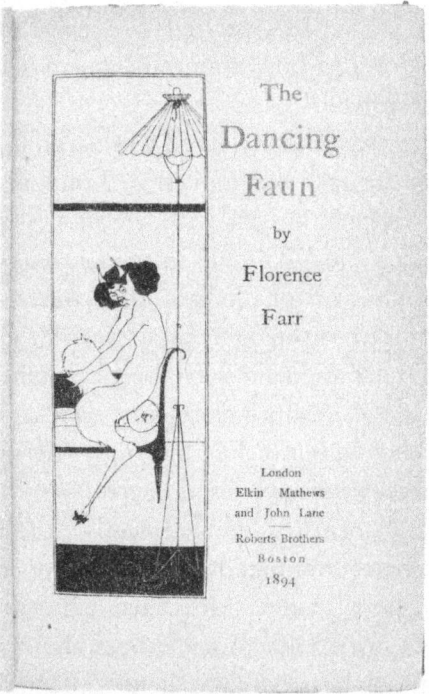

Inside page from Florence Farr's novel *The Dancing Faun.* The illustration by Aubrey Beardsley is a caricature of American expatriate and fellow member of the Aesthetic movement James McNeill Whistler as a domesticated satyr.

She modeled the novel's heroine, in part, on herself as a strong-willed actress who at one point asks in anger but not without logic, "Why should there be one law for men and another for women?" Male writers of the time generated debate by turning their attention to that same question. "The theme of many pens and tongues," was how Henry James put it in a piece about Henrik Ibsen and *Hedda Gabler.* English novelist and poet George Meredith became noted for his feminist sympathies. Mark Twain—an indisputable American product— spent the year between 1896 and 1897 living in Chelsea with his wife, Olivia, and dropped his objections to women's suffrage. In a lecture for the Fabian Society, George Bernard Shaw defended Henrik Ibsen's plays, which put incendiary issues of marriage and sexuality before the British public. The nonfiction output of H. G. Wells—another in Henry James's carefully tended and constantly growing circle of friends—included works of commentary on the hypocrisy of men's expectations of women.

H. G. Wells was a friend of British novelist George Gissing, whose novel *The Odd Women* features a multifaceted depiction of women by way of one of its characters, Mary Barfoot. She trains young women in her school in clerical skills, and her rhetoric of the New Woman inspires her students and emphasizes how words matter. "I want to do away with that common confusion of the words womanly and woman-ish, and I see very clearly that this can only be effected by an armed movement, an invasion by women of the spheres which men have always forbidden us to enter." Gissing's heroine Barfoot undermines the basic assumptions about Ruskin's "angel in the house" and suggests a new type of woman, no longer relegated to a realm apart from men but active in every sphere of life.

Other men were not as convinced. Harry Quilter pushed back against what he considered a concerning trend. Quilter occupied himself with traveling, collecting works of art, and periodically writing articles; in one, he noted that New Women exhibited a "determination, as settled as it is illogical and futile, to retain both the old privileges and the new concessions, to claim at once the rights of an equal, the immunities of a dependent and the respect due to a superior." Quilter insisted that the gains made by women of economic and educational opportunities would come at a cost: women would pay a price for their new social status by relinquishing cherished dispensations. Another distressed by the progressive advancement of women was publisher Leonard Smithers. He commissioned Aubrey Beardsley to illustrate a book of Aristophanes's antiwar play *Lysistrata* (411 BC), wherein women withhold sex unless men abandon the long war against Sparta. Beardsley's erotic drawings depicted what happened after neither of the two sexes refused to heed the other's threats: the women turned to public masturbation and, as a result, the men were burdened with enormous and erect phalluses that threaten to topple them over. By the time peace is restored, the power women have exacted from men has descended into something sordid and vulgar. Beardsley's illustrations satirized men's fear of female superiority at the same time as they took aim at the New Women.

In an era of cultural ferment, it wasn't only men who were alienated by the concept of the New Women. Queen Victoria, the founder of modern nursing, Florence Nightingale, and the writer, traveler, and archaeologist Gertrude Bell—all paradoxically emblematic of the New Women—opposed the concepts behind it.

Despite the backlash it suffered, the New Woman as a cultural icon did what it had set out to do. By the time the 1890s were drawing to a close, the authority of men was no longer absolute.

CHAPTER FORTY-FIVE

Eugenics, revisited.

To consider eugenics beyond the toxicity of its Nazi ideology is impossible, but it would be a mistake to contemplate the eugenics movement in isolation. It began with a crosscurrent of esoteric thinkers in Britain who sought to establish a biological connection between inherited characteristics and abilities linked to social class and race. Francis Galton was not considered controversial in 1883 when, following the ethics of impartial observation born of science, he proposed applying Darwinian theories to humans as a method of improving the population's living standards. The Eugenics Education Society was founded by some of the leading intellectual and social reformers of the time, including H. G. Wells, Aldous Huxley, and Marie Stopes. Francis Galton served as the society's first president; its remit was concerned with "curing" traits among the poor linked to conditions of alcoholism, tuberculosis, and prostitution (all, it could be easily said, having to do with being poor to begin with). Medical conditions such as the spread of syphilis were also considered, as well as mental conditions such as "feeblemindedness"—a catchall term for those who were believed to lack mental capacity and moral judgment.

John Maynard Keynes was a founding member of the Cambridge Eugenics Society. Like Galton, he was a statistician whose system of deficit finance bears his name. The society promoted views held by prominent scientists and medical professionals, alongside leading members of the Church of England, politicians, social reformers, and educators all apprehensive about the possible overpopulation of the nation. A far more existential threat on British society was the subconscious feeling that British ascendancy could not last forever, or even much longer. The British disaster of the Boer War coincided with America surpassing the British nation in its coal output and overtaking Britain's industrial leadership. Britain was forced out of the old order into an unfamiliar world and, in a time of psychological upheaval, eugenics was not a single thing but a shifting idea whose multiple, many-layered concepts depended on the individual or group assigning them a purpose. With the nation facing economic modernization and problems of social welfare, the discourse on eugenics was manipulated by promoting links between the poor and racially diverse to the nation's possible decline; for others, eugenics offered the promise of scientific intervention. Sympathetic to its possibilities, but critical of its strict focus on heredity, were members of the Fabian Society. Among them was George Bernard Shaw, who called for a greater attention to socioeconomic factors when it came to social well-being.

Appearing in America the same year *Lysistrata* was published in Britain was another book with the same theme. Set in the future, *The Strike of a Sex* is a sleeper-awakes tale in which its narrator discovers that women have banded together and refused to have sex, not to stop a war, as was the case in *Lysistrata,* but to stop being forced to have babies they don't want to have. The author was George Noyes Miller, the cousin of John Humphrey Noyes, the founder of the utopian Oneida Community.[1] An early convert to spiritualism in America, John Noyes promoted reproductive rights for women and was sympathetic to the fraught implications of eugenics.[2] His utopian Oneida Community had successfully instilled a cross-gender solidarity by freeing women from the fear of unwanted pregnancies through encouraging men to practice a type of birth control. Women in the community who wanted children were liberated from the strains of childcare through a system of communal child-rearing.

Intrigued by Francis Galton's papers and books, Noyes became convinced that there was a connection between social improvement and hereditary worth based on mental ability, predisposition to sickness or health, and moral tendencies. Expanding upon Galton's ideas, he explored possible benefits of propagation by way of intentional reproduction rather than haphazard sex. Noyes's "stirpiculture" was a proto-eugenics program of controlled reproduction within the Oneida Community governed by a committee who chose candidates based on spiritual and virtuous qualities. Under those circumstances, what, one might ask, could possibly go wrong?

Mrs. Woodhull has her say on the subject.

"My philosophy has been on the lines of Aristotle, who said, 'The *nature* of everything is best seen in its smallest portions.' My efforts were for the individual or ontogenic development of humanity as the only basis upon which to frame any laws—that by understanding and giving the proper attention to this the *quality* of the whole must of necessity ultimately reach a higher standard . . . Active not passive aid is what I demanded from woman. She must be appreciated as the architect of the human race. Men are what their mothers make them. Their intelligence or ignorance has the power to teach them to revere or desecrate womanhood . . . I pleaded for the intellectual emancipation and the redemption of womanhood from sexual slavery—insisting that social evils could only be eliminated by making your daughters the peers of your sons—that the greatness of a nation depends upon its mothers. I denounced as criminal the ignorant marriages which were filling the world with their hereditary consequences of woe, shame, and every manner of crime. The theme of my public work was that I would make it a criminal offence to allow persons to marry in ignorance of parental responsibility . . . I considered the work I was then doing as a necessary part of the evolution of thought—as initiatory to my reformatory work . . . The greatest luxury is being given the time to draw up one's accounts without evasion. I know I shall not please all your ears when I say that I took solace in the ideology of eugenics . . . but go home with me, and see the desolations and devastation of ill-breeding. It is my son who should have been my pride and joy, but has never been blessed by the dawning of reasoning. This is because I knew no better than to surrender my maternal functions to a drunken man, I am cursed to this living death."

CHAPTER FORTY-SIX

Falling out.

While Victoria was retreating from social reform, Tennie continued to fling herself into periodic activity on its behalf. Her largesse was lavishly given to various causes but could be just as easily withdrawn. In 1898, she announced her intentions to build a home for unwed mothers that she would fund by launching a private bank in London, Lady Cook & Co., Ltd. The venture never materialized. The same year, she sailed for New York, where she made it known that she would establish an American counterpart to Queen Alexandra's House, the home she founded in London that offered residency for young women artists. She told the press that she was in the process of purchasing a four-story house at 137 West 131st Street, which she intended to have remodeled specifically for that purpose. The project never got off the ground. After learning that her husband was ailing, she returned to London and discovered that, in her absence, his relatives had been circulating a rumor that his marriage to her was not legally binding—an argument, no doubt, fed by the entanglements of her short-lived marriage in Chicago some thirty-three years before. As soon as Sir Francis recovered from his illness, Tennie took the precaution of remarrying him in a civil ceremony and, to forestall any future litigation, she instructed her solicitors to negotiate a widow's dowry.

Eight months later, on February 17, 1901—shortly after his eighty-fourth birthday—Sir Francis died. Tennessee Claflin (now Lady Cook) was left an income for life from her husband's investments to add to her prenegotiated and sizable dowry. She was a millionaire in her own right. Sir Francis's Monserrate castle in Portugal, two-thirds of his property, and his art collection went to his eldest son, who was one year older than Tennie.[1] His daughter and her issue received a payment outright and incomes for life. The remainder of the estate went to his younger son.

For some part of the year, Tennie housed herself in Monserrate Castle in Sintra, where she founded and supported a number of free schools for the poor. When not in Portugal, she stayed at Doughty House in London with her stepchildren. With no children of her own, Tennie adopted her American grandniece, Utica Celestia, and arranged for her to be presented to Queen Victoria. Utica remained in England and married Thomas Beecham, the heir to the Beecham pharmaceutical company, which had made its fortune concocting England's most popular laxative. Thomas would become the revered conductor of the Royal Philharmonic Orchestra and would be knighted by the queen. It was an impressive tally: three American Claflin women married three of the wealthiest men in England.

Despite the money and glamor, all was not right. For reasons known only to Victoria and Tennie, the bond that had connected them since childhood snapped. Victoria was sixty-three when she wrote to fifty-six-year-old Tennie, "My darling blessed sister, I long to come and see you. How is it that our lives cannot be brought together now in our remaining years of life . . . after all of the trials we two have passed through hand in hand, suffered every hardship, how could we be separated now?"

Separated they most certainly were, and separated they would remain.

Victoria conveyed her decision to close *The Humanitarian* in a manner she saw fit, explaining that "after a career of nearly ten years, the decision was not taken without serious thought. The mental strain in carrying on a magazine of its nature from month to month was very great. There were other causes, on which it is unnecessary to dwell, combined to make the strain even greater still." Never one to waste the opportunity to promote herself, she added that "the many of the subjects which I dealt with in its pages have come to be freely discussed on the platform and in the Press. And it must be said that, at the time I first dealt with them, it required courage."

Perhaps Victoria thought that, at the same time she closed *The*

Humanitarian, moving from London would bring a clean break, or that the country would offer a better environment for Byron, who, now middle-aged, still required full-time attention. It might have been for both reasons that she decided to relocate to Bredon's Norton, an idyllic village beside the River Avon, twenty miles from London, where she took charge of Norton Park, bequeathed to her by her husband and recognized to be one of the most beautiful estates in England. Her installment there was announced in the June 1901 issue of *Country Life* with a seven-page spread of photographs. Its pictures show a wide circular gravel drive that passed through an arch over which was chiseled the date 1585, which led up to the entrance to the ivy-covered, Tudor-style house complete with pitched gables, mullioned windows, and enormous fireplaces. Above the front door was stained glass inlaid with Victoria's cherished word, "KISMET." The center hall resembled a hunting lodge with its dark wood paneling, diamond-patterned floor made of black slate and pale grey stone, and deer antlers set on the thirteen-foot-high walls. Floor-to-ceiling bookshelves lurched upward in the library. A round table situated in the middle of the room featured pamphlets that detailed the history of the estate and Victoria's self-invented genealogy. Displayed in her study were past photographs of her and John Martin pictured with the few important personages John had managed to hold on to after marrying Victoria. There were no photos of Byron and not many of Zula.

So lost in the shadow of her famous mother was Zula, it's impossible to get a sense of her beyond Victoria's meager accounts. At one point, she aspired to become an actress; at another, an editor. She put her mind to writing plays: two were published at her own expense and promptly ignored by theater producers. Zula made peace with the arrangement she had with Victoria: she would never want for money as long as she remained unmarried. By conveying the Norton Park estate as well to Zula, Victoria tethered her daughter to her side. Any resentment Zula might have felt about the control her mother exerted over her life was unspoken. She appeared content in her role as Victoria's full-time companion and enjoyed a comfortable life on the country estate she would one day inherit. Her infrequent adventures away from the estate coincided with Victoria's interests. When Victoria took a shine to what was then a plaything of the rich, the automobile, mother and daughter became the first women to drive through England and then France, which, to Victoria's delight, paved the way for the Prince of Wales to pay a call at Norton to talk motor cars with her.

CHAPTER FORTY-SEVEN

Ending the past.

Queen Victoria died January 22, 1901, at the age of eighty-one.[1] Given her advanced age and the decades she had sat on the throne, you would have thought that there had been ample opportunity to decide what should happen once she passed away. That was far from the case. Her instructions were that she not be embalmed but when the undertaker arrived, it was not with the expected coffin but with a tape measure. While her courtiers were deciding how to go about measuring the queen's regal body with the dignity it required, infighting broke out over who should oversee the state funeral. It seemed that the only people in the palace who had a precise understanding of their remit were the household servants. In their possession was an extensive list of items that the queen wished to be placed in the casket, including—but not limited to—rings of sentimental value, the cast of Albert's hand and his favorite cloak, and a pocket handkerchief that had belonged to her personal attendant, John Brown, whom she referred to as "my faithful Brown, that friend who was more devoted to me than anyone."[2]

With no photographs as a reference guide and few among those in the royal inner circle still alive to describe the previous funeral procession of William IV, the queen's predecessor, it fell upon the two ceremonial dignitaries, the fifteenth Duke of Norfolk and the lord chamberlain, to agree on what the queen's funeral procession should look like. Henry James reported the immeasurably vast sea of mourners who stood in the pouring rain to witness it. Having worn black from head to toe for decades in honor of her beloved husband's early death, the queen had chosen to wear white when laid to rest next to him on the grounds of Frogmore in Windsor.

During the course of her reign, the nation managed to reform its political system without a revolution, unlike its ancient enemy, France, despite the fact that Victoria's government had been largely aristocratic men, products of that unique British phenomenon, the British public school system. In return for the lashings its headmasters had happily inflicted, the schools—along with the church and the class system—ensured a sense of brotherhood among boys who would one day dictate the course of events in Great Britain.

Politics and law were male by default, but there was a still half-enfranchised public waiting for resolutions on some fifteen suffrage bills having to do with the rights of women. Millicent Fawcett organized and was leading the National Union of Women's Suffrage Societies, a nonparty federation formed from what had been disparate women's organizations. While Fawcett put her faith in an evolutionary process through representative parliamentary government, others argued that, for the past forty years, suffragettes had used conventional means to press the cause to no avail. Among them was Mrs. Emmeline Pankhurst, who, in 1903, convinced that all constitutional methods had been exhausted, founded the Women's Social and Political Union—an organization established to take a more militant path.

Elizabeth Cady Stanton and Susan B. Anthony—intent on dissociating the movement in America from Victoria's nonstop scandals—had omitted her name in their three-volume, 889-page account of the suffrage movement in America. Victoria, known as a former feminist firebrand, showed no interest in the crusade for women's suffrage in Britain. She failed even to support the active Women's Suffrage Society in the nearby borough of Cheltenham. Tennie was another matter. She contributed to the Women's Social and Political Union.

"Terrorism is, in fact, the only argument that Parliament understands," declared Emmeline Pankhurst's daughter, Christabel, who came to believe that the governing body would have to be lifted by its neck before it would acknowledge the injustice of its decisions. Her tactics—meant to generate as much publicity as possible—included staging clashes with the police in front of Parliament. With the motto of "deeds not words," the campaigns quickly intensified. Windows were smashed, first at the government buildings in Westminster, and later in shops and hotels in the West End.

When detonating postboxes and cutting telephone wires added to the catalog of protest actions, a number of the militants were arrested and subsequently went on hunger strikes. From solitary confinement, Pankhurst composed a dramatization of her experiences using a contraband pencil on prison-issue toilet paper.

CHAPTER FORTY-EIGHT

A parting of ways.

The escalation of the indiscriminate violence promoted by Emmeline Pankhurst's Women's Social and Political Union alienated the uncommitted and moderate supporters of suffrage, with *The Manchester Guardian* referring to "the small body of misguided women who profess to represent the noble and serious cause of political enfranchisement of women, but in fact do their utmost to degrade and hinder it."

George Bernard Shaw continued to point out the constructive logic of giving women the vote. Insisting that it would "set free a beneficial flood of politicians and social energy, which would be taken up by the government," Shaw signed a petition, along with other male advocates that included Thomas Hardy and James M. Barrie, which was published in the London *Times*. Tennie, who maintained a full travel schedule even in her late sixties, was seen at rallies in London's Hyde Park and, while in New York, took the press on a junket to Ludlow Street Jail to show them the cell she and Victoria had occupied after Anthony Comstock accused them of pornography. She went to Washington and was rebuffed when she attempted to vote in the presidential election in 1908, won by William Howard Taft.

While Tennie was routinely using her influence to further the cause of women's suffrage, Victoria concentrated instead on the Bredon's Norton estate. Estates were as important to the English landed gentry as factories were to American industrialists. Victoria managed hers well: there was a staff of efficient servants who kept the manor house in a constant state of readiness for visitors. The grounds showcased clipped hedges, bedded plants, and weeded walking paths named after poets. Victoria secured a telephone exchange and provided phones to the farmers. She had streetlights installed, improved the postal service, converted one of the barns on the estate into a village hall, and restored the cottages in the village.

Victoria had a history of latching on to new scientific and social theories. It was no different when it came to the issue of educating the young. The Church of England was the most powerful agent for social welfare in the countryside. Victoria chose the local vicar and paid his salary and for his house, but she was benevolent only to a point; she refused to renew the Church of England's lease for the local building located on the estate that housed the village grade school so that she and Zula could run the school themselves. Having assumed that because she owned the building, she could dictate what went on inside the classroom without anyone's permission, Victoria based her educational program on the Froebel method, which stressed practical training and the development of character.[1] When the local authorities refused to allow her the use of public funds for this purpose, Victoria paid for the teachers and provided a bus to collect the children. By 1909, the school was closed.

Victoria's altruism did not come with a great deal of humility. Like muscle memory, her self-regard returned in the form of a regular written series with *The Manor House Causeries,* which reported her pursuits—one specifically on the latest practices in scientific agriculture and the tendency toward specialization. Convinced that small-acreage farms made the prospect of farming more suitable for women, Victoria decided to start a Women's Agricultural College that offered instruction in gardening, poultry keeping, and dairying. Her idea was that any house in the village that became vacant would be acquired to accommodate the increased number of women workers. After the training was over, the college would assist in finding women permanent farming on small rented plots of land, which would enable them to remain in the community. The experiment was neither successful nor long-lived.

By 1900, it had been thirty-one years since Victoria was active in women's suffrage. Her time now was spent on her feudal kingdom of Bredon's Norton. She created a private club utilizing the manor house and the estate facilities to offer country recreation for those primarily from London. Its next incarnation was a retreat for artists and writers.

When that scheme petered out, she changed it into the headquarters for the Ladies' Automobile Club, and, in 1912, it became the location for the Women's Aerial League of Great Britain.

A year later, in 1913, Emily Davison ran onto the Epsom racecourse on Derby Day holding suffragette symbols, and, knocked down by King George V's horse, died a martyr to the cause. The suffragettes responded with even more aggressive acts of destruction. Pankhurst's instructions were that human life was not to be endangered, and so bombs were placed in empty churches and libraries usually at night, while destruction in broad daylight was limited to paintings in museums. The National Gallery was closed for two weeks after Velázquez's masterpiece, *Rokeby Venus,* was slashed.

The protests, the acts of defiance, the violence . . . none forced the issue of women's rights. That achievement would be brought about by another war. The year was 1914.

CHAPTER FORTY-NINE

History rhymes.

One in ten who died fighting what Britons called the "Great War" were under the age of nineteen. Some six thousand among all troops were killed daily. Six weeks was the average life expectancy in the trenches. Soldiers didn't have the protection of metal helmets the first year. The only defense against gas attacks were cloths soaked in their own urine. The position in Washington was that the war was Europe's business, so in an act of solidarity with his country of adoption, Henry James took British citizenship.

Victoria sent cables to Washington urging Congress to intervene. She donated vegetable seeds to the village for people to grow their own food. She provided for the village Land Army. She furnished cottages in the village for Belgian refugees. Her "Manor House Club" was where recruiting speeches were made, children were trained in social services, and tea was served to wounded soldiers from the Red Cross hospital. The fetes and programs organized in the club reflected Victoria's eccentric reach. Pageants included a tableau representing the "Signing of the Treaty of Ghent," and another, the "Landing of the *Mayflower*." There was a talk on Hindu cults, and one by the archbishop of Beirut pleading the cause of oppressed Armenians. An exhibit of great authors stood alongside examples of butter making. When America finally showed a willingness to fight alongside its allies, the stars and stripes waved over Bredon's Norton.

The militant suffragette movement was suspended while the war bled away almost an entire generation of men. Women filled the gaps in a workforce that had been left bare. Factories were altered to produce battle equipment and ammunitions; working conditions were grueling and hazardous. Employed day after day, week after week, month after month, year after year, women redefined what it meant to be female beyond the roles of wives and mothers. When the war ended in 1918, men returning were confronted by the dissatisfaction of women who—having been allowed to work and live independently for the first time—were forced back into low-paying roles or denied the option to work at all.

Women had changed radically during the span of those four years, not only in the way they were meant to act, but in how they looked. Every aspect of their dress and form became the opposite of what it had been. Straight shift dresses called for deliberately flat chests; lower-waisted skirts required narrow hips. Smoking—previously considered inappropriate for women—promised weight loss. Cigarette sales among women rocketed. The status quo between men and women had been engineered for stability. Tectonic plates ground against one another, causing the surface to ripple. The war had blurred boundaries: nice girls were invited into nightclubs and sat down next to the distinctly not so nice girls.

London, too, was changing. After the war, there was widespread demolition without thought given to anything of the past. Churches in the financial district were torn down to make way for banks. Over half of those employed in London were in finance, law, and public administration. A third of London's registered workforce was female, all of whom were underpaid. Many were still crowded in workshops in attics or belowground, but an increasing number of single women found roles as ancillary clerks in one of the growing number of department stores. Consumerism blossomed. Selfridges on Oxford Street in Mayfair introduced the idea of shopping as an experience with their motto, "The customer is always right." Harrods in Knightsbridge boasted of the first "moving staircase" and provided a free glass of brandy for any of its more adventurous customers to make it to the top.

When not residing in Portugal during the war, Tennie divided her time in London between Doughty House and her flat in South Kensington. Her wartime causes had proven fairly absurd (at one time, she announced the formation of an Amazon army), but she continued to support the women's movement.

Tennessee Claflin died in 1923 at the age of seventy-seven, without mending the rift with her sister. She lived long enough to see the ratification of the Nineteenth Amendment to the Constitution in 1920 that gave women the right to vote. Obliterating any recollection of scandal or questionable incident that had marked her life, her obituary in the London *Times* gave generous credit to her "serious campaign" for women's rights in America. It referred to her time as a magnetic healer there as an "admirable career." It praised her as someone well ahead of her time and cited her natural gift for public speaking. Across the Atlantic Ocean, *The New York Times* ran a column-long obituary that depicted the success story of Lady Cook, citing her as a "banker and journalist." No one could question the accuracy of the newspaper's claim that Tennie was crucial "as an advocate of woman's rights," for, by then, Elizabeth Cady Stanton and Susan B. Anthony were long gone.

In death, Tennie managed to appropriate the kind of positive press send-off Victoria was expecting for herself—that of a sober, respected, courageous pioneer in all matters of reform.

CHAPTER FIFTY

Mrs. Woodhull decides to keep the spirits waiting.

Determined to have the final word while she was still able, Victoria returned to the project of writing her autobiography. Inconveniently, she had altered her own story so often and to such a degree that it was impossible for her to find a way to convey a coherent narrative. She left the task to her loyal daughter and, instead, began to prepare for her afterlife.

With no intention of lying among the dead in a graveyard—and having divided her life equally between America and Great Britain—Victoria's instructions were that her ashes be scattered in the Atlantic Ocean. Whatever monies were left after Zula had passed were to be donated to the Society for Psychical Research in London, a learned society founded in 1882 whose purpose was to investigate mesmeric, psychical, and "spiritualist" phenomena from a scientific perspective.

By the time Victoria reached her late eighties, all that Demosthenes had foretold was seen to have been true. She had survived husbands, lovers, mentors, her detractors in America, and those of her British contemporaries, most of whom had been looking at a false reflection of themselves in the mirror while the imperial power was vanishing.

Convicted of robbing the city of millions of dollars, William "Boss" Tweed died in 1878 at the age of fifty-five in Ludlow Street Jail, the very jail in which Victoria had been incarcerated on obscenity charges brought against her by Anthony Comstock.

Fittingly, Phineas Taylor Barnum, a onetime hoaxer, became a politician before dying in 1891.

William Avery Rockefeller Sr., known as Devil Bill, died in 1906 at the age of ninety-five and left behind two sons with a remit to increase the family's wealth.

When Theodore Tilton died in 1907, his family made no effort to bring his body back from France for burial in America.

Mark Twain, who returned to America after living in London between 1896 and 1897, wrote of the unforgiving aging process in his autobiography: "It's sad to go to pieces like this, but we all have to do it." He died in 1910.

Anthony Comstock died in 1915, not before he had Margaret Sanger indicted for planning to open a birth-control clinic; secured the conviction of some 2,500 people on morals charges; and proudly claimed to have been responsible for driving fifteen people to suicide.

Richard.

That had been Mr. Garnett's first name. According to his 1906 obituary, he remained the keeper of the printed books at the British Library until his retirement in 1899. He married. There were children. Among the books he wrote were biographies of Thomas Carlyle, John Milton, and William Blake. He was also the author of histories of Italian and English literature. His poem "Where Corals Lie" had been set to music by Edward Elgar. I am convinced that, to the very last, Mr. Garnett thought of Mrs. Woodhull as a puzzle that had withheld the satisfying clicking sound of its pieces falling neatly into place. It is my hope that, despite the unpleasantness she habitually caused others, he was willing to acknowledge her fortitude and, begrudgingly, he had decided that her recklessness added up to something resembling integrity.

•　　•　　•

It is said that humans process information through pattern recognition, and that the smallest number allowing us to recognize a pattern is three. In point of fact, the most impactful method of conveying an image or a concept is the use of three brief adjectives, back-to-back. "Dark, damp, dirty" is an example; the Churchillian "blood, sweat and tears" is another. The technique is equally successful in creating a lasting impression of an individual.

It's impossible to convey Victoria Woodhull with just three adjectives. Having had two continents in her crosshairs and very few inhibitions restraining her, she went from rags to riches, riches to rags, then back to riches. Living the equivalent of several lives—all featuring outrageous plot twists—she remained a maverick to the core, dealing equally well in truths and falsehoods. She used seduction, bad faith, and deception to get what she wanted. What she wanted was often beyond belief but almost always what she got.

Keeping her death at bay, Victoria scribbled "the deeper I delve for the sure footing, the higher I reach for the light, the more convinced I am that only here and there do we find an instrument capable of responding to the hungry heart's desire for Truth. Whoever I am, whatever I have done, belongs to the spirits."

She should have added, "But not yet."

Victoria Woodhull was greedy for more life, even as her grape-colored veins branched over her swollen legs; even after stiffness in her joints set in; even when the cold weather returned the painful bouts of rheumatism she had known as a child. She became paranoid about germs and insisted that her drinking water be boiled first and that there be six feet between her and any visitor. Operating under the misapprehension that lying down in bed might give death an advantage, she took to sleeping erect in a straight-back chair.

In old age, moments of piercing clarity can accompany a vagueness of recollection. Victoria's disjointed memories may have taken her back to the libel suit. It was some thirty-five years before, but she would have surely remembered Sir Charles Russell, the barrister who defended the British Museum and its trustees against her. He made the mistake of not paying close attention to her testimony. Had he given a moment of thought to her admission of enduring a deprived and abusive childhood, he might have paid heed to the fact that people who survive emotional damage have already proven that they can shift the ground beneath them. He also made light of her—another mistake, for nothing stills mockery more than the nagging thought that one shouldn't have mocked at all.

That was then. Now, her body, which at one time pulsed, dictated, enjoyed, demanded, forbade everything. Her eyes, hooded by drooping lids, looked at nothing in particular while her lips moved in a soundless monologue until she drew her last breath on June 9, 1927, eleven years short of a century after she had drawn her first.

In a single, exquisitely weightless moment of tranquility—when the chair dissolved beneath her and she existed in both life and death— one would like to believe that Victoria's mind's eye saw everything she had been. A child clairvoyant born dirt-poor in an obscure American outpost. A self-styled survivor. A professional provocateur who provided no shortage of material for those wanting to be provoked. An ambitious attention seeker who sought out the glare of publicity. A polarizing figure threatening the social order. A smasher of things. A destroyer of convention. A sexual opportunist. An ardent feminist. A cause. An effect. A committed capitalist chasing profit. A trigger. A progressive visionary reconceptualizing the world around her, who brought to the fore issues we still grapple with today. A person whose good and less good instincts cohabited in her character. Someone who, against all odds, might well have convinced a man like Richard Garnett to think again about almost everything.

Timeline

1687: Hans Sloane sails from Britain for Jamaica to be the personal physician to its new governor. During his relatively short stay in the Caribbean, he collects one thousand specimens of plants—eight hundred of which are unknown to British academics. He marries Elizabeth Langley Rose, the wealthy sugar plantation heiress.

Sloane and his wife return to Britain. He expands his collection beyond plants with an eclectic assortment of objects and books.

1753: Sir Hans Sloane, one of the greatest collectors of his time, bequeaths his vast collection to the nation. An act of Parliament creates the world's first free, national, and public museum, the British Museum, with Sloane's collection as its nucleus.

1759: The British Museum opens in a seventeenth-century London mansion, Montagu House.

1818: Frederick Douglass is born enslaved as Frederick Augustus Washington Bailey in 1818 at a plantation in Talbot County, Maryland.

1838: Carrying false identification papers and dressed in a sailor's uniform provided by a free Black seaman, Frederick Douglass boards a train traveling north and escapes from slavery in Maryland.

Victoria Claflin is born dirt-poor in the small hamlet of Homer, Ohio. Her father is an itinerant con artist; her illiterate mother names her after England's Queen Victoria, whose coronation has just taken place.

1845: Victoria's younger sister, Tennessee Celeste Claflin (known as Tennie) is born in Homer.

1848: The discovery of gold in California sets off a frenzied gold rush; the next year, hopeful prospectors, called "forty-niners," pour into the state.

1849: Karl Marx arrives in London, a thirty-one-year-old stateless refugee, exiled from three other countries for his political writings.

1850: The British Museum opens its completed building on London's Great Russell Street.

1851: The Claflin family take to the road when the townspeople in Homer threaten to tar and feather Victoria's father, Buck. Victoria and Tennie perform at revival meetings to support the family. Buck promotes them initially as child clairvoyants, and then as faith healers.

1853: To escape her abusive father, fourteen-year-old Victoria marries twenty-eight-year-old alcoholic, morphine addict, and quack doctor Canning Woodhull. They move to Chicago.

1854: Victoria gives birth to a mentally handicapped baby boy she names Byron.

The Republican Party is founded.

1857: The British Museum Reading Room is opened, but members of the public wishing access are required to apply in writing.

1858: Having realized that her marriage was a mistake and, with no legal recourse to divorce, Victoria makes the headstrong decision to leave Chicago, and, after insisting that she was guided by visions, she strikes out with her husband and infant son on a tortuous journey to San Francisco, where she works as an actress.

Buck places ads in Cincinnati newspapers promoting Tennie as "the wonderful child with the clairvoyant eye." Her earnings support the extended Claflin family.

Victoria and her own family leave San Francisco for New York.

1861: Victoria's second child, a healthy daughter to be named Zulu, is born.

Liberal Republican Abraham Lincoln sworn in as American president.

America's Civil War begins when Confederate troops fire on Union soldiers at Fort Sumter, South Carolina.

1863: Lincoln signs the Emancipation Proclamation, freeing slaves within the rebellious states.

1864: Victoria sets herself up as a "spiritualist physician" in a hotel in St. Louis, Missouri, where she is consulted professionally by Colonel James Harvey Blood, a war veteran in his early thirties who was the president of the local Society of Spiritualists and had just been appointed St. Louis's city auditor. They divorce their respective spouses and, in Dayton, Ohio, sign a document stating their "intention to marry."

1865: While the death toll from the Civil War climbs to horrifying numbers, institutional religion fails to comfort, and the spiritualist movement fills the gap in the United States, before taking hold in England.

Victoria and Tennie travel on their own by wagon through Tennessee, Arkansas, and Missouri and get rich charging fees as spiritualists.

Confederate General Robert E. Lee surrenders to Union General Ulysses S. Grant.

President Abraham Lincoln is assassinated by John Wilkes Booth.

Karl Marx, a political exile in London, begins to collaborate with German thinker Friedrich Engels, also in London. Under a false name, Marx uses the library at the British Museum while developing *The Communist Manifesto*.

1868: In Pittsburgh, Victoria insists that she has had a vision of Demosthenes, who instructs her to move to New York, where a house will be waiting for her.

In St. Louis, Missouri, Victoria is consulted professionally by Colonel James Harvey Blood, a war veteran in his early thirties who was the president of the local Society of Spiritualists. They divorce their respective spouses and, in Dayton, Ohio, sign a document stating their "intention to marry."

Victoria and Tennie meet Cornelius Vanderbilt in New York. At the time, he is America's richest man.

1869: Taking advantage of the Wall Street crash, Victoria makes a fortune shorting gold. Victoria and Tennie establish Woodhull, Claflin & Company, a Wall Street brokerage firm. They are the first women to do so.

1870: The sisters launch a newspaper, *Woodhull & Claflin's Weekly*.

Victoria and her family move to a mansion on New York's Thirty-Eighth Street.

She meets Stephen Pearl Andrews, a utopian reformer, and announces that she will stand for president in 1872.

Victoria sends a petition to Congress on behalf of women's suffrage and is invited to put her case to the Judiciary Committee of the House of Representatives in Washington, DC.

1871: She presents her memorial (petition) on suffrage to the House Judiciary Committee and lectures in Washington, DC, on "Constitutional Equality."

She lectures on "The Great Social Problems of Labor and Capital" in New York City.

Victoria's mother, Roxanna, brings a lawsuit against Victoria's husband, Colonel Blood, in New York.

Victoria meets Theodore Tilton, social reformer.

She publishes a call for the Equal Rights Party and becomes president of the American Association of Spiritualists in addition to assuming the leadership of Section 12 of the International Workingmen's Association of New York.

The *Weekly* is the first to publish Karl Marx's manifesto in America.

Victoria lectures widely on "The Principles of Social Freedom, Involving the Question of Free Love, Marriage, Divorce and Prostitution." Her book *The Origins, Tendencies and Principles of Government* is published.

Tennie—also divorced—writes a book of her own entitled *Constitutional Equality a Right of Woman*.

1872: Victoria's nomination for the U.S. presidency by the National Suffrage Convention in Washington, DC, is unsuccessful.

Canning Woodhull dies in New York City.

Victoria is nominated for the U.S. presidency by the Equal Rights Party in New York.

She publishes revelations about Henry Ward Beecher's affairs in the *Weekly*.

Victoria and Tennie are arrested in New York for an obscenity charge made by Anthony Comstock.

Ulysses S. Grant is reelected president of the United States.

Woodhull and Claflin's Weekly is suspended.

1873: Financial markets collapse. Woodhull, Claflin & Company brokerage firm is dissolved.

Obscenity trial begins; Victoria and Blood are found not guilty.

1877: Victoria leaves the United States for England, bringing her children and Tennie.

1881: Having settled in London, she publishes a special UK edition of the *Weekly* repudiating the charges of her past radical social and political opinions reported by the American press.

1883: Victoria meets and marries John Biddulph Martin in London. He is an established British banker—a man not only of wealth, but of considerable culture and charm. They live at 17 Hyde Park Gate in an impressively large house with an entrance fashioned after a Pompeian villa.

1885: Tennie zeros in on the even wealthier Francis Cook, an elderly widower. She convinces him that his deceased wife has sent a message from the spirit world advising him to marry Tennie. As the second Mrs. Cook, Tennie moves into Doughty House, a magnificent residence that overlooks the Thames.

1892: Victoria launches *The Humanitarian* in London, and then in New York, as a platform for a bid to run in the 1894 presidential race.

She is nominated for the U.S. presidency by the Kansas delegation of the Equal Rights Party.

1893: She lectures in New York on "The Scientific Propagation of the Human Race."

1894: Victoria Woodhull's libel suit against the British Museum comes to trial. It concludes with her being awarded £1 in damages but obliges her to pay the museum's legal costs of £508.

1897: John Martin dies in the Canary Islands, leaving his entire estate to Victoria.

   She retreats to the English village of Bredon's Norton, where she builds a village school with the purpose of reforming English educational methods.

   Interested in aviation, she announces that she will give a cash prize to any man or woman who would fly the Atlantic to any point in the British Isles or make the same flight in the opposite direction.

1906: Mr. Garnett dies in London at the age of seventy-one.

1914: Britain enters World War I; Victoria lobbies the U.S. government to do the same.

1918: Women in Britain over thirty who meet a property qualification are allowed to vote.

1919: The Nineteenth Amendment legally guarantees American women the right to vote.

1923: Tennie, age seventy-seven, dies in Britain.

1927: At the age of eighty-eight, Victoria Woodhull dies in Britain, where she has spent the last fifty years of her life.

Acknowledgments

This book's primary sources and additional reading section records the debts I owe to previous books, pamphlets, essays, and articles concerning Victoria Woodhull.

I am especially grateful to Robin Holland-Martin, who was generous with his time and referred me to valuable material from the Martin family archives.

Institutions and libraries that enabled my research were the Boston Museum's Manuscript Collection, the British Museum Library, the British Museum Archives, the National American Woman Suffrage Association Collection at the Library of Congress in Washington, DC, the London Library, The New York Historical Society, the New York Public Library's Manuscripts and Archives Division, the New York Society Library, and the private library at the Athenaeum Club in London.

Continued support came from Denise Alay, Hanna al-Shaykh, Lionel Barber, Ann Louise Bardach, Mustafa Baygun, Jadranka Beresford-Peirse, Charles Bingham-Newland, Paul Bogaards, Peter Brown, Brenda Brod, Sally Clarke, Sara Colleton, Sean Collinsworth, Pete Czernin, Pamela D'Arc, Blythe Danner, Annabel Davis-Goff, Andrea Del Corno, Nicolette Donen, Peter Eyre, Ralph Fiennes, Susannah Fiennes, Carol Fitzgerald, Violet Fraser, John Fulvio, Aharoni Ghiora, Vincent Giroud, Victoria Greenwood, Jamanda Haddock, Dominic Hobson, Cecilia Mendez Hodes, Judy Joo, Helena Joseph, Henry Keswick, Antonia La Rocca, Ned Mackay, Peter Mandelson, Kim McCarty, Michael McCarty, Edward Miller, Robert Noel, Christopher Noey, Deborah Owen, Emily Pope, Robert Pounder,

Alan Roxburgh, Amy Ryan, Patricia Shea, Sally Bedell Smith, Pauw Steyl, Kristin Scott Thomas, Pascal Volle, Monia Von Opel, Lisa Immordino Vreeland, Angus Wilkie, Marta Wohrle, Andrea Wong, and Johanna Zwirner.

I am thankful once again for Thomas Gebremedhin, a masterful editor, and for the perceptive judgments of my agent, Lynn Nesbit.

Notes

Chapter Six

1. James Braid, a Scottish surgeon, would later propose the term "hypnotism" for the state that Franz Anton Mesmer would place his patients in.
2. The practice of tar and feathering was first referred to in 1189, when England's Richard the Lionheart decreed that anyone sailing with his army of Crusaders to Jerusalem who had stolen onboard "shall be first shaved, then boiling pitch shall be poured upon his head, and a cushion of feathers shook over it so that he may be publicly known; and at the first land where the ships put in he shall be cast on shore."

Chapter Nine

1. Horace Greeley advanced Ralph Waldo Emerson's writing career and served as a literary agent for Henry David Thoreau.
2. Greeley's written dispatches featured his interview in Salt Lake City with the Mormon leader Brigham Young.

Chapter Ten

1. Fraudsters have enjoyed a long history in America, some storied in its literature, such as Sinclair Lewis's *Elmer Gantry* and Flannery O'Connor's *Wise Blood*. Examples of hucksters in the financial sector: Bernie Madoff, the admitted mastermind of the largest known Ponzi scheme in history; Sam Bankman-Fried, who stole $8 billion from customers of the now-bankrupt FTX cryptocurrency exchange he founded. A con man in politics of near mythic proportions was Congressman George Santos, who devised and executed a scheme to steal the personal identity and financial information of contributors to his campaign, and then charged contributors' credit cards repeatedly, without their authorization. Donald Trump—with his vast number of alleged acts of fraud—has triumphed in combining all three: literature, finance, and politics. Until recently, there were very few—if any—examples of women who have cheated on a large scale, not because women are more moral than men, but because they have not often been in a position of exerting institutional power.

Chapter Eleven

1. The exact date of birth for Zulu Maud Woodhull varies: a ship's passenger recorded her birthday as April 28, 1863, but most sources have her born April 1861.
2. First Lady Mary Todd Lincoln hosted séances in the White House. Attending at least one was her husband, whose own religious philosophy was anything but certain.

Chapter Thirteen

1. The Oneida Community was dissolved in 1881 and, in an ironic reversal of its socialist practices, converted itself to a joint-stock company, which became the silverware manufacturer Oneida Limited, one of the largest in the world.

Chapter Fourteen

1. Cornelius Vanderbilt's plan was to bring together his railroad lines and build a central terminal at Forty-Second Street, which today is Grand Central Terminal.
2. General Robert E. Lee's last two campaigns in Virginia saw his army starving, not from want of produce in Confederate territory, but due to a lack of factory facilities to repair the railways that could have otherwise been transporting that produce.

Chapter Eighteen

1. Thomas Nast was considered the father of the American political cartoon. His cartoons touched on virtually every issue of the era, including slavery, the Civil War, and Reconstruction. He created the modern version of Santa Claus (based on the traditional German Sankt Nikolaus), as well as the political symbol of the elephant for the Republican Party.

Chapter Nineteen

1. When the Scottish explorer David Livingstone became lost in the African jungles during his quest to discover the source of the Nile, an American by the name of James Gordon Bennett agreed to pay the expenses of locating him. Bennett's agreement with the rescue expedition's leader, Henry Morton Stanley, was that, in exchange for covering all costs, Stanley would provide Bennett's paper with an exclusive eyewitness account. When, finally, Henry Stanley found whom he had been looking for, he offered an Englishman's discreetly polite greeting, "Dr. Livingstone, I presume?"

Chapter Twenty

1. Harriet Beecher Stowe's emotive novel *Uncle Tom's Cabin; or, Life Among the Lowly* became more than just an American phenomenon. One million copies of its first publication were sold in England, ten times the number of any work except the Bible. She insisted that she had taken dictation from God when she wrote it. It should be noted that while women were not immune to understanding the horrors of slavery, they were also not oblivious to the ways they could profit from it. Although women were required by law to relinquish property and money to the men they married, exceptions were made

for slaves. To be sure, slavery was largely the business of men, but research by economists at The Ohio State University found that women were buyers or sellers of 30 percent of all transactions at the slave market in New Orleans, and 38 percent of those involved female slaves.

Chapter Twenty-One

1. Between 1400 and 1900, more than 12.5 million captive Africans were transported to the Americas by way of the Middle Passage.
2. For fear that they were infectious, children were refused admittance to ordinary hospitals in London. There was no children's hospital before Hans Sloane became a founding governor of London's Foundling Hospital.
3. Descriptions of the brutal treatment of slaves have been gathered from Sloane's journals, quoted in various sources, and featured on the Wikipedia entry for him.

Chapter Twenty-Four

1. Whether or not individual states could choose their own governance and thus supersede federal law was to become a major issue of the post–Civil War Reconstruction period.

Chapter Twenty-Eight

1. On file in Moscow's Marx-Engels-Lenin Institute is the issue of the *Weekly* that featured Marx's *Communist Manifesto*.

Chapter Thirty-One

1. The epithet "Comstockery" came to be synonymous with moralist censorship. Comstock became one of America's most ideological and extreme enforcers of public morality: during the course of his campaigns, fifteen tons of books were destroyed and some four thousand arrests were made.
2. The Comstock laws against family planning remained unchallenged until Margaret Sanger was arrested in 1916 for opening up the first birth-control clinic in America. It wasn't until the 1918 Crane decision that women were legally allowed to use birth control.
3. William Howe's defense would be used in obscenity cases in Britain in a landmark censorship case concerning the English translations of the "obscene" novels by French author Émile Zola.
4. While Victoria is commonly cited as the first woman to run for president, she was not old enough to be elected. That was not the case with Belva Ann Bennett Lockwood (October 24, 1830–May 19, 1917). Lockwood was a lawyer, author, and politician active in the women's rights movements who ran in 1884 and, again, in 1888, on the ticket of the National Equal Rights Party. Thus, Lockwood was the first woman to appear on official ballots.

Chapter Thirty-Three

1. James Abbott McNeill Whistler wasn't the only fellow American artist living in the bohemian community that was Chelsea. John Singer Sargent, a nomadic expatriate who grew up in Europe, would settle there.

Chapter Thirty-Four

1. Sir Thomas Gresham (1519–79) was regarded as the father of British bank-ing. He became involved in the trade of financing in the 1540s and arranged funding for Henry VIII and Queen Elizabeth I. The grasshopper emblem (featured on his family crest) was used to identify his banking premises on London's Lombard Street. At the end of the seventeenth century, the Martins became associated with the bank referred to as "The Grasshopper," and, over the next six generations, its operations would be run by the sons of sons of the Martin family.

Chapter Thirty-Six

1. Sir Leslie Stephen might have provided Henry James with the details of Victoria Woodhull's life. Father to Virginia Woolf and Vanessa Bell, author, critic, historian, biographer, early humanist activist, Sir Leslie was the editor of the London-based *Cornhill Magazine,* a monthly literary publication that ran an excerpt of James's *The Siege of London.* Stephen and his family lived at 22 Hyde Park Gate, a few doors down from what would become Victoria and John Martin's home.

Chapter Thirty-Eight

1. The First International Eugenics Congress, which met in London in 1912, was chaired by Major Leonard Darwin, the son of Charles Darwin. Attendees included Dr. Alexander Graham Bell and Sir Winston Churchill. In 1921, the Second International Eugenics Congress was held at New York's American Museum of Natural History. The darker threads that collected at the edges of what began as a mainstream idea appeared in Adolf Hitler's writings, includ-ing *Mein Kampf.*

Chapter Forty-Two

1. The 17 Hyde Park Gate mansion survived the London Blitz and was converted into six separate flats.

2. During the years he'd been seeking fame as a writer, Twain was on the lookout for investment opportunities, and, after purchasing a typesetting machine, he founded his own publishing company in 1884 and advanced Henry Ward Beecher $5,000 to write his autobiography. Beecher died after spending the money and left behind a barely begun manuscript. This was not the only example of Twain's failed enterprises—truth be told, none of the investments he made netted his hoped-for windfall. Twain was, however, astute with the strategies he employed to protect the Mark Twain brand. His figure remained slender past middle age and, though his shock of red hair was beginning to grey and his eyebrows began to resemble plumage, he was instantly identifi-able as Mark Twain. His speeches and lectures—welcoming, expansive, and entertaining on so many levels—produced a steady stream of income.

Chapter Forty-Three

1. William Booth, founder and first general of the Salvation Army, described London's degrading living conditions: "Talk about Dante's Hell, and . . . the

torture-chamber of the lost!...The man who walks with open eyes...through the shambles of our civilisation needs no such fantastic images of the poet to teach him horror."

2. While serving as lord rector of the University of St. Andrews in Scotland, John Stuart Mill made the now-famous—and often wrongly attributed—remark delivered at his inaugural address that "bad men need nothing more to compass their ends, than that good men should look on and do nothing."

3. Britain's parliamentary government was then (and it is today) composed of three elements: the queen (or king), the House of Commons, and the House of Lords, whose members were lifelong and unelected. In 1895, the House of Lords was composed of hereditary and representative peers, four law lords together with retired law lords, as well as two archbishops and twenty-four senior bishops of the Anglican Church. Despite this illustrious display, the House of Commons was then (as it is today) the most influential of the three elements.

Chapter Forty-Five

1. By the time *The Strike of a Sex* was published, the Oneida Community had been dissolved.

2. In 1895, Connecticut passed the first eugenics marriage laws, which stated that "feebleminded, imbecilic, and epileptic men and women under 45 years of age" could not marry. The law was repealed in 1967. In 1897, Michigan was the first state to introduce a mandatory sterilization bill for the castration of criminals and degenerates. It failed to pass. In 1907, Indiana passed the first mandatory sterilization law. It was struck down by the Indiana Supreme Court in 1921.

Chapter Forty-Six

1. Francis Cook's art collection was held in a family trust for four generations and partly dispersed in the years following World War II: a portrait attributed to Titian was presented to London's National Gallery. Forty pictures by van Dyck were sold to a Dutch dealer in 1940 and fell into Nazi hands; some of them have never been recovered.

Chapter Forty-Seven

1. Queen Victoria's sixty-three-year reign produced quite a few of the most notable figures in English history: Robert Browning, Alfred Lord Tennyson, Anthony Trollope, John Stuart Mill, Charles Darwin, John Ruskin, Matthew Arnold, Christina Rossetti, Algernon Charles Swinburne, William Morris, the Brontës, Karl Marx, George Eliot, George Meredith, Oscar Wilde, Thomas Carlyle, George Bernard Shaw, Charles Dickens, Francis Galton, Benjamin Disraeli, William Blake, William Gladstone, Arthur Conan Doyle, David Livingstone, Lewis Carroll, Elizabeth Gaskell, William Wordsworth, Alexander Graham Bell, William Butler Yeats, Thomas Hardy, and Rudyard Kipling.

2. John Brown, who was Scottish, was Prince Albert's gillie in Scotland, acting as his attendant on hunting expeditions. At Prince Albert's instigation, Brown's

role changed to permanent leader of the queen's pony. After the prince's death in 1861, Brown became a friend of the queen. The exact nature of their relationship was the subject of speculation.

Chapter Forty-Eight

1. Friedrich Froebel was a German educator who believed that a child's education should take into account the whole of that child.

Primary Sources and Additional Reading

Prologue

Delbourgo, James. *Collecting the World: The Life and Curiosity of Hans Sloane*. Viking Penguin, 2018.

Sloane, Hans. *A Voyage to the Islands Madera, Barbados, Nieves, S. Christophers and Jamaica, with the Natural History of the Herbs and Trees, Four-Footed Beasts, Fishes, Birds, Insects, Reptiles, &c. of the Last of Those Islands*. Legare Street Press, 2021.

Chapter One

Harris, P. R. *The History of the British Museum Library, 1753–1973*. The British Museum, 1998.

Chapter Two

Tocqueville, Alexis de. *De la démocratie en Amérique (Democracy in America)*. Saunders and Otley, 1835–1840.

Trollope, Frances. *The Domestic Manners of the Americans*. First published in 1832; republished by the Folio Society, 1974.

Chapter Three

McCrimmon, Barbara. "Victoria Woodhull Martin Sues the British Museum for Libel." *The Library Quarterly: Information, Community, Policy* 45, no. 4 (October 1975): 355–72. http://www.jstor.com/stable/4306559.

Chapter Four

Original editions from the archives of the British Library, formerly the British Museum Library.

Commercial Court of New England and Wales. "Charles Arthur Russell, 1st Baron Russell of Killowen (1832–1900)." https://www.commercialcourt.london/ca-russell.

McCrimmon, Barbara. "Richard Garnett as Censor." https://www.jstor.org/stable/42554233.

Chapter Five

Wight, Charles Henry. *Genealogy of the Claflin Family*. William Green, 1903.

Chapter Six

Barnum, P. T. *The Life of P. T. Barnum, Written by Himself.* Kindle, 2000.

Inglis, Brian. *Trance: A Natural History of Altered States of Mind.* Grafton Books, 1989.

Mesmer, Franz, G. F. Frankau, et al. *Mesmerism: The Discovery of Animal Magnetism.* English Translation of Mesmer's historic *Mémoire sur la découverte du Magnétisme Animal.* Kindle, 2016.

Weisberg, Barbara. *Talking to the Dead: Kate and Maggie Fox and the Rise of Spiritualism.* Harper San Francisco, 2004.

Chapter Seven

Beaude, Ann. *Radical Spirits: Spiritualism and Women's Rights in Nineteenth-Century America.* Indiana University Press, 1989.

Moore, Laurence. *In Search of White Crows: Spiritualism, Parapsychology, and American Culture.* Oxford University Press, 1986.

Tischner, Rudolf. *Telepathy and Clairvoyance.* Harcourt Brace & Co., 1925.

Chapter Eight

Andreas, Alfred Theodore. *The History of Chicago: Ending with the Year 1857.* Legare Street Press, 2023.

The Book of Mormon. Seven major editions have been published by the Church of Jesus Christ of Latter-Day Saints.

Jesse, Dean C., ed. *The Personal Writings of Joseph Smith.* Deseret Books, 1984.

Chapter Nine

Brands, H. W. *The Age of Gold: The California Gold Rush and the New American Dream.* Doubleday, 2002.

Brown, Dee. *Bury My Heart at Wounded Knee: An Indian History of the American West.* Holt, Rinehart & Winston, 1970.

Popova, Maria. "From the Gold Rush to Silicon Valley: How Mark Twain Became the Steve Jobs of His Day." *The Marginalian* (blog). https://www.themarginalian.org/2014/04/02/mark-twain-bohemians-tarnoff/.

Seitz, Don C. *Horace Greeley.* Bobbs-Merrill, 1926.

Twain, Mark. "The Celebrated Jumping Frog of Calaveras County." https://www.youtube.com/watch?v=6cpJZjAph8E.

White, Steward Edward. *The Forty-Niners: A Chronicle of the California Trail and El Dorado.* Yale University Press, 1918.

Chapter Ten

Collier, Peter. *The Rockefellers: An American Dynasty.* Kindle. Originally published in 1976.

Crane, Stephen. *The Red Badge of Courage.* Jonathan Cape, 1940.

Lent, Jeffrey. *In the Fall.* Atlantic Monthly Press, 2000.

McFerson, James. *The War That Forged a Nation: Why the Civil War Still Matters.* Oxford University Press, 2015.

Winik, Jay. *April 1865: The Month That Saved America.* Harper Perennial, 2002.

Chapter Eleven

Gabriel, Mary. *Notorious Victoria: The Life of Victoria Woodhull, Uncensored*. Algonquin Books of Chapel Hill, 1991.

Chapter Twelve

Katz, Neal. *Outrageous: The Victoria Woodhull Saga*. Vol. 1, *Rise to Riches*. Top Reads Publishing, 2015.

Leach, William. *True Love and Perfect Union: The Feminist Reform of Sex and Society*. Basic Books, 1980.

Chapter Thirteen

Demosthenes. *Orations*. https://www.loebclassics.com/view/LCL238/1930/volume .xml.

Klaw, Spencer. *Without Sin: The Life and Death of the Oneida Community*. Penguin/Allen Lane, 1993.

Passet, Joanne Ellen. *Sex Radicals and the Quest for Women's Equality*. University of Illinois Press, 2003.

Sears, Hall D. *The Sex Radicals: Free Love and High Victorian America*. Regents Press, 1977.

Chapter Fourteen

Auchincloss, Louis. *The Vanderbilt Era: Profiles of a Gilded Age*. Charles Scribner's Sons, 1989.

Lane, Wheaton. *Commodore Vanderbilt: An Epic of the Steam Age*. Alfred A. Knopf, 1942.

Nevin, Allan. *The Emergence of Modern America: 1865–1878*. The Macmillan Co., 1927.

Chapter Fifteen

McCabe, John. *Lights and Shadows of New York*. National Publishing, 1872.

Renehan, Howard J. Jr. *Commodore: The Life of Cornelius Vanderbilt*. Basic Books, 2007.

Wicker, Elmus. *The Banking Panics of the Gilded Age*. Cambridge University Press, 2006.

Chapter Sixteen

Caplan, Sheri J. *Petticoats and Pinstripes: Portraits of Women in Wall Street's History*. Praeger, 2012.

Clews, Henry. *Fifty Years in Wall Street*. Irving Publishing, 1908.

Chapter Seventeen

Robb, George. *Ladies of the Ticker: Women and Wall Street from the Gilded Age to the Great Depression*. University of Illinois Press, 2017.

Chapter Eighteen

Ackerman, Kenneth D. *Boss Tweed: The Rise and Fall of the Corrupt Politician Who Conceived the Soul of Modern New York*. Kindle. Originally published in 1995.

Briggs, Asa, and John Callow. *Marx in London*. Lawrence and Wishart, 2008.

George, Henry. *Progress and Poverty: An Inquiry into the Cause of Increase of Want with an Increase of Wealth: The Remedy*. Aziloth, 2016.

Halloran, Fiona Deans. *Thomas Nast: The Father of Modern Political Cartoons.* University of North Carolina Press, 2013.

Love, Marriage and Divorce and the Sovereignty of the Individual: A Discussion by Stephen Pearl Andrews, William James, and Horace Greeley. Stringer and Townsend, 1853.

Lynch, D. T. *"Boss" Tweed.* Boni & Liveright, 1927.

Marx, Karl. *The Classics of Marxism.* Well Red Publications, 2013.

Stern, Madeleine. *The Pantarch: A Biography of Stephen Pearl Andrews.* University of Texas Press, 1968.

Chapter Nineteen

Underhill, Lois Beachy. *The Woman Who Ran for President.* Bridge Works Publishing, 1995.

Woodhull, Victoria. "Great Political Issue of Constitutional Equality." Speech reprint. Woodhull, Claflin and Co., 1871.

Woodhull, Victoria. "The Origin, Tendencies and Principles of Government; or, A Review of the Rise and Fall of Nations from Early Historic Time to the Present." Woodhull, Claflin and Co., 1871. https://onlinebooks.library.upenn.edu /webbin/book/lookupid?key=olbp44236.

Chapter Twenty

Davis, Sue. *The Political Thought of Elizabeth Cady Stanton: Women's Rights and the American Political Traditions.* New York University Press, 2008.

Douglass, Frederick. *Narrative of the Life of Frederick Douglass, an American Slave. Written by himself.* Electronic edition. https://docsouth.unc.edu/neh/douglass /douglass.html.

Fritz, Jean. *Harriet Beecher Stowe and the Beecher Preachers.* Scholastic, 1994.

Griffith, Elizabeth. *In Her Own Right: The Life of Elizabeth Cady Stanton.* Oxford University Press, 1984.

Papachristou, Judith. *Women Together: A History in Documents of the Women's Movement in the United States.* Alfred A. Knopf, 1976.

Stowe, Harriet Beecher. *Uncle Tom's Cabin.* Black & White Publications, 2015.

Chapter Twenty-One

Morgan, Kenneth. *Slavery and the British Empire: From Africa to America.* Oxford University Press, 2007.

Pettinger, Alasdair. *Frederick Douglass and Scotland, 1846: Living an Antislavery Life.* Edinburgh University Press, 2019.

Scanlan, Padraic X. *Slave Empire: How Slaves Built Modern Britain.* Little, Brown, 2020.

Chapter Twenty-Two

Frisken, Amanda. *Victoria Woodhull's Sexual Revolution: Political Theater and the Popular Press in Nineteenth-Century America.* University of Pennsylvania Press, 2004.

Hudson, Frederick. *Journalism in America.* Harper & Brothers, 1873.

Chapter Twenty-Three

Banfield, Susan. *The Fifteenth Amendment: African American Men's Right to Vote.* Enslow, 1998.

Butler, Benjamin. *Autobiography and Personal Reminiscences of Major-General Benjamin Butler.* A. M. Thayer & Co., 1892.

Greene, Meg. *Into the Land of Freedom: African Americans in Reconstruction.* Learner Publications Company, 2004.

Harper, Ida Husted. *The Life and Work of Susan B. Anthony.* Bobbs-Merrill, 1899.

James, Edward, Janet Williams James, and Paul Boyer, eds. *Stormy Ben Butler.* Macmillan, 1954.

Lutz, Alma. *Created Equally: A Biography of Elizabeth Cady Stanton, 1815–1902.* John Day, 1940.

Woodhull, Victoria C. "Address to the Judiciary Committee of the U.S. House of Representatives—Jan. 11, 1871." https://awpc.cattcenter.iastate.edu/2020/12/15/address-to-the-judiciary-committee-of-the-u-s-house-of-representatives-jan-11-1871/.

Chapter Twenty-Four

Bolt, Christine. *The Women's Movements in the United States and Britain from the 1790s to the 1920s.* Harvesting Wheatsheaf, 1993.

Chaucer, Geoffrey. *The House of Fame.* Translated by A. S. Kline, 2007. https://www.poetryintranslation.com/PITBR/English/Fame.php.

Congressional Reports on Women's Suffrage. "Constitutional Equality the Logical Result of the XIV and XV Amendments, Which Not Only Declare Who Are Citizens, but Also Define Their Rights, One of Which Is the Right to Vote Without Regard to Sex." Woodhull, Claflin & Co., 1871.

Midorikawa, Emily. *Out of the Shadows: Six Visionary Women in Search of a Public Voice.* Counterpoint Press, 2021.

Woodhull, Victoria Claflin. "The Origin, Tendencies and Principles of Government." Woodhull, Claflin & Co., 1891. https://www.gutenberg.org/ebooks/67127.

Chapter Twenty-Five

Brody, Miriam. *Victoria Woodhull: Free Spirit for Women's Rights.* Oxford University Press, 2004.

Davis, Paulina Wright. *A History of the National Woman's Rights Movement, for Twenty Years, with the Proceedings of the Decade Meeting Held at Apollo Hall, October 20, 1870.* Journeymen Printers' Co-Operative Association, 1871; Kraus Reprint, 1971.

Fitzpatrick, Ellen. *The Highest Glass Ceiling: Women's Quest for the American Presidency.* Harvard University Press, 2016.

Woodhull, Victoria. "Social Problem of Labor & Capital." Speech delivered at New York's Cooper Institute, May 8, 1871. Journeymen Printers' Co-Operative Association, 1871.

Chapter Twenty-Six

Applegate, Debby. *The Most Famous Man in America: The Biography of Henry Ward Beecher.* Doubleday, 2006.

Beecher, Rev. William C., Samuel Scoville, assisted by Mrs. Henry Ward Beecher. *A Biography of Henry Ward Beecher.* Charles Webster & Company, 1888.

Hedrick, Joan. *Harriet Beecher Stowe: A Life.* Oxford University Press, 1994.

Hibben, Paxton. *Henry Ward Beecher: An American Portrait.* Oxford University Press, 1927.

Scott, Jeremy. *The Women Who Dared to Break the Rule.* One World, 2019.

Chapter Twenty-Seven

Greer, William Wilson. *A Dirty Year: Sex, Suffrage, and Scandal in Gilded Age New York.* Chicago Review Press, 2020.

Shaplen, Robert. *Free Love and Heavenly Sinners: The Story of the Great Henry Ward Beecher Scandal.* Knopf, 1954.

Tilton, Theodore. *The Golden Age Tracts.* No. 3, *Victoria C. Woodhull. A Biographical Sketch.* New York, 1871.

Chapter Twenty-Eight

Johnston, Johanna. *The Terrible Siren.* First published in 1928; republished by Arno Press, 1972.

Marx, Karl, with Frederick Engels, *The Manifesto of the Communist Party.* 1848.

Pearl, Stephen Andrews. *The Basic Outline of Universology.* Dion Thomas, 1872.

Woodhull, Victoria C. "A New Constitution for the United States of the World, Proposed by Victoria C. Woodhull for the Consideration of the Constructors of Our Future Government." Woodhull, Claflin and Co., 1872.

Chapter Twenty-Nine

Johnston, Joanna. *Mrs. Satan: The Incredible Saga of Victoria C. Woodhull.* G. P. Putnam's Sons, 1967.

Chapter Thirty

Hibben, Paxton. *Henry Ward Beecher: An American Portrait.* George H. Doran Company, 1927.

Marberry, M. M. *Vicky: A Biography of Victoria C. Woodhull.* Funk & Wagnalls, 1967.

Rugoff, Milton. *The Beechers: An American Family in the Nineteenth Century.* Harper & Row, 1981.

Chapter Thirty-One

Broun, Heywood, and Margaret Leech. *Anthony Comstock: Roundsman of the Lord.* Albert and Charles Boni, 1927.

Comstock, Anthony. *Tips for the Young.* Funk & Wagnalls, 1884.

Turnbull, Charles. *Outlawed: How Anthony Comstock Fought and Won the Purity of a Nation.* Scott Matthew Dix, 2013.

Chapter Thirty-Two

Smith, Arthur D. Howden. *Commodore Vanderbilt.* Philip Allan & Co., 1920.

Waller, Altina. *The Reverend Beecher and Mrs. Tilton: Sex and Class in Victorian America.* University Massachusetts Press, 1982.

Chapter Thirty-Three

Flanders, Judith. *The Victorian City.* St. Martin's Press, 2012.

Jenkins, Simon. *A Short History of London: The Creation of a World Capital.* Viking Penguin, 2019.

Norton, Graham. *Victorian London*. Macdonald, 1969.
Paterson, Michael. *Voices from Dickens' London*. David & Charles, 2006.

Chapter Thirty-Four
Fawcett, Millicent Garrett. *What I Remember*. G. P. Putnam's Sons, 1925.
Picard, Liza. *Victorian London: The Life of a City 1840–1870*. Weidenfeld & Nicolson, 2005.

Chapter Thirty-Five
Burke's Peerage. https://www.burkespeerage.com.
Metcalf, Priscilla. *Victorian London*. Cassell & Company, 1972.
Tocqueville, Alexis de. *Voyages en Angleterre et Irlande*. Gallimard, 1982.

Chapter Thirty-Six
Edel, Leon. *Henry James: The Conquest of London, 1870–1881*. Lippincott, 1962.
James, Henry. *The Bostonians*. Macmillan & Co., 1921.
James, Henry. *The Europeans*. Houghton, Osgood & Co., 1879.
James, Henry. *The Great Short Stories of Henry James: The Siege of London*. Dial Press, 1944.
James, Henry. *London Stories*. Tabb House, 1989.
James, Henry. *The Siege of London*. *The Cornhill Magazine*, January–February 1883.

Chapter Thirty-Seven
Hofstadter, Richard. *Social Darwinism in American Thought, 1860–1915*. University of Pennsylvania Press, 1944; revised, Beacon, 1955.
Martin, John Biddulph. *The Grasshopper in Lombard Street*. Simpkin Marshall Hamilton Kent & Co., 1892.
Woodhull, Victoria. "A Speech on the Principles of Social Freedom." Blackfriars Printers, 1894.

Chapter Thirty-Eight
Galton, Francis. *Inquiries into Human Faculties and Their Development*. Macmillan, 1883.
Gillham, Nicholas Wright. *A Life of Sir Francis Galton: From African Exploration to the Birth of Eugenics*. Oxford University Press, 2001.
Perry, Michael. *Lady Eugenics: Feminist Eugenics in the Speeches and Writings of Victoria Woodhull*. Inkling Books, 2005.
Woodhull, Victoria, and Lady Tennessee Claflin Cook. *The Human Body the Temple of God; or, The Philosophy of Sociology*. Published by the authors, 1890. https://onlinebooks.library.upenn.edu/webbin/book/lookupid?key=olbp89391.

Chapter Thirty-Nine
Brough, James. *The Vixens: A Biography of Victoria and Tennessee Claflin*. Simon and Schuster, 1918.
Kingsbury, Ida. *Sir Francis Cook and Monserrate*. The British Historical Society of Portugal, 1976. https://www.bhsportugal.org/library/articles/sir-francis-cook-and-monserrate.

Chapter Forty

Goldsmith, Barbara. *Other Powers: The Age of Suffrage, Spiritualism, and the Scandalous Victoria Woodhull.* Knopf, 1998.

Martin, Victoria Woodhull. *The Argument for Women's Electoral Rights, Under Amendments XIV and XV of the Constitution of the United States: A Review of My Work at Washington, D.C., in 1870–1871.* Norman, 1887.

Stanton, Elizabeth Cady, Susan B. Anthony, and Matilda Joslyn Gage, eds. *The History of Woman Suffrage.* Fowler & Wells, 1882.

Chapter Forty-One

Martin, Victoria Woodhull. *The Human Body the Temple of God; or, The Philosophy of Sociology.* 1890.

Chapter Forty-Two

Booth, William. *The Darkest England and the Way Out.* First published in 1890; republished by Book Jungle, 2008.

Mayhew, Henry. *London Labor and the London Poor.* 1851, Project Gutenberg Ebook.

Morris, Jan. *Pax Britannica.* Faber and Faber, 1998.

Pakenham, Thomas. *The Boer War.* Weidenfeld & Nicolson, Ltd., 1997.

Sala, George Augustus. *Twice Around the Clock.* Richard Marsh, 1862.

Schlesinger, Max. *Sauntering In and About London.* Gutenberg Ebook.

Chapter Forty-Three

Aiken, Diane. "Victorian Prostitution." British Literature Wiki. February 10, 2012. https://sites.udel.edu/britlitwiki/victorian-prostitution/.

Earland, Ada. *Ruskin and His Circle.* G. P. Putnam's Sons, 1910.

Logan, Deborah Anna. *Fallenness in Victorian Women's Writing: Marry, Stitch, Die, or Do Worse.* University of Missouri Press, 1998, ebook.

Mill, John Stuart. *On Liberty and the Subjection of Women.* Penguin Classics, 2006.

Rose, Phyllis. *Parallel Lives: Five Victorian Marriages.* Vintage Books, 1984.

Rugoff, Milton. *American's Gilded Age: Intimate Portraits from an Era of Extravagance and Change, 1850–1890.* Henry Holt & Co., 1989.

Ruskin, John. *Sesame and Lilies.* First published in 1865. Create Space Independent Publishing Platform, Nov. 2014.

Ruskin, John. *Unto This Last and Other Writings.* Penguin Classics, 1985.

Strachey, Lytton. *Queen Victoria.* Harcourt, Brace & Co., 1921.

Twain, Mark, and Charles Dudley Warner. *The Gilded Age.* American Publishing Co., 1873.

Chapter Forty-Four

Farr, Florence. *The Dancing Faun.* University of California Library, 1994.

Gettman, Royal A. *George Gissing and H. G. Wells: Their Friendship and Correspondence.* Rupert Hart-Davis, 1961.

Heilmann, Ann, and Stephane Forward, eds. *Sex, Social Purity and Sarah Grand.* Routledge Press, 2000.

Chapter Forty-Five

Carpenter, Carl M., ed. *Selected Writings of Victoria Woodhull: Suffrage, Free Love, and Eugenics.* University of Nebraska Press, 2010.

English Heritage. "Eugenics in Britain." https://www.english-heritage.org.uk/visit /blue-plaques/blue-plaque-stories/eugenics/#:~:text=Founding%20Eugenics &text=The%20eugenics%20movement%20in%20Britain,Eugenics%20and %20the%20Eugenics%20Society.

Eugenics Archives. "Timeline." https://www.eugenicsarchives.ca/timeline.

Martin, Victoria C. Woodhull. *The Rapid Multiplication of the Unfit.* The Women's Anthropological Society of America, 1891.

Miller, George Noyes. *The Strike of a Sex: A Novel.* G. W. Dillingham, 1890.

Noyes, John Humphrey. *Home Talks, 1875.* Edited by Alfred Barron and George Noyes Miller. Kessinger Publishing, 2010.

Chapter Forty-Six

Cook, Lady. *Essays on Social Topics: 1845–1923.* The Roxburghe Press, 1886–1923.

Chapter Forty-Seven

Baird, Julia. *Victoria: The Queen. An Intimate Biography of the Woman Who Ruled an Empire.* Deckle Edge, 2016.

Pankhurst, Emmeline. *A Suffragette, My Own Story.* First published in 1914; available from Hesperus Press, 2016, and on Kindle.

Papachristou, Judith. *Women Together: A History in Documents of the Women's Movement in the United States.* Alfred A. Knopf, 1976.

Richards, Stewart. *The Curtain Down at the Death of Queen Victoria: In the Words of Those Who Were There.* The History Press, 2019.

Terras, Melissa, and Elizabeth Crawford, eds. *Millicent Garrett Fawcett, Selected Writings.* UCL Press, 2022.

Chapter Forty-Eight

Bogdanor, Vernon. *The Strange Survival of Liberal Britain: Politics and Power Before the First World War.* Biteback Publishing, Ltd., 2022.

Parry, Jonathan. *The Rise and Fall of Liberal Government in Victorian Britain.* Yale University Press, 1983.

Chapter Forty-Nine

Stinchcombe, Owen. *The American Lady of the Manor, Bredon's Norton; The Later Life of Victoria Woodhull Martin.* Published by the author, 2000.

Chapter Fifty

Garnett, Richard. *Review of Essays of an Ex-Librarian.* The Athenaeum, 1901.

Havelin, Kate. *Fearless Feminist: Victoria Woodhull.* Twenty-First Century Books, 2007.

Miller, Lisa. *Visions of Heaven: A Journey Through the Afterlife.* Time Books, 2014.

Woodhull, Victoria, with an introduction by Ian Randal Strock. *Victoria C. Woodhull: Ideas Ahead of Her Time.* Gray Rabbit Publishing, 2018.

Illustration Credits

About the Author

EDEN COLLINSWORTH was president of Arbor House Publishing Company and a founder of the Los Angeles–based monthly magazine *Buzz,* before becoming a vice president at Hearst Corporation. She served as the chief of staff at the EastWest Institute, a global think tank. After writing a bestselling book in China, she launched Collinsworth & Associates, a Beijing-based consulting company that specialized in intercultural communication. Collinsworth is the author of *What the Ermine Saw, Behaving Badly, I Stand Corrected,* and *It Might Have Been What He Said.*